NOW THERE'S AN EASY WAY
TO COUNT CALORIES

Nearly a million readers of *The All-in-One Calorie Counter* can attest to the advantages of having such a valuable source at their fingertips. Now, well-known nutrition expert, Jean Carper has completely revised and updated this book with the latest information available from food manufacturers and the U. S. Department of Agriculture. This convenient and important handbook contains over 5,500 entries on just about every kind of food imaginable—including the top fast-food chain foods.

AN INVALUABLE BOOK
IF YOU ARE CONCERNED
ABOUT YOUR WEIGHT.

D0666791

Bantam Books by Jean Carper
Ask your bookseller for the books you have missed

THE ALL-IN-ONE CALORIE COUNTER
THE ALL-IN-ONE CARBOHYDRATE GRAM
  COUNTER
THE ALL-IN-ONE LOW FAT GRAM COUNTER
THE BRAND NAME NUTRITION COUNTER

The All-In-One Calorie Counter

Revised Edition

By Jean Carper

BANTAM BOOKS
TORONTO · NEW YORK · LONDON · SYDNEY

THE ALL-IN-ONE CALORIE COUNTER

A Bantam Book / published by arrangement with
Workman Publishing Co., Inc.

PRINTING HISTORY

Bantam edition / January 1974

2nd printing	.... May 1974	8th printing	...... August 1977
3rd printing	.... August 1974	9th printing	...... October 1977
4th printing	.... April 1975	10th printing	.... January 1978
5th printing	.. December 1975	11th printing	...... January 1979
6th printing	.... July 1976	12th printing	.... May 1979
7th printing	.. November 1976	13th printing	. November 1979

Revised Bantam edition / July 1980
15th printing ...... September 1980
16th printing .... June 1981

All rights reserved.
Copyright © 1974, 1980 by Jean Carper.
This book may not be reproduced in whole or in part, by
mimeograph or any other means, without permission.
For information address: Bantam Books, Inc.

ISBN 0-553-20339-8

Published simultaneously in the United States and Canada

Bantam Books are published by Bantam Books, Inc. Its trade-
mark, consisting of the words "Bantam Books" and the por-
trayal of a bantam, is Registered in U.S. Patent and Trademark
Office, and in other countries. Marca Registrada. Bantam
Books, Inc., 666 Fifth Avenue, New York, New York 10103.

PRINTED IN THE UNITED STATES OF AMERICA

25 24 23 22 21 20 19 18 17

Contents

Introduction

"Counting calories is not just the best way to long-term weight maintenance—it's the only way," says Harvard nutritionist Dr. Jean Mayer. It is that unit of energy— the calorie—which determines how much weight you put on and take off, he says. And certainly there are hundreds of thousands of successful calorie-counting dieters who would agree. Take in fewer calories than you burn up each day, and you're bound to shed pounds.

But how to do it? Unfortunately, there aren't any mysterious secrets for making dieting actually fun. But in this book you'll find loads of information that I hope will take some of the monotony out of dieting, enable you to eat some foods on your diet you never dreamed possible, and clear up some misconceptions you may have about which foods are high in calorie content and which aren't. For example, many calorie-conscious persons avoid potatoes and spaghetti like the plague (which by themselves are fairly low in calories) and load up on "protein" foods like beef (which is comparatively much higher in calories).

With potatoes and pasta, it is not the basic food itself but the way they are prepared or the embellishments that make the calorie difference. A medium-sized boiled potato weighs in with only 104 calories, whereas only 10 French fries have 137 calories. Of course, if you want to splurge occasionally and eat French fries or load up your baked potato with butter and sour cream cheese sauce, why shouldn't you as long as you consider the calorie difference?

And why shouldn't you eat a Mars bar if you want one? Or a slice of Sara Lee's rich cake? Or Jeno's piz-

za? If you don't exceed your daily limit. Dieting—even
if you are counting calories—doesn't have to be a
Monklike experience—ascetic and uninteresting. Of
course, overindulging in these goodies at the expense
of well-balanced nutrition is not in your best interest.

The only stumbling block may be that you don't
know how many calories are present in these products.
For unlike pure, fresh foods, when the ingredients get
into a company chef's kitchen, they are all mixed any
which way according to the company's special recipe.
Only the company can tell you how many calories are
in their foods. And that's the kind of information you
will find in this book: a comprehensive listing of not
only all common "generic-type" foods, but commercially prepared foods—from Durkee's appetizer frozen
puff pastries to Mrs. Paul's frozen zucchini sticks.

You'll see that the number of calories in similar
grocery products can vary greatly, and you'll find that
simple knowledge can trim calories off a product
quickly. For example, it is almost startling to realize
that if you use a 7 ounce can of Chicken of the Sea
white tuna complete with oil, you accumulate 507
calories—but if you drain off the oil before use, you're
left with only 328 calories—a saving of 179 calories!

If you've bought or are thinking of buying this book,
you're probably already committed to losing weight, so
there's no use wasting time telling you why you should
reduce, or all the terrible medical problems that may
confront you if you don't. But there are some facts
about calories that you may find valuable. A calorie
is a unit of energy in foods. Technically, it is the
amount of heat needed to raise the temperature of one
liter (about a quart) of water by one degree. The body
constantly takes in calories through food and expends
them through activity.

Theoretically, if you took in precisely as many
calories in a day as you used up in energy, you wouldn't
lose or gain a smidgen of an ounce that day. But when
you take in more calories than your body can use, you
store them as fat. The rule of thumb is that a mod-

erately active person needs about 15 calories per day per pound of body weight to "stay as you are." That is, if you weigh 120 pounds and want to stay that way, you should consume about 1800 calories a day. If you're happy at 150 pounds, you take in 2250 calories a day. Now if you want to get rid of some of that stored fat by counting calories, the calorie intake should dip below that. How much you want to lose and how fast is up to you.

According to the American Medical Association there are about 3500 calories in each stored pound of fat. So if you want to take off a pound, you have to get rid of that 3500 calories somehow. One way you can do it is to shave 500 calories a day for seven days off your caloric intake. Thus, if you're 120 pounds and want to take off a pound a week, you would cut your regular 1800 calorie daily count to 1300; and if you weigh 150, you'd go down from 2250 calories daily to 1750. It's an easy formula and you can work it out for yourself according to your own weight and diet aims.

As far as giving you the basic facts necessary to follow your diet, you'll find in this book the calorie counts on all kinds of foods—both fresh and processed (by brand name, of course)—from A to Z. Included are not only the usual brands you see everyday on grocery shelves and on TV commercials, but also the "house brands" of the A & P and Safeway supermarkets—such as Ann Page from A & P and Lucerne from Safeway. (If you wonder why we didn't include other major supermarkets, it's because, though we asked, they did not make such information available.) And there's a whole special section on fastfoods—everything from Big Mac's to Dairy Queen sundaes—valuable information, not found in any other popular book to my knowledge.

A word about the figures in the book: This book was first published in 1974 and has been an enormous success. Dozens of people have written to say how much it helped them lose weight, and it is used in organized weight-loss clinics. It has sold over 7 hundred thousand copies. Since the original publication, some of the calorie counts have changed due to new analyses or reformulation of products, and new products have been introduced. Thus, new figures were gathered in 1979 for this complete revision. Of course, some of the calorie counts are the same or similar, since the calories in many basic foods, such as milk, cheese, bread, as well as alcoholic drinks, don't change much. And a few companies did not have any new information. But I would estimate that fully two-thirds to three-fourths of the figures are brand new. For example, the baby food companies have eliminated most or all of the sugar in their fruits and vegetables, in some cases reducing the calories in a jar of baby food by 100 per cent. Many companies now have their products analyzed in a laboratory instead of "calculating" the calories from the food's recipe as they did in the past. That means in some cases slightly altered figures.

All of the figures bearing brand names in this book were provided by food companies and are the latest the company had available. If some of your favorite products are missing, it is because the company does not have the information or did not provide it.

In some cases the information from the company has been translated from 100 gram units or other serving sizes (for example to one slice of bacon or one slice of bread) to make it easier for you. This translation may account for some minor variations in figures.

Within the last few years more companies have started putting nutritional information on their products, although they are not required by the federal government to do so, unless they make specific nutritional claims for the food. However, if they do label, they must provide the information in a standardized form. Still, it is difficult to make comparisons among various brand name foods without running all around the supermarket. Thus, another benefit of this book:

you can pick out the lower calorie items *before* you go shopping.

Most calorie counts, now that companies have done more analyses, should remain exceedingly stable over the years. However, occasionally a food maker will change the composition of a product, severely changing the calorie count. For example, during the lifetime of this book, some soft drink companies came out with saccharin-sweetened drinks that slashed the sugar and thus the calorie count to virtually nothing. Diet Rite, for example, instead of having 48 calories per 8 fluid ounces, as listed in the book, had only one, and advertised that fact. Many readers wrote in to ask which was correct.

This happens only rarely, but in such cases of conflict, you can believe the calorie information on the label. The accuracy of a food company's labeling is regulated by the federal Food and Drug Administration, and a company would be subject to severe penalties for putting out a label that was grossly inaccurate.

Also, some manufacturers have asked me to point out that their figures are the best average calculations or analyses they have on specific products, but because of normal variations beyond their control, there may be ever-so-slight variations from batch to batch from the same manufacturer. Even such factors as seasonal conditions or soil composition may influence final food nutritional values.

All of the calorie counts without any brand name or company attribution are from the U.S. Department of Agriculture. And here, too, some calculations were done to make sure the figures were in the most convenient form.

To sum up, the new revised *All-In-One Calorie Counter* will provide you with the latest, most accurate data available about fresh foods, processed foods and fastfoods.

Jean Carper
January, 1980

How To Use This Book

The most important organizational fact about the *All-In-One Calorie Counter,* as you will quickly see, is that it is alphabetized for easy use according to food categories. That is, you don't have to look in the front of the book under B for bean soup and then flip to the T's to find out if tomato soup is lower in calories. It runs through the alphabet, starting with appetizers and ending with yogurt. All the breads are listed together in the B section, all the fruits are grouped together under F, the vegetables under V, and so on. Simply by looking at the Table of Contents in the front of the book, you can quickly spot which category a food is in and turn directly to that section. You'll then find the foods alphabetized within the sections. Some foods, to be sure, just don't fit easily into categories, and rather than force them into some artificial grouping, we've listed them alphabetically too, even though there may be only one or two of a kind; for example, baking powder and cornstarch have listings of their own. And for the first time we've included a special Fast-Foods section at the end of the book.

In other words, the book is akin to a dictionary—with headings at the top of each page, too, to help you out. If you get stuck and can't decide where a food might be, just consult the index.

We have tried to standardize the language and food serving sizes as much as possible to make them useful, but here again we haven't strained the point.

We have tried to be realistic. For example, under cereals, you won't find all of them in either 1-cup or ½-cup portions. The reason: simply because they are not really comparable. A person may easily sit down to an 8-ounce cup of puffed rice, but rarely to a full 8-ounce cup of the heavier All-bran. A more realistic portion for bran is ⅓ of a cup. Therefore, we have followed the manufacturers' recommendations and provided single serving sizes they believe appropriate.

For some items, for example, frozen pies, we've given the calorie content for the entire pie. Often the producer provides the information in portions of 1/6 of a pie. But it seemed to us that a person who wanted to eat only ⅛ of a pie when we had given figures for only a 1/6 wedge would have to go through the laborious procedure of first figuring out the total calorie content of the whole pie and then dividing by eight. Consequently we've stated the calorie count of the entire pie. A person can then cut it anyway he wants and figure accordingly; he's not tied down to a single serving size arbitrarily decided by us.

Whenever you see the word "prepared" the figures are based on the assumption that the food has been prepared according to the manufacturer's directions. If you alter the preparation, for example, by adding meat drippings instead of water to a gravy mix or using milk when water is called for on the package or adding other embellishments of your own, you must figure these extras in. Whenever milk is called for in a preparation, we assume it is whole milk—not skim or nonfat or condensed milk. If you use any of the latter —either raising or lowering the calorie content in the finished product—you will have to make provision for it.

In most cases companies prefer to tell you how many calories are in the finished prepared product— for example, a cup of pudding from pudding mixes, because it's rare that the powder would be used in any other way. But in some instances you will find the calorie count for the dry mix only—*before* preparation. That way, if you want to add another ingredient to your mix, you're free to do so and add up the extra calories. Also on this note: whenever you merely add water to a mix, you're not adding calories—for example, when you make a Lipton's soup. If you use the dry soup mix in any other fashion, say as a dip mix, you have the same calorie count in the dry mix as in the cup of prepared soup.

In keeping with our determination to make this book easy to use, we've taken due note of the power of identity of brand names. Whenever possible, without interfering with the organization, we've used brand names for quick identification. Thus, when you look up a certain cookie, cracker or cereal, you don't have to peruse the whole list searching for a description of your cookie. We don't have Cheez-Its listed under "crackers, cheese;" we have it simply alphabetized under Cheez-Its. And we have Oreo cookies under O and not under "chocolate creme sandwich." The same goes for Franken Berry cereal (under F in the cereal section). Of course, it was not always possible to do this without creating a chaotic organization, and in many cases the only identifying factor is a description of the product (chocolate chip cookies, for example) and the name of the manufacturer.

Within the listings, we repeat the measurements frequently, even though they are the same, rather than place the portion size at the head of a section which may be a page or two back. However, on items like cookies and crackers and frozen "TV" dinners, where the portion size is not confusing—one cookie or cracker or a complete dinner—we've simply noted the portion at the head of the section. This has also been done on fairly short listings.

To avoid confusion, whenever possible, we have stated the measurement in the most easily used terms: cups and tablespoons and fluid ounces for liquids and items such as canned fruits and vegetables; and weight ounces for items like cheese and frozen fish fillets.

Despite our best efforts, there's no way we can save you from doing some figuring on your own, simply because no one, including yourself, wants to eat the same amount of a certain food at every sitting. And, of course, when you use your own recipes, there's no way possible that we could give figures on the finished product, because home recipes vary greatly just as do recipes for commercially prepared foods. If you're whipping up your own tapioca pudding, we can tell you how many calories are in the dry tapioca, in the eggs, milk and sugar, and you'll have to take it from there. Only you know how much of an ingredient you really use.

For doing your own conversions, here's an equivalency table that may be of help:

1 tablespoon = 3 teaspoons
2 tablespoons = 1 fluid ounce
4 tablespoons = ¼ cup
5⅓ tablespoons = ⅓ cup
16 tablespoons = 1 cup
1 cup = 8 fluid ounces
     = ½ pint
2 cups = 1 pint
2 pints = 1 quart
1 pound = 16 ounces

Happy calorie counting!

Abbreviations

art	artificial
diam	diameter
fl	fluid
in	inch
lb	pound
med	medium
oz	ounce
pkg	package
swt	sweetened
tbsp	tablespoon
tsp	teaspoon
unswt	unsweetened
w	with
wo	without

Appetizers

	CALORIES
Frozen	
Cheese straws: 1 piece / **Durkee**	29
Frankfurter: 1 piece / **Durkee** Franks-n-Blankets	45
Puff pastry: 1 piece	
Beef puffs / **Durkee**	47
Cheese puffs / **Durkee**	59
Chicken puffs / **Durkee**	49
Chicken liver puffs / **Durkee**	48
Shrimp puffs / **Durkee**	44

Baby Food

BAKED GOODS

	CALORIES
Biscuits, teething: 1 piece / Gerber	50
Cookies, animal shaped: 1 cookie / Gerber	30
Cookies, arrowroot: 1 cookie / Gerber	30
Pretzel: 1 pretzel / Gerber	23
Toast, zwieback: 1 piece / Gerber	30

STRAINED BABY FOODS

Cereal: 1 jar

High protein w applesauce and bananas / Gerber	120
Mixed w apples and bananas / Heinz	90
Mixed w applesauce and bananas / Beech-Nut	85
Mixed w applesauce and bananas / Gerber	110
Mixed w fruit / Beech-Nut	110
Oatmeal w apples and bananas / Heinz	100
Oatmeal w applesauce and bananas / Gerber	100
Oatmeal w fruit / Beech-Nut	73
Rice w apples and bananas / Beech-Nut	86
Rice w apples and bananas / Heinz	100
Rice w applesauce and bananas / Gerber	110

CALORIES

Cereal, dry: ½ oz

Barley / **Gerber**	60
Barley / **Heinz**	50
High protein / **Gerber**	50
High protein / **Heinz**	50
High protein w apple and orange / **Gerber**	60
Mixed / **Gerber**	60
Mixed / **Heinz**	50
Mixed w banana / **Gerber**	60
Oatmeal / **Gerber**	60
Oatmeal / **Heinz**	50
Oatmeal w banana / **Gerber**	60
Rice / **Gerber**	60
Rice / **Heinz**	50
Rice w banana / **Gerber**	60

Formula, meat base: 2 tbsp / Gerber
Infant Formula   40

Fruits and Desserts: 1 jar

Apple betty / **Beech-Nut**	69
Apple blueberry / **Gerber**	90
Apple raspberry / **Gerber** Strained Fruits	90
Apples and apricots / **Beech-Nut**	58
Apples and cranberries w tapioca / **Heinz**	130
Apples and pears / **Heinz**	70
Applesauce	
Beech-Nut	59
Gerber	60
Heinz	70
and apricots / **Gerber**	110
and apricots / **Heinz**	100
and cherries / **Beech-Nut**	72
w pineapple / **Gerber**	60
and raspberries / **Beech-Nut**	59
Apricots w tapioca / **Beech-Nut**	64
Apricots w tapioca / **Gerber**	100

	CALORIES
Apricots w tapioca / **Heinz**	70
Bananas	
w pineapple / **Beech-Nut**	70
w pineapple and tapioca / **Gerber**	100
w pineapple and tapioca / **Heinz**	80
w tapioca / **Beech-Nut**	66
w tapioca / **Gerber**	100
w tapioca / **Heinz**	90
Cottage cheese w pineapple / **Gerber**	100
Dutch apple dessert / **Gerber**	100
Fruit dessert / **Gerber**	100
Fruit dessert / **Heinz**	90
Fruit dessert w tapioca / **Beech-Nut**	64
Hawaiian delight / **Gerber**	120
Orange-pineapple dessert / **Beech-Nut**	64
Peach cobbler / **Gerber**	100
Peach cobbler / **Heinz**	100
Peach melba / **Beech-Nut**	59
Peaches / **Beech-Nut**	58
Peaches / **Gerber**	110
Peaches / **Heinz**	120
Pears	
Beech-Nut	64
Gerber	70
Heinz	70
and pineapple / **Beech-Nut**	77
and pineapple / **Gerber**	60
and pineapple / **Heinz**	80
Pineapple dessert / **Beech-Nut**	66
Pineapple-orange dessert / **Heinz**	90
Plums w tapioca / **Beech-Nut**	74
Plums w tapioca / **Gerber**	120
Plums w tapioca / **Heinz**	70
Prunes w tapioca / **Beech-Nut**	109
Prunes w tapioca / **Gerber**	110
Prunes w tapioca / **Heinz**	110
Pudding	
Cherry vanilla / **Gerber**	100

CALORIES

Custard / **Heinz**	110
Custard, apple / **Beech-Nut**	90
Custard, chocolate / **Gerber**	120
Custard, vanilla / **Gerber**	120
Orange / **Gerber**	120
Tutti-frutti / **Heinz**	90

Juices: 1 can

Apple / **Beech-Nut**	52
Apple / **Gerber**	60
Apple / **Heinz**	60
Apple-cherry / **Beech-Nut**	47
Apple-cherry / **Gerber**	70
Apple-cherry / **Heinz**	60
Apple-grape / **Beech-Nut**	53
Apple-grape / **Gerber**	60
Apple-grape / **Heinz**	70
Apple-peach / **Gerber**	60
Apple-plum / **Gerber**	60
Apple-prune / **Heinz**	70
Mixed fruit / **Beech-Nut**	55
Mixed fruit / **Gerber**	70
Orange / **Beech-Nut**	54
Orange / **Gerber**	70
Orange / **Heinz**	70
Orange-apple / **Beech-Nut**	52
Orange-apple / **Gerber**	80
Orange-apple-banana / **Gerber**	70
Orange-apple-banana / **Heinz**	70
Orange-apricot / **Gerber**	60
Orange-banana / **Beech-Nut**	56
Orange-pineapple / **Beech-Nut**	59
Orange-pineapple / **Gerber**	70
Prune-orange / **Beech-Nut**	64
Prune-orange / **Gerber**	90

Main Dishes: 1 jar

Beef
Beech-Nut	120
Beech-Nut High Meat Dinner	125
Gerber	100
w beef hearts / **Gerber**	90
and noodles / **Beech-Nut**	68
and noodles w vegetables / **Gerber**	70
w vegetables / **Gerber** High Meat Dinner	100
Cereal and egg yolks / **Gerber**	70
Cereal, egg yolks and bacon / **Beech-Nut**	107
Cereal and egg / **Heinz**	70

Chicken
Beech-Nut	106
Beech-Nut High Meat Dinner	83
Gerber	130
Noodle / **Beech-Nut**	55
Noodle / **Gerber**	70
w vegetables / **Beech-Nut**	54
w vegetables / **Gerber** High Meat Dinner	100
Cottage cheese w bananas / **Heinz**	90
Cottage cheese w pineapple / **Gerber** High Meat Dinner	160
Egg yolks / **Beech-Nut**	190
Egg yolks / **Gerber**	180
Egg yolks / **Heinz**	170
Grits w egg yolks / **Gerber**	70

Ham
Beech-Nut	112
Beech-Nut High Meat Dinner	135
Gerber	110
w vegetables / **Gerber** High Meat Dinner	100
Lamb / **Beech-Nut**	122
Lamb / **Gerber**	100
Liver, beef / **Gerber**	90

CALORIES

Macaroni and cheese / **Gerber**	80
Macaroni, tomato sauce, beef / **Beech-Nut**	80
Macaroni w tomatoes and beef / **Gerber**	60
Pork / **Gerber**	120
Soup, chicken, cream of / **Gerber**	80
Turkey	
Beech-Nut	105
Beech-Nut High Meat Dinner	111
Gerber	130
and rice / **Beech-Nut**	65
and rice w vegetables / **Gerber**	70
w vegetables / **Gerber**	
High Meat Dinner	120
Veal	
Beech-Nut	112
Beech-Nut High Meat Dinner	90
Gerber	90
w vegetables / **Gerber** High Meat Dinner	90
Vegetables	
and bacon / **Beech-Nut**	80
and bacon / **Gerber**	100
and beef / **Beech-Nut**	75
and beef / **Gerber**	70
and chicken / **Gerber**	60
and ham / **Beech-Nut**	72
and ham / **Gerber**	60
and lamb / **Beech-Nut**	70
and lamb / **Gerber**	70
and liver / **Beech-Nut**	55
and liver / **Gerber**	60
and turkey / **Gerber**	60

Vegetables: 1 jar

Beans, green / **Beech-Nut**	35
Beans, green / **Gerber**	35
Beans, green / **Heinz**	35
Beets / **Gerber**	50
Beets / **Heinz**	40

CALORIES

Carrots / **Beech-Nut**	36
Carrots / **Gerber**	30
Carrots / **Heinz**	35
Corn, creamed / **Beech-Nut**	90
Corn, creamed / **Gerber**	80
Corn, creamed / **Heinz**	80
Garden vegetables / **Beech-Nut**	55
Garden vegetables / **Gerber**	50
Mixed / **Gerber**	60
Mixed / **Heinz**	60
Peas / **Beech-Nut**	67
Peas / **Gerber**	60
Peas, creamed / **Heinz**	70
Spinach, creamed / **Gerber**	60
Squash / **Beech-Nut**	28
Squash / **Gerber**	40
Squash / **Heinz**	50
Sweet potatoes / **Beech-Nut**	70
Sweet potatoes / **Gerber**	90
Sweet potatoes / **Heinz**	80

Yogurt: 1 jar

w mixed fruit / **Beech-Nut**	74
w peach-apple / **Beech-Nut**	68
w pineapple / **Beech-Nut**	79

JUNIOR BABY FOODS

Cereal: 1 jar

Mixed cereal w applesauce and bananas / **Gerber**	180
Oatmeal w applesauce and bananas / **Gerber**	170
Rice cereal w mixed fruit / **Gerber**	180

Fruits and Desserts: 1 jar

Apple betty / **Beech-Nut**	115
Apple blueberry / **Gerber**	160

CALORIES

Apple raspberry / Gerber	150
Apples and apricots / Beech-Nut	96
Apples and cranberries / Heinz	130
Apples and pears / Heinz	120
Applesauce	
Beech-Nut	98
Gerber	90
Heinz	110
and apricots / Gerber	200
and apricots / Heinz	170
and cherries / Beech-Nut	120
w pineapple / Gerber	100
and raspberries / Beech-Nut	98
Apricots w tapioca / Beech-Nut	106
Apricots w tapioca / Gerber	160
Apricots w tapioca / Heinz	140
Banana dessert / Beech-Nut	136
Bananas w pineapple and tapioca /	
Beech-Nut	117
Bananas w pineapple and tapioca / Gerber	170
Bananas w tapioca / Gerber	150
Cottage cheese w pineapple / Gerber	210
Dutch apple dessert / Gerber	180
Fruit dessert / Gerber	160
Fruit dessert / Heinz	140
Fruit dessert w tapioca / Beech-Nut	106
Hawaiian delight / Gerber	200
Peach cobbler / Gerber	170
Peach melba / Beech-Nut	98
Peaches / Beech-Nut	96
Peaches / Gerber	170
Peaches / Heinz	200
Pears	
Beech-Nut	106
Gerber	110
Heinz	120
and pineapple / Beech-Nut	128
and pineapple / Gerber	110
and pineapple / Heinz	130

CALORIES

Pineapple-orange dessert / **Heinz**	150
Plums w tapioca / **Beech-Nut**	124
Plums w tapioca / **Gerber**	200
Prunes w tapioca / **Beech-Nut**	180
Prunes w tapioca / **Gerber**	180
Pudding	
Cherry vanilla / **Gerber**	170
Custard / **Heinz**	190
Custard, apple / **Beech-Nut**	150
Custard, chocolate / **Gerber**	210
Custard, vanilla / **Gerber**	210
Tropical fruit dessert / **Beech-Nut**	106
Tutti-frutti / **Heinz**	150

Main Dishes: 1 jar

Beef	
Beech-Nut	120
Beech-Nut High Meat Dinner	125
Gerber	100
and noodles / **Beech-Nut**	121
and noodles w vegetables / **Gerber**	120
and rice w tomato sauce / **Gerber**	
Toddler Meals	150
Stew / **Gerber** Toddler Meals	110
w vegetables / **Gerber**	
High Meat Dinner	100
Cereal and egg yolk / **Gerber**	110
Cereal, egg yolks and bacon / **Beech-Nut**	183
Cereal and eggs / **Heinz**	110
Chicken	
Beech-Nut	106
Beech-Nut High Meat Dinner	83
Gerber	150
Noodle / **Beech-Nut**	87
and noodles / **Gerber**	110
Stew / **Gerber** Toddler Meals	150
Sticks / **Gerber**	130
w vegetables / **Beech-Nut**	87
w vegetables / **Gerber**	130

CALORIES

Cottage cheese w bananas / **Heinz**	150
Ham / **Beech-Nut** High Meat Dinner	112
Ham / **Gerber**	120
Ham casserole w green beans and potatoes / **Gerber** Toddler Meals	140
Ham w vegetables / **Gerber** High Meat Dinner	100
Lamb / **Beech-Nut**	122
Lamb / **Gerber**	100
Lasagna, beef / **Gerber** Toddler Meals	140
Macaroni and beef / **Beech-Nut**	128
Macaroni and cheese / **Gerber**	130
Macaroni, tomato, beef / **Gerber**	110
Meat sticks / **Gerber**	130
Peas, split w ham / **Gerber**	150
Peas, split w vegetables and ham / **Beech-Nut**	145
Spaghetti, tomato sauce / **Beech-Nut**	128
Spaghetti w tomato sauce and beef / **Gerber**	140
Spaghetti and meatballs / **Gerber** Toddler Meals	130
Turkey	
Beech-Nut	106
Beech-Nut High Meat Dinner	111
Gerber	120
and rice w vegetables / **Beech-Nut**	85
and rice w vegetables / **Gerber**	110
Sticks / **Gerber**	130
w vegetables / **Gerber**	120
Veal	
Beech-Nut	112
Beech-Nut High Meat Dinner	90
Gerber	100
w vegetables / **Gerber**	100
Vegetables	
and bacon / **Beech-Nut**	134
and bacon / **Gerber**	170
and beef / **Beech-Nut**	115
and beef / **Gerber**	120

	CALORIES
and chicken / Gerber	110
and ham / Gerber	120
and lamb / Beech-Nut	113
and lamb / Gerber	110
and liver / Beech-Nut	87
and liver / Gerber	90
and turkey / Gerber	110
and turkey casserole / Gerber Toddler Meals	150

Vegetables: 1 jar

Beans, green / Beech-Nut	60
Beans, green, creamed / Gerber	80
Carrots / Beech-Nut	60
Carrots / Gerber	60
Carrots / Heinz	60
Corn, creamed / Gerber	120
Corn, creamed / Heinz	140
Mixed / Gerber	90
Peas, creamed / Heinz	130
Spinach, creamed / Gerber	100
Squash / Beech-Nut	47
Squash / Gerber	60
Sweet potatoes / Beech-Nut	117
Sweet potatoes / Gerber	140
Sweet potatoes / Heinz	130

Yogurt: 1 jar

w mixed fruit / Beech-Nut	124
w peach-apple / Beech-Nut	112
w pineapple / Beech-Nut	132

Baking Powder

	CALORIES
Canned, 1 tsp / Most brands	5

Beer, Ale, Malt Liquor

	CALORIES
12 fluid ounces	
Ale / Red Cap	160
Beer	
Andeker	160
Black Label	148
Budweiser	150
Busch	146
Coors	138
Goebel	145
Grenzquell	150
Hamms	138
Heidelberg	143
Michelob	163
Michelob Light	134
Miller's	150
Miller's Lite	96
Natural Light	110
Old Milwaukee	144
Olympia	140
Olympia Gold Light	70

	CALORIES
Pabst Blue Ribbon	150
Pabst Extra Light	70
Pabst Light	100
Rheingold	159
Schlitz (Regular)	148
Schlitz (Repeal)	121
Schlitz Light	96
Stag	151
Stroh Bock	157
Stroh Bohemian	148
Stroh Bohemian 3.2	126
Stroh Light	115
Stroh Light 3.2	115
Tuborg USA	148
Malt Liquor / **Budweiser**	160
Malt Liquor / **Schlitz**	175

Biscuits

	CALORIES
Refrigerator: 1 biscuit	
Ballard Oven Ready	50
Hungry Jack Butter Tastin	95
Hungry Jack Flaky	90
Merico	55
Merico Butter-Me-Not	90
Merico Texas Style	85
1869 Brand	105
Pillsbury Country Style	50
Pillsbury Prize	65
Baking powder / **1869 Brand**	105
Baking powder, prebaked / **1869 Brand**	100
Baking powder / **Tenderflake** Dinner	60

  CALORIES

Buttermilk
    Hungry Jack Extra Rich   65
    Hungry Jack Flaky   80
    Hungry Jack Fluffy   100
    1869 Brand   105
    Prebaked / **1869 Brand**   100
    Pillsbury   50
    Pillsbury Big Country   90
    Pillsbury Extra Lights   55
    Tenderflake Dinner   55
Corn bread / **Pillsbury**   95

Bread

                                          CALORIES

**1 slice unless noted: an average slice
weighs about one ounce**

Bran / **Brownberry**   75
Brown, plain, canned: ½-in slice / **B & M**   78
Brown, raisin, canned: ½-in slice / **B & M**   78
Cinnamon raisin / **Thomas'**   60
Corn and molasses / **Pepperidge Farm**   70
English muffin style / **Mrs. Wright's**   55
French
    Earth Grains / 1 oz   70
    Mrs. Wright's   65
    Pepperidge Farm   75
    Wonder   75
    Sourdough: 1 oz / **Earth Grains**   75
Garlic, frozen / **Stouffer's**   80
Gluten / **Thomas' Glutogen**   30
Gluten, frozen / **Thomas' Glutogen**   30
Grecian style w sesame seeds / **Mrs. Wright's**   95
Hollywood Light   70

	CALORIES
Hollywood Dark	70
Honey bran / **Pepperidge Farm**	58
Honey Wheatberry / **Arnold**	90
Honey Wheatberry / **Pepperidge Farm**	60
Italian: 1 oz / **Pepperidge Farm**	75
Italian / **Mrs. Wright's**	95
Meal	
Colonial Country / 6 oz	75
Kilpatrick's Country / 1 oz	75
Manor Country / 1 oz	75
Rainbo Country / 1 oz	75
Roman Meal	70
Naturél / **Arnold**	65
Nut / **Brownberry**	85
Oatmeal / **Brownberry**	80
Oatmeal / **Pepperidge Farm**	65
Profile Dark	75
Profile Light	75
Protein / **Thomas'** Protogen	45
Protein, frozen / **Thomas'** Protogen	55
Pumpernickel	
Arnold	75
Earth Grains / 1 oz	70
Pepperidge Farm Family	75
Pepperidge Farm Party	23
Raisin / **Arnold** Tea	75
Raisin / **Pepperidge Farm**	75
Raisin cinnamon / **Brownberry**	85
Raisin nut / **Brownberry**	95
Rye	
Arnold Melba Thin	50
Arnold Soft	75
Brownberry Extra Thin	65
Earth Grains Light / 1 oz	75
Earth Grains Party / 1 oz	75
Pepperidge Farm Family	80
Pepperidge Farm Party	18
Wonder	75

CALORIES

Jewish / **Pepperidge Farm**	85
Jewish, seeded / **Arnold**	75
Jewish, unseeded / **Arnold**	75
Seedless / **Pepperidge Farm**	80
Sourdough / **DiCarlo**	70
Vienna w poppy seeds / **Mrs. Wright's**	55
Wheat	
Arnold American Granary	70
Arnold Bran'nola	90
Arnold Brick Oven Whole Wheat	
(small family)	60
Arnold Brick Oven Whole Wheat 16 oz size	65
Arnold Brick Oven Whole Wheat 32 oz size	80
Arnold Melba Thin Whole Wheat	40
Brownberry	85
Brownberry Great Grains	70
Brownberry Sandwich Dark	75
Buckwheat	75
Colonial / 1 oz	75
Colonial Honey Grain / 1 oz	75
Earth Grains Berry / 1 oz	75
Earth Grains Earth / 1 oz	70
Earth Grains 100% Whole Wheat / 1 oz	70
Earth Grains Very Thin / 1 oz	80
Fresh Horizons	50
Home Pride Butter Top Wheat	75
Home Pride Wheatberry	70
Kilpatrick's / 1 oz	75
Kilpatrick's Honey Grain / 1 oz	75
Light Wheat Fiber	55
Manor / 1 oz	75
Manor Honey Grain / 1 oz	75
Mrs. Wright's Grain Belt	80
Pepperidge Farm 1½ lb	90
Pepperidge Farm Very Thin Whole Wheat	40
Pepperidge Farm Whole Wheat 1 lb	70
Pritikin 100% Whole Wheat	65
Rainbo / 1 oz	75

	CALORIES
Rainbo Honey Grain / 1 oz	75
Thomas' Whole Wheat	50
Wonder	75
Wonder Whole Wheat	70
Cracked wheat: 1 oz / **Earth Grains**	75
Cracked wheat / **Pepperidge Farm**	70
Cracked wheat / **Wonder**	75
Dark style / **Mrs. Wright's** Special Formula	50
Granola bran / **Mrs. Wright's**	75
Honey bran / **Mrs. Wright's**	85
Light style / **Mrs. Wright's** Special Formula	50
Sprouted wheat / **Pepperidge Farm**	65
Wheat germ / **Pepperidge Farm**	60

White

Arnold Brick Oven 16 oz size	65
Arnold Brick Oven 32 oz size	85
Arnold Brick Oven (small family)	65
Arnold Country	95
Arnold Hearthstone Country	70
Arnold Melba Thin	40
Brownberry Extra Thin	70
Brownberry Sandwich	75
Butternut	75
Colonial / 1 oz	75
Colonial Butter / 1 oz	75
Colonial Contour / 1 oz	75
Earth Grains Very Thin / 1 oz	80
Fresh Horizons	50
Hart's	75
Hearthstone	85
Hillbilly	70
Home Pride Butter Top White	75
Homestyle	75
Kilpatrick's / 1 oz	75
Kilpatrick's Butter / 1 oz	75
Kilpatrick's Contour / 1 oz	75
Light White Fiber	55
Manor / 1 oz	75
Manor Butter / 1 oz	75

Manor Contour / 1 oz	75
Millbrook	75
Mrs. Karl's	75
Mrs. Wright's	80
Mrs. Wright's Butter and Egg	75
Mrs. Wright's Low Sodium	50
Mrs. Wright's Sandwich Bread Country Style (thin sliced)	65
Ovenjoy 16 oz	65
Ovenjoy 22 oz	75
Ovenjoy 24 oz	80
Ovenjoy Sandwich Bread 22 oz size	60
Ovenjoy Sandwich Bread 24 oz size	65
Pepperidge Farm Family	75
Pepperidge Farm Sandwich	65
Pepperidge Farm Thin Sliced	75
Pepperidge Farm Toasting	85
Pepperidge Farm Unsliced / 1 oz	85
Pepperidge Farm Very Thin	40
Rainbo / 1 oz	75
Rainbo Butter / 1 oz	75
Rainbo Contour / 1 oz	75
Safeway 16 oz size	70
Safeway (thin sliced) 16 oz size	65
Safeway (thin sliced) 24 oz size	70
Sweetheart	75
Weber's	75
Weight Watchers	35
Wonder	75
Wonder Low Sodium	70
w buttermilk / **Mrs. Wright's**	80
w buttermilk / **Mrs. Wright's** Sandwich Bread (thin sliced)	65
w buttermilk / **Wonder**	75
Refrigerator, to bake / **Pillsbury** Hotloaf	90

BREAD CRUMBS

Bread crumbs: 1 cup / **Contadina**	411

BREAD MIXES

	CALORIES
Prepared: 1 loaf unless noted	
Applesauce spice / **Pillsbury**	1920
Apricot nut / **Pillsbury**	1760
Banana / **Pillsbury**	1920
Blueberry nut / **Pillsbury**	1760
Cherry nut / **Pillsbury**	1920
Corn: 1 pkg / **Aunt Jemima** Easy Mix	1320
Corn: 1 pkg / **Pillsbury**	1280
Cranberry / **Pillsbury**	1920
Date / **Pillsbury**	2080
Nut / **Pillsbury**	1920
Oatmeal raisin / **Pillsbury**	1920

BREADSTICKS

1 stick	
Stella D'Oro	40
Stella D'Oro Dietetic	43
Onion / **Stella D'Oro**	42
Sesame / **Stella D'Oro**	56
Sesame / **Stella D'Oro** Dietetic	57

STUFFING MIXES

Chicken & Herb: 1 oz / **Pepperidge Farm** Pan Style	110
Chicken-flavored, prepared w butter: ½ cup / **Stove Top**	170
Chicken-flavored, prepared: ½ cup cooked w butter / **Uncle Ben's** Stuff'n Such	198
Chicken-flavored, prepared: ½ cup cooked wo butter / **Uncle Ben's** Stuff'n Such	123
Corn bread: 1 oz / **Pepperidge Farm**	110
Corn bread, prepared w butter: ½ cup / **Stove Top**	170

CALORIES

Corn bread, prepared: ½ cup cooked w butter / **Uncle Ben's** Stuff'n Such	205
Corn bread, prepared: ½ cup cooked wo butter / **Uncle Ben's** Stuff'n Such	129
Cube: 1 oz / **Pepperidge Farm**	110
Pork-flavored, mix, prepared w butter: ½ cup / **Stove Top**	170
Sage, prepared: ½ cup cooked w butter / **Uncle Ben's** Stuff'n Such	198
Sage, prepared: ½ cup cooked wo butter / **Uncle Ben's** Stuff'n Such	124
Seasoned: 1 oz / **Pepperidge Farm**	110
Seasoned: 1 oz / **Pepperidge Farm** Pan Style	110
Seasoned white bread: 1 oz / **Mrs. Cubbinson's**	101
w rice, prepared w butter: ½ cup / **Stove Top**	180

CROUTONS

¼ cup unless noted

Artificial bacon / **Bel Air**	40
Caesar Salad / **Brownberry**	45
Cheddar cheese: 1 oz / **Pepperidge Farm**	130
Cheese / **Brownberry**	45
Cheese and garlic / **Bel Air**	50
Cheese-garlic: 1 oz / **Pepperidge Farm**	140
Croutettes: .7 oz dry mix / **Kellogg's**	70
Garlic / **Bel Air**	40
Italian cheese / **Bel Air**	50
Onion and garlic / **Brownberry**	45
Onion-garlic: 1 oz / **Pepperidge Farm**	140
Plain / **Bel Air**	30
Plain: 1 oz / **Pepperidge Farm**	140
Seasoned / **Bel Air**	45
Seasoned / **Brownberry**	45
Seasoned: 1 oz / **Pepperidge Farm**	140
Toasted / **Brownberry** "Buttery"	45

Butter and Margarine

CALORIES

Butter

Regular: ½ cup (¼ lb stick)	815
1 tbsp	100
Whipped: ½ cup	540
1 tbsp	65

Margarine

Imitation: 1 tbsp

Mazola diet	50
Mrs. Filbert's diet soft	50
Parkay diet	50
Weight Watchers	50

Regular and Soft: 1 tbsp

Blue Bonnet	100
Blue Bonnet Diet	50
Blue Bonnet Soft	100
Chiffon	100
Chiffon Soft	100
Coldbrook	100
Coldbrook Soft	100
Dalewood	100
Empress	100
Empress Soft	100
Fleischmann's	100
Fleischmann's Diet	50
Fleischmann's Parve	100
Fleischmann's Soft	100
Holiday	100

CALORIES

Mazola	100
Meadowlake	100
Mrs. Filbert's	100
Mrs. Filbert's Soft	100
Nucoa	100
Nucoa Soft	90
Parkay	100
Swift Allsweet	100

Spread: 1 tbsp

Blue Bonnet	80
Coldbrook	80
Fleischmann's	80
Mrs. Filbert's Spread 25	64
Parkay light	70

Whipped: 1 tbsp

Blue Bonnet Whipped stick and Soft	70
Chiffon Soft	70
Fleischmann's Soft	70
Mrs. Filbert's Soft	70

Cakes

FROZEN DESSERT CAKES

CALORIES

1 whole cake unless noted

Banana / **Pepperidge Farm**	1120
Banana / **Sara Lee**	1442
Banana nut, layer / **Sara Lee**	1864
Black Forest / **Sara Lee**	1624
Boston Creme / **Pepperidge Farm**	1080
Cheesecake	
Mrs. Smith's	1230
Cream cheese, small / **Sara Lee**	861
Cream cheese, large / **Sara Lee**	1440
Cream cheese, cherry / **Sara Lee**	1284
Cream cheese, French / **Sara Lee**	2192
Cream cheese, French, strawberry /	
Sara Lee	2064
Cream cheese, strawberry / **Sara Lee**	1284
Chocolate / **Pepperidge Farm**	1240
Chocolate / **Sara Lee**	1377
Chocolate Bavarian / **Sara Lee**	2280
Chocolate 'n Cream / **Sara Lee**	1672
Chocolate fudge / **Pepperidge Farm**	1800
Chocolate fudge / **Pepperidge Farm Half Cakes**	900
Chocolate, German / **Pepperidge Farm**	1600
Chocolate, German / **Sara Lee**	1229
Coconut / **Pepperidge Farm**	1800
Coconut / **Pepperidge Farm Half Cakes**	900
Crumbcake, blueberry / **Stouffer's**	210

CALORIES

Crumbcake, chocolate chip / **Stouffer's**	227
Crumbcake, French / **Sara Lee**	172
Crumbcake, French / **Stouffer's**	200
Cupcake, cream-filled / **Stouffer's**	240
Cupcake, yellow / **Stouffer's**	190
Devil's food / **Pepperidge Farm**	1800
Devil's food / **Sara Lee**	1496
Double chocolate, layer / **Sara Lee**	1712
Golden / **Pepperidge Farm** Half Cakes	900
Golden / **Sara Lee**	1442
Golden, layer / **Pepperidge Farm**	1800
Lemon Bavarian / **Sara Lee**	2176
Lemon coconut / **Pepperidge Farm**	1120
Mandarin orange / **Sara Lee**	1648
Orange / **Sara Lee**	1442
Pound cake	
Plain / **Sara Lee**	1320
Plain: 1 oz / **Stouffer's**	125
Apple nut / **Pepperidge Farm**	
Old Fashioned	1300
Banana nut / **Sara Lee**	1170
Butter / **Pepperidge Farm**	
Old Fashioned	1300
Carrot / **Pepperidge Farm**	
Old Fashioned	1600
Chocolate / **Pepperidge Farm**	
Old Fashioned	1300
Chocolate / **Sara Lee**	1220
Chocolate Swirl / **Sara Lee**	1300
Family size / **Sara Lee**	1905
Home style / **Sara Lee**	1090
Raisin / **Sara Lee**	1270
Cherry shortcake / **Mrs. Smith's**	2340
Strawberry 'n Cream / **Sara Lee**	1704
Strawberry shortcake / **Mrs. Smith's**	1830
Strawberry shortcake / **Sara Lee**	1544
Vanilla / **Pepperidge Farm**	1900
Walnut / **Sara Lee**	1688

MIXES

**Prepared according to package directions:
1 whole cake unless noted**

Angel food	
Betty Crocker	1560
Betty Crocker One-Step	1680
Duncan Hines	1680
Pillsbury	1680
Chocolate / **Betty Crocker**	1680
Confetti / **Betty Crocker**	1800
Lemon custard / **Betty Crocker**	1680
Raspberry / **Pillsbury**	1680
Strawberry / **Betty Crocker**	1800
Apple raisin / **Duncan Hines**	2280
Apple raisin, spicy / **Duncan Hines**	
Moist and Easy	1620
Applesauce raisin / **Betty Crocker**	
Snackin' Cake	1800
Banana / **Betty Crocker**	3240
Banana / **Duncan Hines** Supreme	2400
Banana / **Pillsbury Plus**	3120
Banana nut / **Duncan Hines** Moist and Easy	1800
Banana walnut / **Betty Crocker**	
Snackin' Cake	1800
Bundt cake	
Chocolate macaroon / **Pillsbury**	3960
Fudge nut crown / **Pillsbury**	3480
Lemon blueberry / **Pillsbury**	3360
Marble / **Pillsbury**	3960
Pound / **Pillsbury**	3720
Triple fudge / **Pillsbury**	3600
Butter / **Duncan Hines**	3240
Butter / **Pillsbury Plus**	2680
Butter brickle / **Betty Crocker**	3120
Butter fudge / **Duncan Hines**	3240
Butter pecan / **Betty Crocker**	3120
Cheesecake / **Pillsbury** No Bake	3120

	CALORIES
Cheesecake / **Jell-O**	2000
Cheesecake / **Royal**	1840
Cherry / **Duncan Hines**	2280
Cherry chip / **Betty Crocker**	2280
Chocolate / **Betty Crocker** Pudding Cake	1380
Chocolate / **Duncan Hines**	2400
Chocolate almond / **Betty Crocker** Snackin' Cake	1890
Chocolate chip / **Betty Crocker** Snackin' Cake	1980
Chocolate chip / **Duncan Hines**	1710
Chocolate chip, double / **Duncan Hines**	1620
Chocolate, dark / **Pillsbury Plus**	3120
Chocolate fudge / **Betty Crocker**	3240
Chocolate fudge / **Betty Crocker** Snackin' Cake	1980
Chocolate, German / **Betty Crocker**	3240
Chocolate, German / **Pillsbury Plus**	3120
Chocolate, milk / **Betty Crocker**	3120
Chocolate, sour cream / **Betty Crocker**	3240
Chocolate, sour cream / **Duncan Hines**	2400
Chocolate, Swiss / **Duncan Hines**	2400
Chocolate w chocolate frosting / **Betty Crocker** Stir n' Frost	1680
Coconut pecan / **Betty Crocker** Snackin' Cake	1980
Cupcake / **Flako**	150
Date nut / **Betty Crocker** Snackin' Cake	1890
Devil's food / **Betty Crocker**	3240
Devil's food / **Duncan Hines**	2400
Devil's food / **Pillsbury Plus**	3240
Fudge marble / **Duncan Hines**	2400
Fudge marble / **Pillsbury Plus**	3240
Gingerbread / **Betty Crocker**	1890
Gingerbread: 3-in square / **Pillsbury**	190
Lemon	
Betty Crocker	3240
Betty Crocker Pudding Cake	1380
Duncan Hines	2400
Pillsbury Plus	3240
w lemon frosting / **Betty Crocker** Stir n' Frost	1380

CALORIES

Lemon chiffon / **Betty Crocker**	2280
Marble / **Betty Crocker**	3360
Orange / **Betty Crocker**	3240
Orange / **Duncan Hines**	2400
Pineapple / **Duncan Hines**	2400
Pineapple upside-down w topping / **Betty Crocker**	2430
Pound / **Betty Crocker**	2280
Spice / **Betty Crocker**	3240
Spice / **Duncan Hines**	2400
Spice w vanilla frosting / **Betty Crocker** Stir n' Frost	1620
Spice raisin / **Betty Crocker** Snackin' Cake	1800
Strawberry / **Betty Crocker**	3240
Strawberry / **Duncan Hines**	2400
Strawberry / **Pillsbury**	3120
Streusel cake	
Cinnamon / **Pillsbury**	4080
Devil's food / **Pillsbury**	3960
Fudge marble / **Pillsbury**	4080
German chocolate / **Pillsbury**	3960
Lemon / **Pillsbury**	4200
White	
Betty Crocker	2400
Duncan Hines	2280
Pillsbury Plus	3000
Sour cream / **Betty Crocker**	2400
Yellow	
Betty Crocker	3240
Betty Crocker Butter Recipe	2880
Duncan Hines	2400
Pillsbury Plus	3120
w chocolate frosting / **Betty Crocker** Stir n' Frost	1380

COFFEE CAKES

CALORIES

1 whole cake

Almond, frozen / **Sara Lee**	1352
Almond, frozen / **Sara Lee** Coffee Ring	1106
Apple, frozen / **Sara Lee** Danish	1176
Apple cinnamon, mix, prepared / **Pillsbury**	1880
Blueberry, frozen / **Sara Lee** Coffee Ring	1080
Blueberry, frozen / **Sara Lee** Danish	1136
Butter pecan, mix, prepared / **Pillsbury**	2480
Butter streusel, frozen / **Sara Lee**	1393
Cherry, frozen / **Sara Lee** Danish	1050
Cinnamon streusel, mix, prepared / **Pillsbury**	2000
Cinnamon streusel, frozen / **Sara Lee**	1232
Coffee cake, mix, prepared / **Aunt Jemima** Easy Mix	1360
Maple crunch, frozen / **Sara Lee** Coffee Ring	1157
Pecan, small, frozen / **Sara Lee**	764
Pecan, large, frozen / **Sara Lee**	1320
Raspberry, frozen / **Sara Lee** Coffee Ring	1090
Sour cream, mix, prepared / **Pillsbury**	2160

SNACK CAKES

Big Wheels: 1 cake / **Hostess**	170
Brownie, small / **Hostess**	150
Brownie, large / **Hostess**	240
Choco-Diles: 1 cake / **Hostess**	250
Creamies, chocolate: 1 pkg / **Tastykake**	256
Creamies, spice: 1 pkg / **Tastykake**	272
Crumb cake: 1 cake / **Hostess**	130
Cupcakes	
Buttercream filled: 1 pkg / **Tastykake** Cup	240
Chocolate: 1 cake / **Hostess**	160
Chocolate: 3½ oz / **Rainbo**	350
Chocolate: 1 pkg / **Tastykake**	200
Chocolate, cream filled: 1 pkg / **Tastykake**	244
Orange: 1 cake / **Hostess**	150
Devil Dog's: 1 piece / **Drake's**	171

	CALORIES
Ding Dongs: 1 cake / **Hostess**	170
Donuts: 1 donut unless noted	
Hostess plain	110
Hostess Crunch	100
Hostess Enrobed	130
Cinnamon / **Hostess**	110
Powdered / **Hostess**	110
Sugar: 2½ oz / **Rainbo** Gem	310
Filled Twins: 3 oz / **Rainbo**	300
Funny Bones: 1¼ oz cake / **Drake's**	
Family Pkg	164
Ho Ho's: 1 cake / **Hostess**	120
Juniors, chocolate: 1 pkg / **Tastykake**	307
Juniors, coconut: 1 pkg / **Tastykake**	330
Juniors, Koffee Kake: 1 pkg / **Tastykake**	313
Juniors, lemon: 1 pkg / **Tastykake**	297
Koffee Kake, cream filled: 1 pkg / **Tastykake**	247
Krimpets, butterscotch: 1 pkg / **Tastykake**	192
Krimpets, jelly: 1 pkg / **Tastykake**	168
Krimpies, chocolate: 1 pkg / **Tastykake**	252
Krimpies, vanilla: 1 pkg / **Tastykake**	239
Macaroon, fudge: 1 cake / **Hostess**	210
Oatmeal cake, creme filled: 2 oz / **Frito-Lay**	257
Oatmeal raisin: 1 pkg / **Tastykake** Bars	267
Orange Treats: 1 pkg / **Tastykake**	229
Pound, marble: 1 cake / **Drake's**	186
Pound, plain: 1 cake / **Drake's**	181
Pound, raisin: 1 cake / **Drake's**	323
Ring Ding: 1 piece / **Drake's**	366
Ring Ding Jr: 1⅓ oz cake / **Drake's** Family Pkg	186
Sno Balls: 1 cake / **Hostess**	140
Suzy Q / **Hostess**	240
Suzy Q, chocolate: 1 cake / **Hostess**	225
Tandy Takes, chocolate: 1 pkg / **Tastykake**	181
Tandy Takes, peanut butter: 1 pkg / **Tastykake**	190
Tasty Klairs, chocolate: 1 pkg / **Tastykake**	435
Teens, chocolate: 1 pkg / **Tastykake**	225
Tempty, chocolate cream: 1 pkg / **Tastykake**	196

CALORIES

	CALORIES
Tempty, lemon: 1 pkg / **Tastykake**	259
Tiger Tails: 1 cake / **Hostess**	430
Twinkies: 1 cake / **Hostess**	140
Twinkies, devil's food: 1 cake / **Hostess**	140
Yankee Doodles: 1 cake / **Drake's**	125
Yodels: ⅞ oz cake / **Drake's**	134

Candy

CALORIES

	CALORIES
Breath candy: 1 piece	
Breath Savers, sugar free / **Life Savers**	7
Certs Clear	8
Certs Pressed	6
Chewels	10
Clorets Mints	6
Dentyne Dynamints	2
Trident Mints	8
Butter mints: 1 piece / **Kraft**	8
Butterscotch: 1 piece / **Rothchilds**	19
Caramels: 1 piece / **Kraft**	35
Caramel Nip: 1¾ oz / **Pearson**	220
Chocolate and chocolate-covered bars:	
1 oz unless noted	
Ghirardelli	150
w almonds / **Ghirardelli**	154
Hershey's	160
w almonds / **Hershey's**	160
Nestlé's	150
w almonds / **Nestlé's**	150
Baby Ruth: 1 bar	260
Butterfinger: 1 bar	220
Choco'Lite / **Nestlé's**	150
Choc-O-Roon: 2 oz / **Frito-Lay**	286

CALORIES

Chunky, regular	130
Chunky, pecan	130
Crisp / **Ghirardelli**	150
Crunch / **Nestlé's**	150
Forever Yours	128
Golden Almond / **Hershey's**	160
Kit Kat: 1.1 oz	160
Krackel	160
Marathon	132
Mars Almond	138
Milky Way	130
Mint / **Ghirardelli**	158
Mr. Goodbar: 1.3 oz	210
$100,000 / **Nestlé's**	140
Rally: 1.5 oz	210
Reggie: 1 bar	290
Snickers	130
Snik Snak Sticks	150
Special Dark Bar: 1.2 oz / **Hershey's**	190
3 Musketeers	123
Tootsie Roll	116
Chocolate and chocolate-covered bits	
Hershey-ets: 1.1 oz	140
Kisses: 1 oz / **Hershey's**	150
M & M's, plain: 1 oz	140
M & M's, peanut: 1 oz	144
Raisinets: 1 oz	115
Rolo: 1 piece	28
Chocolate Parfait: 1¾ oz / **Pearson**	240
Chocolate Toffee: 1 piece / **Rothchilds**	22
Coffee Nip: 1¾ oz / **Pearson**	220
Coffioca: 1¾ oz / **Pearson**	240
Cough drops: 1 drop / **Beech-Nut**	10
Cough drops: 1 drop / **Pine Bros.**	8
Good and Plenty: 1 box	136
Good 'n Fruity: 1 box	136
Hard candies	
Life Savers, all flavors: 1 drop	9

Life Savers Sugar Nothings, all flavors: 1 tablet	8
Licorice Nip: 1¾ oz / **Pearson**	220
Lollipops: 1 lollipop	
Fruit: .35 oz size / **Life Savers**	44
Fruit: .5 oz size / **Life Savers**	63
Swirled: .35 oz size / **Life Savers**	44
Swirled: .5 oz size / **Life Savers**	63
Vanilla: .35 oz size / **Life Savers**	44
Vanilla: .5 oz size / **Life Savers**	63
Marshmallow: 1 piece / **JETS**	24
Marshmallows, miniature: 12 pieces / **Kraft**	24
Mint: 1 drop / **Life Savers**	7
Mint Parfait: 1¾ oz / **Pearson**	240
Peanut Bar: 1 oz / **Munch**	150
Peanut Butter Bar: 1¾ oz / **Frito-Lay**	274
Peanut Butter Cup: 1 piece / **Reese's**	95
Peanut candy, canned: 1 oz / **Planters** Old Fashioned	140
Sour Bites: 1 tablet / **Life Savers**	4
Starburst Fruit Chews: 1 oz	114
Toffee: 1 piece / **Rothchilds** Creamy	22

DIETETIC CANDY

Chocolate bars	
Almond: ¾ oz bar / **Estee**	110
Almond: 1 section of 3 oz bar / **Estee**	37
Bittersweet: 1 section of 3 oz bar / **Estee**	38
Crunch: ⅝ oz bar / **Estee**	90
Crunch: 1 section of 2½ oz bar / **Estee**	30
Fruit and nut: 1 section of 3 oz pkg / **Estee**	37
Milk: ¾ oz bar / **Estee**	110
Milk: 1 section of 3 oz pkg / **Estee**	37
Chocolates, boxed: 1 piece	
Peanut butter cups / **Estee**	45
Raisins, chocolate covered / **Estee**	6
T.V. Mix / **Estee**	9
Estee-Ets, plain / 1 piece	6

CALORIES

Estee-Ets, peanut / 1 piece	7
Gum drops, fruit: 1 piece / **Estee**	3
Gum drops, licorice: 1 piece / **Estee**	3
Hard candies: 1 piece	
Assorted / **Estee**	12
Cough / **Estee**	12
Creme / **Estee**	12
Peppermint / **Estee**	12
Mint candies: 1 piece	
Assorted / **Estee** 5 Pak	4
Assorted fruit / **Estee** 5 Pak	4
Peppermint / **Estee**	4
Sour cherry / **Estee**	4
Sour lemon / **Estee**	4
Sour orange / **Estee**	4
Spearmint / **Estee**	4

Cereals

DRY READY-TO-SERVE

CALORIES

Measurements vary according to what
companies consider appropriate one-
serving sizes. The servings generally are
one ounce in weight.

All-bran: 1/3 cup / **Kellogg's**	70
Alpha-Bits: 1 cup / **Post**	110
Apple Jacks: 1 cup / **Kellogg's**	110
Boo Berry: 1 cup / **General Mills**	110
Bran, plain, added sugar, defatted	
wheat germ: 1/2 cup	90

Bran, plain, added sugar, malt extract:	
½ cup	75
Bran Buds: ⅓ cup / Kellogg's	70
Bran Chex: ⅔ cup / Ralston Purina	110
Bran Flakes 40%: ⅔ cup / Kellogg's	90
Bran Flakes 40%: ⅔ cup / Post	90
Buc Wheats: ¾ cup / General Mills	110
Cap'n Crunch: ¾ cup	121
Cap'n Crunch's Crunchberries: ¾ cup	120
Cap'n Crunch's Peanut Butter: ¾ cup	127
Cheerios: 1¼ cup / General Mills	110
Chocolate Crazy Cow: 1 cup / General Mills	110
Cocoa Krispies: ¾ cup / Kellogg's	110
Cocoa Pebbles: ⅞ cup / Post	120
Cocoa Puffs: 1 cup / General Mills	110
Concentrate: ⅓ cup / Kellogg's	110
Cookie Crisp, chocolate chip: 1 cup /	
Ralston Purina	110
Cookie Crisp, vanilla wafer: 1 cup /	
Ralston Purina	110
Corn Chex: 1 cup / Ralston Purina	110
Corn flakes: 1 cup / General Mills Country	110
Corn flakes: 1 cup / Kellogg's	110
Corn flakes: 1¼ cup / Post Toasties	110
Corn flakes: 1 cup / Ralston Purina	110
Corn flakes: 1 cup / Safeway	110
Corn flakes, sugar-coated: ⅔ cup /	
Kellogg's Frosted	110
Corn Total: 1 cup / General Mills	110
Corny-Snaps: 1 cup / Kellogg's	120
Count Chocula: 1 cup / General Mills	110
Country Morning: ⅓ cup / Kellogg's	130
Country Morning w raisins and dates:	
⅓ cup / Kellogg's	130
Cracklin' Bran: ⅓ cup / Kellogg's	110
Crispy Rice: 1 cup / Ralston Purina	110
Family Style: ½ cup / C.W. Post	140
Family Style w raisins: ½ cup / C.W. Post	130

CALORIES

Franken Berry: 1 cup / **General Mills**	110
Froot Loops: 1 cup / **Kellogg's**	110
Frosty O's: 1 cup / **General Mills**	110
Fruit Brute: 1 cup / **General Mills**	110
Fruity Pebbles: ⅞ cup / **Post**	120
Golden Grahams: 1 cup / **General Mills**	110
Grape-Nuts: ¼ cup / **Post**	110
Granola: 1 oz / **Nature Valley**	130
Granola w cinnamon and raisins: 1 oz / **Nature Valley**	130
Granola w coconut and honey: 1 oz / **Nature Valley**	130
Granola w fruit and nuts: 1 oz / **Nature Valley**	130
Grape-Nut Flakes: ⅞ cup / **Post**	100
Heartland, plain: 1 oz	120
Heartland, coconut: 1 oz	130
Heartland, raisin: 1 oz	120
Honeycomb: 1⅓ cup / **Post**	110
Kaboom: 1 cup / **General Mills**	110
King Vitaman: ¾ cup	120
Kix: 1½ cup / **General Mills**	110
Life: ⅔ cup	105
Lucky Charms: 1 cup / **General Mills**	110
Mini-Wheats: about 5 biscuits / **Kellogg's**	100
Mini-Wheats, frosted: about 4 biscuits / **Kellogg's**	110
Oat flakes, fortified: ⅔ cup / **Post**	110
Pep: ¾ cup / **Kellogg's**	100
Product 19: ¾ cup / **Kellogg's**	110
Quaker 100% Natural: ¼ cup	139
Quaker 100% Natural w apples and cinnamon: ¼ cup	135
Quaker 100% Natural w raisins and dates: ¼ cup	134
Quisp: 1⅙ cup	121
Raisin bran: ¾ cup / **Kellogg's**	120
Raisin bran: ½ cup / **Post**	90
Raisin bran: ½ cup / **Ralston Purina**	100

	CALORIES
Raisin bran: ½ cup / **Safeway**	100
Rice: 1 cup / **Safeway** Crispy Rice	110
Rice, frosted: 1 cup / **Kellogg's**	110
Rice, puffed: ½ oz / **Malt-O-Meal**	50
Rice, puffed: 1 cup / **Quaker**	55
Rice Chex: 1⅛ cup / **Ralston Purina**	110
Rice Krinkles, frosted: ⅞ cup / **Post**	110
Rice Krispies: 1 cup / **Kellogg's**	110
Safeway Tasteeos: 1¼ cup	110
Special K: 1¼ cup / **Kellogg's**	110
Strawberry Crazy Cow: 1 cup / **General Mills**	110
Sugar Corn Pops: 1 cup / **Kellogg's**	110
Sugar Frosted Flakes: ¾ cup / **Ralston Purina**	110
Sugar Smacks: ¾ cup / **Kellogg's**	110
Super Sugar Crisp: ⅞ cup / **Post**	110
Toasty O's: 1 oz	110
Total: 1 cup / **General Mills**	110
Trix: 1 cup / **General Mills**	110
Wheat, puffed: ½ oz / **Malt-O-Meal**	50
Wheat, puffed: 1 cup / **Quaker**	54
Wheat, shredded: 1 biscuit / **Quaker**	52
Wheat Chex: ⅔ cup / **Ralston Purina**	110
Wheaties: 1 cup / **General Mills**	110

TO BE COOKED

Measurements vary

Barley, pearled: ¼ cup uncooked (1 cup cooked) / **Quaker** Scotch Brand	172
Barley, pearled: ¼ cup uncooked (¾ cup cooked) / **Quaker** Scotch Brand Quick	172
Farina: 1 cup cooked / **H-O** Cream Enriched	120
Farina: ⅔ cup / **Pillsbury**	80
Farina: ⅔ cup prepared w milk and salt / **Pillsbury**	200
Farina: 1/6 cup uncooked / **Quaker** Hot 'n Creamy	101

CALORIES

Grits: ¼ cup uncooked / **Albers**	150
Grits: 1 packet / **Quaker** Instant Grits Product	79
Grits: 1/6 cup uncooked / **3-Minute Brand** Quick	100
Grits, hominy, white: 3 tbsp / **Aunt Jemima** Quick Enriched	101
Grits, hominy, white: 3 tbsp / **Aunt Jemima** Regular	101
Grits, hominy, white: 3 tbsp / **Quaker** Quick	101
Grits, hominy, white: 3 tbsp / **Quaker** Regular	101
Grits w artificial cheese flavor: 1 packet / **Quaker** Instant Grits Product	104
Grits w imitation bacon bits: 1 packet / **Quaker** Instant Grits Product	101
Grits w imitation ham bits: 1 packet / **Quaker** Instant Grits Product	99
Malt-O-Meal Chocolate: 1 oz uncooked (about ¾ cup cooked)	100
Malt-O-Meal Quick: 1 oz uncooked (about ¾ cup cooked)	100
Oats and oatmeal	
H-O Old Fashioned: ¾ cup cooked	140
H-O Quick: ¾ cup cooked	130
Harvest Quick: 1 oz uncooked	110
Quaker Old Fashioned: ⅓ cup uncooked	109
Quaker Quick: ⅓ cup uncooked	109
Ralston Purina: 1 oz uncooked	110
Ralston Purina Quick: 1 oz uncooked	110
Safeway Quick: ⅓ cup uncooked	100
3-Minute Brand Quick: 1 oz uncooked	110
Instant: 1 packet / **H-O**	105
Instant: ½ cup uncooked / **H-O**	130
Instant: ¾ cup cooked / **H-O** Regular	130
Instant: 1 packet / **H-O** Sweet and Mellow	150
Instant: 1 packet / **Quaker** Regular	105
Instant: 1 packet / **3-Minute Brand** Stir 'n Eat	110

	CALORIES
Instant w apple and brown sugar: 1 packet / **3-Minute Brand** Stir 'n Eat	120
Instant w apples and cinnamon: 1 packet / **Quaker**	134
Instant w bran and raisins: 1 packet / **Quaker**	153
Instant w cinnamon and spice: 1 packet / **Quaker**	176
Instant w maple and brown sugar: 1 packet / **H-O**	165
Instant w maple and brown sugar: 1 packet / **Quaker**	163
Instant w raisins and spice: 1 packet / **H-O**	165
Instant w raisins and spice: 1 packet / **Quaker**	159
Ralston: 1 oz uncooked / **Ralston Purina**	100
Ralston: 1 oz uncooked / **Ralston Purina** Instant	100
Rye: ¼ cup uncooked / **Con Agra** Cream of Rye	90
Whole wheat: ⅓ cup uncooked (⅔ cup cooked) / **Quaker** Pettijohns	100

Cheese

CALORIES

1 oz unless noted

American

	CALORIES
Pimento / **Borden**	105
Processed / **Borden**	105
Processed / **Borden** Made In Wisconsin	104

CALORIES

Processed: 1 slice / **Borden** Single Slices	67
Processed / **Kraft** Singles	90
Sliced: 1 slice / **Lucerne** 24 Single Slices	53
Sliced: 1 slice / **Safeway**	73
American-flavored, processed, single wrap slices / **Kraft** Light 'n Lively	60
Blue / **Borden Bleu**	105
Blue / **Casino**	100
Brick / **Casino**	110
Brick, slices / **Kraft**	110
Brie, Danish / **Tiny Dane**	100
Camembert / **Borden**	85
Cheddar / **Borden** Longhorn	113
Cheddar / **Borden** Wisconsin Old Fashioned	113
Cheddar / **Kraft** Cracker Barrel	110
Colby / **Borden**	111
Colby, low sodium / **Swift Pauly**	110
Farmer's	
Dutch Garden	100
Friendship	38
Wispride	100
Salt free / **Friendship**	38
Bulk: ½ cup / **Breakstone**	200
Midget: ½ cup / **Breakstone**	150
Fondue / **Swiss Knight**	60
Gouda / **Borden** Dutch Maid	86
Gruyere / **Borden**	101
Gruyere, plain / **Swiss Knight**	100
Liederkranz / **Borden**	86
Limburger / **Borden** Dutch Maid	97
Limburger / **Mohawk Valley**	100
Monterey Jack / **Borden**	103
Monterey Jack / **Casino**	100
Monterey Jack / **Kraft**	100
Mozzarella / **Borden**	96
Muenster, slices / **Kraft**	100
Pimento / **Borden** Made In Wisconsin	104
Pizza / **Borden**	85

	CALORIES
Provolone / **Borden**	93
Provolone, sharp / **Casino**	90
Provolone, slices / **Kraft**	90
Ricotta / **Borden**	42
Romano / **Casino**	110
Roquefort / **Borden**	105
Scamorze / **Kraft**	70
Skim milk cheese, low fat /	
Swift Pauly Slim Line	60
Swiss	
Natural / **Borden**	104
Natural / **Borden** Imported Switzerland	104
Natural / **Borden** Imported Finland	104
Natural / **Kraft**	100
Processed / **Borden**	101
Processed / **Borden** Made In Wisconsin	100

COTTAGE CHEESE

½ cup unless noted

Creamed	
Borden	121
Friendship / 4 oz	120
Lucerne	120
Meadow Gold	120
w chives / **Borden**	117
w chives / **Lucerne**	120
w fruit salad: 4 oz / **Friendship**	
Calorie Meter	120
w fruit salad / **Lucerne**	150
w pineapple / **Borden**	107
w pineapple: 4 oz / **Friendship**	140
w pineapple / **Lucerne**	150
w vegetable salad / **Borden**	119
w vegetable salad: 4 oz / **Friendship**	
Garden Salad	120
Dry cottage cheese	
Borden	100

	CALORIES
Lucerne	80
Pot style / **Breakstone**	110
Low-fat	
Borden Lite Line	90
Breakstone	90
Friendship Calorie Meter / 4 oz	100
Friendship Pot Style / 4 oz	100
Lucerne Lowfat	100
Viva Lowfat	100
Weight Watchers Lowfat	90
wo salt: 4 oz / **Friendship** Calorie Meter	90
Skim milk, large curd / **Breakstone**	90

CREAM AND NEUFCHATEL CHEESE

1 oz

Cream cheese	
Borden	105
Philadelphia Brand	100
Lucerne	100
w chives / **Borden**	96
w pimento / **Borden**	74
Imitation / **Philadelphia** Brand	50
Cream cheese, whipped	
Philadelphia Brand	100
w bacon and horseradish /	
Philadelphia Brand	90
w blue cheese / **Philadelphia** Brand	100
w chives / **Philadelphia** Brand	90
w onion / **Philadelphia** Brand	90
w pimento / **Philadelphia** Brand	90
w smoked salmon / **Philadelphia** Brand	90
Neufchatel cheese	
Calorie-wise	70
w bacon and horseradish / **Kraft**	70
w blue cheese / **Kraft**	70
w clams / **Kraft**	70
w dill pickles / **Kraft**	70
w garlic and onions / **Kraft**	70

CALORIES

w olive and pimento / **Borden**	81
w onions / **Kraft**	70
w pimento / **Borden**	82
w pineapple / **Kraft**	70
w relish / **Borden**	81

GRATED AND SHREDDED CHEESE

1 oz (= about ⅓ cup or about 5½ tbsp)

American, grated / **Borden**	30
Parmesan, grated / **Borden**	130
Parmesan, grated / **Kraft**	130
Parmesan, grated / **Lucerne**	110
Parmesan and Romano, grated / **Borden**	143
Romano / **Kraft**	130

CHEESE FOODS

1 oz unless noted

American	
Borden	92
Lucerne / 1 slice	60
Lucerne 10 Single Slices / 1 slice	72
Safeway / 1 slice	100
Swift Pauly	90
Blue / **Borden** Blue Brand	82
Blue / **Borden** Vera Blue	91
Blue / **Wispride** Cold Pack	100
Cheddar flavor / **Wispride** Cold Pack	100
Pimento	
Borden	91
Lucerne / 1 slice	60
Safeway / 1 slice	75
Swift Pauly	90
Sweet Munchee / **Swift Pauly**	100
Swiss	
Borden	91

	CALORIES
Lucerne 10 Single Slices / 1 slice	72
Swift Pauly	90
Wispride Cold Pack	100

CHEESE SPREADS

1 oz

American / **Borden**	85
American w bacon / **Borden**	
Cheese 'N Bacon	80
Blue / **Roka**	80
Cheddar flavor, processed / **Wispride**	80
Cheez Whiz	75
w garlic / **Borden**	82
Limburger / **Borden**	82
Smoke-flavored / **Borden**	80
Smoke-flavored / **Squeez-A-Snak**	83
Velveeta, processed / **Kraft**	80

WELSH RAREBIT

Canned: 1 cup / **Snow's**	384
Frozen: 5 oz / **Green Giant** Boil-in-Bag	
Toast Toppers	220
w sherry, canned: 1 cup / **Snow's**	324

Chewing Gum

	CALORIES
1 stick or piece	
Adams Sour	9
Beech-Nut	9
Beechies	6

Bubble
 Bubble Yum   27
 Bubblicious   25
 Care Free, all flavors   8
 Fruit Stripe   10
 Orbit   8
 Trident Stick   7
 Dietetic / **Estee**   3
Chiclets   6
Clorets   6
Dentyne   5
Freshen-Up   10
Fruit, dietetic / **Estee**   3
Fruit Stripe   9
Orbit, all flavors   8
Peppermint, dietetic / **Estee**   3
Spearmint, dietetic / **Estee**   3
Trident   5
Wrigley's, all flavors   10

Chinese Foods

Apple-cinnamon roll, frozen: 1 roll / **La Choy** 38
Bamboo shoots, canned: 8½ oz / **Chun King** 48
Bamboo shoots, canned: 8 oz / **La Choy** 23
Bean sprouts, canned: 16 oz / **Chun King** 80
Bean sprouts, canned: 1 cup / **La Choy** 23
Chop suey
 Beef, frozen: 32 oz / **Banquet**
  Buffet Supper   418
 Beef, frozen: 7 oz / **Banquet** Cookin' Bag 73
 Vegetables, canned: 1 cup / **La Choy** 53

CALORIES

Chow mein, canned: 1 cup unless noted

Beef / **La Choy**	72
Beef / **La Choy** Bi-Pack	83
Chicken / **La Choy**	68
Chicken / **La Choy** Bi-Pack	101
Chicken / **La Choy** 50 oz	93
Meatless / **La Choy**	47
Meatless / **La Choy** 50 oz	46
Mushroom / **La Choy** Bi-Pack	85
Pepper oriental / **La Choy**	89
Pepper oriental / **La Choy** Bi-Pack	89
Pork / **La Choy** Bi-Pack	120
Shrimp / **La Choy**	61
Shrimp / **La Choy** Bi-Pack	110
Vegetables: 16 oz can / **Chun King**	88

Chow mein, frozen

Beef: 1 cup / **La Choy**	97
Chicken: 32 oz / **Banquet** Buffet Supper	345
Chicken: 7 oz / **Banquet** Cookin' Bag	89
Chicken: 1 cup / **La Choy**	108
Chicken wo noodles: 9 oz / **Green Giant** Boil-in-Bag	130
Shrimp: 1 cup / **La Choy**	73

Egg rolls, chicken, frozen: 1 roll / **La Choy**	30
Egg rolls, lobster, frozen: 1 roll / **La Choy**	27
Fried rice, chicken, canned: 1 cup / **La Choy**	418
Fried rice, Chinese style, canned: 1 cup / **La Choy**	414
Fried rice and pork, frozen: 1 cup / **La Choy**	216

Noodles, canned: 1 cup

Chow mein / **La Choy**	306
Ramen-beef / **La Choy**	225
Ramen-chicken / **La Choy**	202
Ramen-oriental / **La Choy**	207
Rice / **La Choy**	260
Wide chow mein / **La Choy**	298

Pea pods, frozen: 1 pkg / **La Choy**	90
Pepper oriental, frozen: 1 cup / **La Choy**	110

CALORIES

Sweet and sour pork, frozen: 1 cup / **La Choy**	245
Vegetables, mixed Chinese, canned:	
1 cup / **La Choy**	35
Water chestnuts, canned: 8½ oz / **Chun King**	119
Won ton, frozen: 1 cup / **La Choy**	92

Chips, Crisps and Similar Snacks

CALORIES

1 oz unless noted

Cheddar Bitz / Frito-Lay	129
Cheese Doodles / **Old London**	133
Cheese Pixies / **Wise**	158
Chee.tos / Frito-Lay	160
Cheez Balls / **Planters**	160
Cheez Curls / **Planters**	160
Corn chips	
Fritos	156
Granny Goose	157
Old London	150
Old London Dipsy Doodles	150
Planters	170
Wise	166
Barbecue-flavored / **Fritos**	150
Barbecue-flavored / **Wise**	160
Corn Nuggets, toasted: 1⅜ oz / **Frito-Lay**	176
Fiesta chips / **Granny Goose**	147
Funyuns	138
Jalapeno Corn Toots / **Granny Goose**	161

CALORIES

Munchos / Frito-Lay	154
Onion-flavored rings / **Old London**	136
Onion-flavored rings / **Wise**	126
Potato chips	
Frito-Lay	158
Frito-Lay Natural Style	157
Frito-Lay Ruffles	155
Granny Goose	161
Planters Stackable	150
Pringles	150
Pringles Country Style	160
Pringles Extra Rippled	150
Wise	160
Wise Ridgies	160
Barbecue-flavored / **Granny Goose**	159
Barbecue-flavored / **Frito-Lay**	157
Barbecue-flavored / **Wise**	160
Green onion-flavored / **Granny Goose**	160
Onion-garlic-flavored / **Wise**	160
Sour cream-and-onion-flavored / **Frito-Lay**	155
Potato sticks, canned: 1½ oz / **O & C**	231
Potato sticks / **Wise** Julienne	136
Puffs-Crunchy, cheese-flavored / **Chee.tos**	156
Rinds, fried	
Bacon / **Wise** Bakon Delites	166
Bacon, barbecue-flavored / **Wise**	
Bakon Delites	160
Pork / **Baken-Ets**	140
Pork / **Granny Goose**	152
Snack Sticks	
Lightly salted / **Pepperidge Farm**	120
Pumpernickel / **Pepperidge Farm**	110
Sesame / **Pepperidge Farm**	120
Whole wheat / **Pepperidge Farm**	110
Taco chips / **Old London**	129
Tortilla chips	
Doritos	137
Granny Goose	139

	CALORIES
Planters Nacho	130
Planter Taco	130
Nacho cheese flavor / **Doritos**	141
Taco flavor / **Doritos**	142
Wheat chips, imitation bacon-flavored / **Bakon-snacks**	150

Chocolate and Chips

For Baking: 1 oz unless noted

	CALORIES
Chips	
Butterscotch-flavored / **Nestlé's** Morsels	150
Chocolate: ¼ cup / **Hershey's**	230
Chocolate / **Nestlé's** Morsels	150
Chocolate-flavored / **Baker's**	130
Chocolate, semi-sweet / **Ghirardelli**	150
Chocolate, semi-sweet / **Hershey's**	150
Chocolate, semi-sweet / **Hershey's Mini**	150
Chocolate, semi-sweet / **Nestlé's** Morsels	150
Peanut butter-flavored / **Reese's**	150
Choco-bake / **Nestlé's**	170
Chocolate / **Ghirardelli** Eagle Bar	151
Chocolate, ground / **Ghirardelli**	163
Chocolate, solid	
Ghirardelli Milk Chocolate Blocks	150
Hershey's	190
German's sweet / **Baker's**	140
Semi-sweet / **Baker's**	130
Unswt / **Baker's**	140

Cocktails

ALCOHOLIC

	CALORIES
Canned: 2 fl oz	
Apricot Sour / Party Tyme	66
Banana Daiquiri / Party Tyme	66
Daiquiri / Party Tyme	65
Gimlet / Party Tyme	82
Gin and Tonic / Party Tyme	55
Mai Tai / Party Tyme	65
Manhattan / Party Tyme	74
Margarita / Party Tyme	66
Martini / Party Tyme	82
Pina Colada / Party Tyme	63
Rum and Cola / Party Tyme	55
Scotch Sour / Party Tyme	65
Screwdriver / Party Tyme	69
Tom Collins / Party Tyme	58
Vodka Martini / Party Tyme	72
Vodka Tonic / Party Tyme	55

NONALCOHOLIC MIXES

Dry: 1 packet	
Alexander / Holland House	69
Banana Daiquiri / Holland House	66
Bloody Mary / Holland House	56
Daiquiri / Holland House	69
Gimlet / Holland House	69
Grasshopper / Holland House	69

	CALORIES
Mai Tai / Holland House	69
Margarita / Holland House	69
Mint Julep / Holland House	67
Pina Colada / Holland House	66
Pink Squirrel / Holland House	69
Screwdriver / Holland House	69
Strawberry Margarita / Holland House	62
Strawberry Sting / Holland House	74
Tequilla Sunrise / Holland House	63
Tom Collins / Holland House	69
Vodka Sour / Holland House	65
Wallbanger / Holland House	65
Whiskey Sour / Holland House	69

Liquid: 1 fl oz unless noted

Amaretto / Holland House	79
Apricot Sour / Holland House	48
Black Russian / Holland House	92
Blackberry Sour / Holland House	50
Bloody Mary / Holland House Regular	10
Bloody Mary / Holland House Extra Tangy	10
Bloody Mary / Holland House Smooth 'n Spicy	6
Cocktail Host / Holland House	47
Collins Mixer: 8 fl oz / Canada Dry	80
Cream of Coconut / Holland House Coco Casa	117
Daiquiri / Holland House	51
Dry Martini / Holland House	10
Gimlet / Holland House	40
Mai Tai / Holland House	33
Manhattan / Holland House	29
Margarita / Holland House	39
Old Fashioned / Holland House	36
Pina Colada / Holland House	60
Strawberry Sting / Holland House	35
Tom Collins / Holland House	67
Whiskey Sour: 8 fl oz / Canada Dry	90
Whiskey Sour / Holland House	55
Whiskey Sour / Holland House Low Calorie	9

Cocoa

	CALORIES
Coca: 1 oz / **Hershey's**	120
Cocoa: 1 tbsp / **Marvel**	30
Cocoa, chocolate flavor: ¾ oz / **Nestlé's**	70
Cocoa	
Mix: 1 oz / **Hershey's**	110
Mix: 3 tbsp / **Hershey's** Instant	80
Mix: 3 tbsp, prepared w 8 oz milk /	
Hershey's Instant	240
Mix: 1 oz / **Nestlé's**	110
Mix: 1 oz / **Ovaltine**	120
Mix: .69 oz / **Ovaltine** Reduced Calorie	80
Mix, all flavors, instant: 1 oz / **Carnation**	112

Coconut

	CALORIES
Fresh	
In shell: 1 coconut	1373
Meat: 1 piece (2 x 2 x ½ in)	156
Meat, shredded or grated: 1 cup	277
Cream, (liquid from grated meat): 1 cup	815
Milk, (liquid from mixture of grated	
meat and water): 1 cup	605
Water, (liquid from coconuts): 1 cup	53

Canned or packaged: ¼ cup
    Plain / **Baker's** Angel Flake   90
    Plain / **Baker's** Premium Shred   100
    Plain / **Baker's** Southern Style   90
    Plain, shredded / **Durkee**   70
    Cookie-coconut / **Baker's**   140

Coffee

	CALORIES
All coffee has about	
2 calories per cup for ground roasted	
4 calories per cup for instant and	
instant freeze-dried	
Chase & Sanborn: 1 cup	2
Decaf Instant: 1 tsp	4
General Foods International: 6 fl oz	
Cafe Francais, swtd, prepared	60
Cafe Vienna, swtd, prepared	60
Orange Cappuccino, swtd, prepared	60
Suisse Mocha, swtd, prepared	60
Nescafé Instant: 1 tsp	4
Nescafé Instant, freeze-dried,	
decaffeinated: 1 tsp	4
Postum (cereal beverage), instant: 6 fl oz	10
Taster's Choice Instant, freeze-dried: 1 tsp	4
Taster's Choice Instant, freeze dried,	
decaffeinated: 1 tsp	4

Condiments

	CALORIES
A.1 Sauce / 1 tbsp	12
Catsup: 1 tbsp / **Del Monte**	15
Catsup: 1 tbsp / **Tillie Lewis**	20
Chili sauce: 1 tbsp / **Heinz**	17
Chutney: 1 tbsp / **Major Grey's**	53
Horseradish: 1 tbsp	2
Cream style	5
Oil style	10
Horseradish, raw: ¼ lb	70
Hot sauce: 1 tsp / **Frank's**	12
Mustard, prepared	
Brown: 1 tbsp / **French's Brown 'n Spicy**	15
Brown: 1 tsp / **Mr. Mustard**	11
Cream salad: 1 tbsp / **French's**	10
Dijon: 1 tsp / **Grey Poupon**	5
w horseradish: 1 tbsp / **French's**	15
w onion: 1 tbsp / **French's**	25
Yellow: 1 tbsp / **French's** Medford	16
Sauce Diable: 1 tbsp / **Escoffier**	20
Sauce Robert: 1 tbsp / **Escoffier**	19
Seafood cocktail: ¼ cup / **Del Monte**	70
Seafood cocktail: 2 oz / **Pfeiffer**	100
Soy sauce: 1 tbsp / **La Choy**	8
Steak sauce: 1 tbsp / **Steak Supreme**	20
Taco sauce: 1 tbsp / **Ortega**	21
Taco sauce: 1 oz / **Old El Paso**	8
Tartar sauce: 1 tbsp	
Best Foods	70
Hellmann's	70
Seven Seas	80

	CALORIES
Tartar sauce, mix: 1 pkg / **Lawry's**	64
Vinegar: 1 fl oz	
Champagne / **Regina**	1
Red wine / **Regina**	1
Red wine w garlic / **Regina**	1
Wine, cooking	
Marsala: 1 fl oz / **Holland House**	35
Red: 1 fl oz / **Holland House**	25
Sauterne: ¼ cup / **Regina**	2
Sherry: 1 fl oz / **Holland House**	40
Sherry: ¼ cup / **Regina**	19
White: 1 fl oz / **Holland House**	25
Worcestershire: 1 tbsp / **French's**	10
Worcestershire, hickory smoke-flavored:	
1 tbsp / **French's** Smoky	10

See also Sauces, Seasonings

Cookies

	CALORIES
1 piece as packaged unless noted	
Adelaide / **Pepperidge Farm**	53
Angel puffs / **Stella D'Oro** Dietetic	17
Angelica Goodies / **Stella D'Oro**	100
Anginetti / **Stella D'Oro**	28
Animal crackers	
Keebler	12
Sunshine	10
Iced / **Sunshine**	26
Barnum's Animals / **Nabisco**	12
Anisette sponge / **Stella D'Oro**	50
Anisette toast / **Stella D'Oro**	46

CALORIES

Applesauce / **Sunshine**	86
Applesauce, iced / **Sunshine**	86
Arrowroot / **Sunshine**	16
Assortment	
Stella D'Oro Hostess with the Mostest	39
Stella D'Oro Lady Stella	37
Aunt Sally, iced / **Sunshine**	96
Big Treat / **Sunshine**	153
Biscos / **Nabisco**	44
Bordeaux / **Pepperidge Farm**	37
Breakfast Treats / **Stella D'Oro**	100
Brown sugar / **Pepperidge Farm**	50
Brussels / **Pepperidge Farm**	57
Butter-flavored / **Nabisco**	23
Butter-flavored / **Sunshine**	23
Buttercup / **Keebler**	24
Cameo creme sandwich / **Nabisco**	68
Capri / **Pepperidge Farm**	85
Chessman / **Pepperidge Farm**	43
Chinese dessert cookies / **Stella D'Oro**	170
Chip-A-Roos / **Sunshine**	63
Chocolate brownie / **Pepperidge Farm**	57
Chocolate chip	
Estee Dietetic	30
Keebler Old Fashioned	80
Keebler Rich 'n Chips	73
Pepperidge Farm	43
Chocolate chip coconut / **Sunshine**	80
Chocolate fudge sandwich / **Sunshine**	72
Chocolate-strawberry wafers, dietetic, single serving	
pkg: 1 pkg / **Estee**	90
Cinnamon sugar / **Pepperidge Farm**	53
Cinnamon toast / **Sunshine**	13
Coconut Bar / **Keebler**	62
Coconut Bar / **Sunshine**	47
Coconut cookies / **Stella D'Oro** Dietetic	47
Coconut Chocolate Drop / **Keebler**	75
Coconut macaroons / **Nabisco**	87

CALORIES

Como Delight / **Stella D'Oro**	150
Cream Lunch / **Sunshine**	45
Crescents, almond-flavored / **Nabisco**	34
Cup Custard, chocolate / **Sunshine**	70
Cup Custard, vanilla / **Sunshine**	71
Danish Wedding / **Keebler**	31
Date-Nut Granola / **Pepperidge Farm**	53
Devilsfood / **Keebler**	64
Dixie Vanilla / **Sunshine**	60
Egg biscuits	
Stella D'Oro	42
Stella D'Oro Dietetic	40
Anise / **Stella D'Oro** Roman	131
Rum and brandy / **Stella D'Oro** Roman	131
Sugared / **Stella D'Oro**	60
Vanilla / **Stella D'Oro** Roman	131
Egg Jumbo / **Stella D'Oro**	43
Fig bar: 2 oz / **Frito-Lay**	189
Fig bar / **Keebler**	71
Fig bar / **Sunshine**	45
French vanilla creme / **Keebler**	93
Fudge Chip / **Pepperidge Farm**	57
Fudge Stick / **Keebler**	42
Fudge Stripes / **Keebler**	57
German chocolate / **Keebler**	85
Ginger snap	
Keebler	24
Nabisco	29
Sunshine	24
Gingerman / **Pepperidge Farm**	33
Golden bars / **Stella D'Oro**	110
Golden Fruit / **Sunshine**	61
Graham crackers	
Sunshine Sweet-Tooth	45
Chocolate-covered / **Keebler** Deluxe	42
Cinnamon: smallest piece when broken on	
score line / **Keebler** Crisp	17
Crumbs: 1 bag / **Sunshine**	420

Honey: smallest piece when broken on score line / **Keebler**	17
Honey / **Nabisco** Honey Maid	30
Honey: 1 entire piece / **Sunshine**	60
Hydrox / **Sunshine**	48
Hydrox, mint / **Sunshine**	48
Hydrox, vanilla / **Sunshine**	50
Irish oatmeal / **Pepperidge Farm**	50
Keebies / **Keebler**	51
Kichel / **Stella D'Oro** Dietetic	8
Krisp Kreem, chocolate / **Keebler**	32
Krisp Kreem, strawberry / **Keebler**	31
Krisp Kreem, vanilla / **Keebler**	31
Lady Joan / **Sunshine**	47
Lady Joan, iced / **Sunshine**	42
LaLanne Sesame / **Sunshine**	15
LaLanne Soya / **Sunshine**	16
Lemon / **Sunshine**	76
Lemon Coolers / **Sunshine**	29
Lemon nut crunch / **Pepperidge Farm**	60
Lemon Thins, dietetic / **Estee**	25
Lido / **Pepperidge Farm**	95
Love Cookies / **Stella D'Oro** Dietetic	110
Mallopuffs / **Sunshine**	63
Mandel toast / **Stella D'Oro**	54
Margherite combination / **Stella D'Oro**	73
Margherite, vanilla / **Stella D'Oro**	73
Marigold sandwich / **Keebler**	91
Milano / **Pepperidge Farm**	63
Mint Milano / **Pepperidge Farm**	70
Molasses crisps / **Pepperidge Farm**	30
Molasses and spice / **Sunshine**	67
Nassau / **Pepperidge Farm**	75
'Nilla wafers / **Nabisco**	18
Nutter Butter / **Nabisco**	69
Oatmeal	
Sunshine	58
Almond / **Pepperidge Farm**	53

Iced / **Keebler** Old Fashioned	81
Iced / **Sunshine**	69
Marmalade / **Pepperidge Farm**	53
Peanut butter / **Sunshine**	79
Raisin / **Nabisco**	77
Raisin / **Pepperidge Farm**	57
Raisin, dietetic / **Estee**	30
Opera Creme Sandwich / **Keebler**	82
Orbit Creme Sandwich / **Sunshine**	51
Oreo / **Nabisco**	50
Orleans / **Pepperidge Farm**	33
Peanut / **Pepperidge Farm**	47
Peanut butter / **Keebler** Old Fashioned	81
Peanut butter wafers / **Sunshine**	33
Peanut creme patties / **Nabisco**	34
Pecan Sandies / **Keebler**	85
Penguin / **Keebler**	93
Penguin, peanut butter / **Keebler**	91
Pfeffernusse / **Stella D'Oro** Spice Drops	44
Pirouette / **Pepperidge Farm**	40
Pirouette, chocolate-laced / **Pepperidge Farm**	40
Pitter Patter / **Keebler**	84
Raisin bar, iced / **Keebler**	80
Raisin Bran / **Pepperidge Farm**	53
Raisin fruit biscuit / **Nabisco**	56
Royal Nuggets / **Stella D'Oro** Dietetic	1
St. Moritz / **Pepperidge Farm**	47
Sandwich	
Estee Dietetic	50
Assortment / **Nabisco** Pride	55
Creme, Swiss / **Nabisco**	52
Creme, chocolate fudge / **Keebler**	99
Creme, lemon / **Keebler**	80
Creme, vanilla / **Keebler**	82
Lemon / **Estee** Dietetic	60
Scotties / **Sunshine**	39
Sesame cookies / **Stella D'Oro** Regina	49
Sesame cookies / **Stella D'Oro** Regina Dietetic	43

CALORIES

Shortbread / **Pepperidge Farm**	65
Shortbread, almond / **Keebler** Spiced Windmill	61
Shortbread, pecan / **Nabisco**	77
Social Tea Biscuit / **Nabisco**	21
Social Tea Sandwich / **Nabisco**	51
Sorrento cookies / **Stella D'Oro**	57
Sprinkles / **Sunshine**	57
Sugar / **Keebler** Old Fashioned	78
Sugar / **Pepperidge Farm**	53
Sugar / **Sunshine**	86
Sugar Rings / **Nabisco**	68
Sunflower Raisin / **Pepperidge Farm**	53
Swedish Kremes / **Keebler**	98
Swiss Fudge / **Stella D'Oro**	64
Tahiti / **Pepperidge Farm**	85
Taste of Vienna / **Stella D'Oro**	85
Toy Cookies / **Sunshine**	13
Vanilla snaps / **Nabisco**	13
Vanilla thins, dietetic / **Estee**	25
Vienna Finger sandwich / **Sunshine**	71
Wafers	
Assorted, dietetic / **Estee**	35
Brown edge / **Nabisco**	28
Chocolate, dietetic / **Estee**	25
Peanut butter-chocolate, dietetic / **Estee**	90
Spiced / **Nabisco**	40
Sugar / **Biscos**	18
Sugar / **Sunshine**	43
Sugar, lemon / **Sunshine**	44
Vanilla / **Keebler**	19
Vanilla / **Sunshine**	15
Vanilla, dietetic / **Estee**	25
Yum Yums / **Sunshine**	83
Zanzibar / **Pepperidge Farm**	37
Zuzu Ginger Snaps / **Nabisco**	16

COOKIE MIXES AND DOUGH

CALORIES

Bar, date, mix, prepared: 1/32 pkg / **Betty Crocker**	60
Bar, Vienna, mix, prepared: 1/24 pkg/ **Betty Crocker**	90
Brownies	
Chocolate chip butterscotch, mix, prepared: 1/16 pkg / **Betty Crocker**	130
Fudge, mix, prepared: 1/24 pkg / **Betty Crocker** Family Size	130
Fudge, mix, prepared: 1/16 pkg / **Betty Crocker** Regular Size	120
Fudge, mix, prepared: 1/24 pkg / **Betty Crocker** Supreme	120
Fudge, mix, prepared: 1 brownie / **Duncan Hines** Double Fudge	140
Fudge, mix, prepared: 1½-in square / **Pillsbury**	65
Fudge, mix, prepared: 1½-in square / **Pillsbury** Family Size	70
Fudge, refrigerator, to bake: 1/16 pkg / **Pillsbury**	110
German chocolate, mix, prepared: 1/16 pkg / **Betty Crocker**	150
Walnut, mix, prepared: 1/16 pkg / **Betty Crocker**	140
Walnut, mix, prepared: 1/24 pkg / **Betty Crocker** Family Size	140
Walnut, mix, prepared: 1½-in square / **Pillsbury**	75
Walnut, mix, prepared: 1½-in square / **Pillsbury** Family Size	75
Butterscotch nut, refrigerator, to bake: 1/36 pkg / **Pillsbury**	53
Chocolate chip, mix, prepared: 1/36 pkg / **Betty Crocker** Big Batch	75
Chocolate chip, refrigerated: 1 cookie / **Merico**	55

Chocolate chip, refrigerator, to bake: 1/36 pkg / **Pillsbury**	53
Fudge, refrigerator, to bake: 1/30 pkg / **Pillsbury**	83
Fudge chip, mix, prepared: 1 cookie / **Quaker**	75
Ginger, refrigerator, to bake: 1/36 pkg / **Pillsbury** Spicy	53
Macaroon, coconut, mix, prepared: 1/24 pkg / **Betty Crocker**	80
Oatmeal, mix, prepared: 1/36 pkg / **Betty Crocker** Big Batch	70
Oatmeal, mix, prepared: 1 cookie / **Quaker**	65
Oatmeal chocolate chip, refrigerator, to bake: 1/36 pkg / **Pillsbury**	56
Oatmeal raisin, refrigerator, to bake: 1/36 pkg / **Pillsbury**	60
Peanut butter, mix, prepared: 1/36 pkg / **Betty Crocker** Big Batch	70
Peanut butter, mix, prepared: 1 cookie / **Quaker**	75
Peanut butter, refrigerator: 1 cookie / **Merico**	60
Peanut butter, refrigerator, to bake: 1/36 pkg / **Pillsbury**	53
Sugar, mix, prepared: 1/36 pkg / **Betty Crocker** Big Batch	65
Sugar, mix, prepared: 1 cookie / **Quaker**	80
Sugar, refrigerator: 1 cookie / **Merico**	50
Sugar, refrigerator, to bake: 1/36 pkg / **Pillsbury**	63

Corn Starch

	CALORIES
1 tbsp	
Argo	35
Duryea's	35
Kingsford's	35

Crackers

	CALORIES
1 cracker unless noted	
Butter-Flavor Thins / **Keebler**	17
Cheese filled: 1½ oz / **Frito-Lay**	203
Cheese Peanut Butter Snax / **Keebler**	14
Cheez-Its: 1 piece / **Sunshine**	6
Che-zo / **Keebler**	5
Club: smallest piece when broken on score line / **Keebler**	15
Flings Curls / **Nabisco**	10
Gold Fish	
Cheddar cheese: 1 oz / **Pepperidge Farm**	140
Lightly salted: 1 oz / **Pepperidge Farm**	140
Parmesan cheese: 1 oz / **Pepperidge Farm**	140
Pizza: 1 oz / **Pepperidge Farm**	140
Pretzel: 1 oz / **Pepperidge Farm**	120
Sesame-garlic: 1 oz / **Pepperidge Farm**	140

	CALORIES
Taco: 1 oz / **Pepperidge Farm**	140
Thins, cheddar cheese: 4 thins / **Pepperidge Farm**	70
Thins, lightly salted: 4 thins / **Pepperidge Farm**	70
Thins, rye: 4 thins / **Pepperidge Farm**	70
Thins, wheat: 4 thins / **Pepperidge Farm**	70
Hi-Ho / **Sunshine**	18
Kavli Flatbread: 1 wafer	35
Matzos: 1 sheet or 1 cracker	
American / **Manischewitz**	122
Egg Matzo / **Manischewitz**	132
Egg 'n' Onion / **Manischewitz**	113
Onion Tams / **Manischewitz**	13
Regular Matzo / **Manischewitz**	109
Tam Tams / **Manischewitz**	14
Tasteas / **Manischewitz**	116
Thin Tea / **Manischewitz**	111
Thins / **Manischewitz**	90
Whole Wheat / **Manischewitz**	124
Melba Toast: 1 piece	
Garlic rounds / **Old London**	9
Onion rounds / **Old London**	10
Pumpernickel / **Old London**	17
Rye, salted / **Old London**	17
Rye, unsalted / **Old London**	18
Sesame, rounds / **Old London**	10
Wheat, salted / **Old London**	17
Wheat, unsalted / **Old London**	18
White / **Old London**	17
White, unsalted / **Old London**	17
White rounds, salted / **Old London**	9
Mixed Suites, green onion: 1 oz / **Pepperidge Farm**	140
Mixed Suites, pretzel-cheese: 1 oz / **Pepperidge Farm**	130
Mixed Suites, sesame-cheese: 1 oz / **Pepperidge Farm**	140

Oyster / **Keebler** Crax	3
Oyster / **Keebler** Zesta Crax	2
Oyster / **Sunshine**	3
Peanut butter: 1½ oz / **Frito-Lay**	214
Ritz / **Nabisco**	16
Ritz Cheeze / **Nabisco**	17
Ry Krisp: 1 triple cracker	23
Ry Krisp, seasoned: 1 triple cracker	26
Saltines and soda crackers	
Export soda: smallest piece when broken on score line / **Keebler**	25
Krispy / **Sunshine**	11
Milk Lunch Biscuit / **Keebler**	27
Premium / **Nabisco**	12
Premium, unsalted tops / **Nabisco**	12
Royal Lunch / **Nabisco**	54
Sea toast / **Keebler**	62
Sunshine	20
Uneeda, unsalted / **Nabisco**	22
Waldorf, low sodium / **Keebler**	16
Zesta / **Keebler**	12
Zesta, unsalted / **Keebler**	14
Shapies, cheese-flavored / **Nabisco**	9
Shapies, cheese-flavored shells / **Nabisco**	10
Sip 'N Chips, cheese-flavored / **Nabisco**	9
Sociables / **Nabisco**	10
Toast	
Bacon / **Keebler**	15
Cheese / **Keebler**	16
Onion / **Keebler**	18
Rye: smallest piece when broken on score line / **Keebler**	17
Sesame / **Keebler**	16
Wheat / **Keebler**	16
Town House / **Keebler**	18
Triangle Thins / **Nabisco**	8
Triscuit / **Nabisco**	21
Twigs / **Nabisco**	14

CALORIES

Waverly Wafers / **Nabisco**	18
Wheat Thins / **Nabisco**	9
Zweiback / **Nabisco**	31

Cream

CALORIES

Half and half (cream and milk, 11.7% fat)

1 cup	324
1 tbsp	20

Light, coffee or table (20.6% fat)

1 cup	506
1 tbsp	32

Light whipping (31.3% fat)

1 cup (about 2 cups whipped)	717
1 tbsp	45

Heavy whipping (37.6% fat)

1 cup (about 2 cups whipped)	838
1 tbsp	53
whipping, in aerosol can: 1 whipped oz / **Lucerne** Real Cream Topping	20

NON-DAIRY CREAMERS

Dry

Carnation Coffee-Mate / 1 packet	17
Coffee Tone / 1 tsp	12
Cremora / 1 tsp	12

Liquid

Coffee Tone Freezer Pack / 1 tbsp	20
Lucerne Cereal Blend / ½ cup	150
Powdered: 1 tsp / **Pet**	10

SOUR CREAM

	CALORIES
Lucerne / 2 tbsp	59
1 cup	475
Lucerne, half and half / 2 tbsp	42
1 cup	335
Sealtest / 2 tbsp	57
1 cup	456
Sealtest, half and half / 2 tbsp	41
1 cup	328
Imitation sour cream / **Borden's** Zest 2 tbsp	49
1 cup	388
Imitation sour cream / **Pet** 1 tbsp	25

Dessert Mixes

	CALORIES
Apple cinnamon, prepared: ⅔ cup / **Pillsbury Appleasy**	200
Apple caramel, prepared: ½ cup / **Pillsbury Appleasy**	160
Apple raisin, prepared: ⅔ cup / **Pillsbury Appleasy**	215

Diet Bars

	CALORIES
All flavors: 1 bar / **Pillsbury** Figurines	137
All flavors: 1 stick / **Pillsbury** Food Sticks	45
Cinnamon: 1 bar / **Carnation** Slender Bars	137
Chocolate: 1 bar / **Carnation** Slender Bars	137
Vanilla: 1 bar / **Carnation** Slender Bars	137

Dinners

FROZEN DINNERS

	CALORIES
Beans and beef patties: 11 oz / Swanson "TV"	500
Beans w franks: 10¾ oz / Banquet	591
Beans w franks: 10¾ oz / Morton	530
Beans w franks: 11¼ oz / Swanson "TV"	550
Beef	
Banquet / 11 oz	312
La Choy	342
Morton / 10 oz	270
Swanson 3 Course / 15 oz	490
Swanson "TV" / 11½ oz	370
Beef, chopped: 11 oz / Banquet	443
Beef, chopped: 11 oz / Morton	340
Beef, sirloin, chopped: 10 oz / Swanson "TV"	460
Beef, sliced: 14 oz / Morton Country Table	540
Beef, sliced: 17 oz / Swanson Hungry-Man	540
Beef steak, chopped: 18 oz / Swanson Hungry-Man	730
Beef tenderloin: 9½ oz / Morton Steak House Dinner	920
Chicken / La Choy	354
Chicken, boneless: 10 oz / Morton	240
Chicken, boneless: 19 oz / Swanson Hungry-Man	730
Chicken breast: 15 oz / Weight Watchers	330
Chicken croquette: 10¼ oz / Morton	410
Chicken, fried	
Banquet / 11 oz	530
Banquet Man Pleaser / 17 oz	1026

CALORIES

Morton / 11 oz	470
Morton Country Table / 15 oz	710
Swanson Hungry-Man / 12 oz	620
Swanson Hungry-Man / 15¾ oz	910
Swanson Hungry-Man Barbecue-flavored / 16 ½ oz	760
Swanson 3 Course / 15 oz	630
Swanson "TV" / 11½ oz	570
Barbecue-flavored: 12 oz / **Swanson** Hungry-Man	550
Barbecue-flavored: 11¼ oz / **Swanson** "TV"	530
Crispy fried: 10¾ oz / **Swanson** "TV"	650
w whipped potatoes: 7 oz / **Swanson** "TV"	360
Chicken w dumplings: 12 oz / **Banquet**	282
Chicken w dumplings: 11 oz / **Morton**	280
Chicken w noodles: 12 oz / **Banquet**	374
Chicken w noodles: 10¼ oz / **Morton**	260
Chicken oriental style: 16 oz / **Weight Watchers**	320
Chop suey, beef: 12 oz / **Banquet**	282
Chow mein, chicken: 12 oz / **Banquet**	282
Enchilada / **El Chico**	680
Enchilada, beef: 12 oz / **Banquet**	479
Enchilada, beef: 15 oz / **Swanson** "TV"	570
Enchilada, cheese: 12 oz / **Banquet**	459
Fish: 8¾ oz / **Banquet**	382
Fish: 9 oz / **Morton**	270
Fish 'n' Chips: 15¾ oz / **Swanson** Hungry-Man	760
Fish 'n' Chips: 10¼ oz / **Swanson** "TV"	450
Flounder: 16 oz / **Weight Watchers**	240
German style: 11¾ oz / **Swanson** "TV"	430
Haddock: 8¾ oz / **Banquet**	419
Haddock: 16 oz / **Weight Watchers**	250
Ham: 10 oz / **Banquet**	369
Ham: 10 oz / **Morton**	440
Ham: 10¼ oz / **Swanson** "TV"	380

	CALORIES
Hash, corned beef: 10 oz / **Banquet**	372
Italian style: 11 oz / **Banquet**	446
Italian style: 13 oz / **Swanson "TV"**	420
Lasagna and meat: 17¾ oz / **Swanson Hungry-Man**	740
Macaroni and beef: 12 oz / **Banquet**	394
Macaroni and beef: 10 oz / **Morton**	260
Macaroni and beef: 12 oz / **Swanson "TV"**	400
Macaroni and cheese: 12 oz / **Banquet**	326
Macaroni and cheese: 11 oz / **Morton**	320
Macaroni and cheese: 12½ oz / **Swanson "TV"**	390
Meat loaf: 11 oz / **Banquet**	412
Meat loaf: 11 oz / **Morton**	340
Meat loaf: 15 oz / **Morton** Country Table	480
Meat loaf: 10¾ oz / **Swanson "TV"**	530
Meatballs: 11¾ oz / **Swanson "TV"**	400
Mexican style: 16 oz / **Banquet**	608
Mexican style combination: 12 oz / **Banquet**	571
Mexican / **El Chico**	820
Mexican style combination: 16 oz / **Swanson "TV"**	600
Noodles and chicken: 10¼ oz / **Swanson "TV"**	390
Pepper oriental / **La Choy**	349
Perch, ocean: 8¾ oz / **Banquet**	434
Perch, ocean: 16 oz / **Weight Watchers**	320
Polynesian style: 13 oz / **Swanson "TV"**	490
Pork, loin of: 11¼ oz / **Swanson "TV"**	470
Queso / **El Chico**	810
Rib eye: 9 oz / **Morton** Steak House Dinner	820
Salisbury steak	
Banquet / 11 oz	390
Morton / 11 oz	290
Morton Country Table / 15 oz	430
Swanson Hungry-Man / 17 oz	870
Swanson 3 Course / 16 oz	490
Swanson "TV" / 11½ oz	500
Saltillo / **El Chico**	790

CALORIES

Shrimp / **La Choy**	325
Sirloin, chopped: 9½ oz / **Morton** Steak House Dinner	760
Sirloin strip: 9½ oz / **Morton** Steak House Dinner	920
Sole: 16 oz / **Weight Watchers**	240
Spaghetti and meatballs: 11½ oz / **Banquet**	450
Spaghetti and meatballs: 11 oz / **Morton**	360
Spaghetti and meatballs: 18½ oz / **Swanson** Hungry-Man	660
Spaghetti and meatballs: 12½ oz / **Swanson** "TV"	410
Swiss steak: 10 oz / **Swanson** "TV"	350
Turbot: 16 oz / **Weight Watchers**	490
Turkey	
Banquet / 11 oz	293
Banquet Man Pleaser / 19 oz	620
Morton / 11 oz	350
Morton Country Table / 15 oz	600
Swanson Hungry-Man / 19 oz	740
Swanson 3 Course / 16 oz	520
Swanson "TV" / 11½ oz	360
Breast: 10 oz / **Weight Watchers**	400
Veal Parmagian: 11 oz / **Banquet**	421
Veal Parmigiana: 10¼ oz / **Morton**	330
Veal Parmigiana: 20½ oz / **Swanson** Hungry-Man	910
Veal Parmigiana: 12¼ oz / **Swanson** "TV"	520
Western: 11 oz / **Banquet**	417
Western Round-Up: 11¾ oz / **Morton**	410
Western style: 17¾ oz / **Swanson** Hungry-Man	890
Western style: 11¾ oz / **Swanson** "TV"	460

DINNER MIXES

Ann Page Beef Noodle Dinner / 1/5 prepared dinner	330

CALORIES

Ann Page Cheeseburger Macaroni Dinner / 1/5 prepared dinner	360
Ann Page Chili Tomato Dinner / 1.6 oz before preparation	150
Ann Page Hash Dinner / 1/5 prepared dinner	300
Ann Page Italian Style Dinner / 2 oz before preparation	210
Ann Page Potato Stroganoff Dinner / 1/5 prepared dinner	320
Dinner Mexicana, Taco Casserole: 1 pkg before preparation / **McCormick**	655
Dinner Mexicana, Taco Casserole: 1 pkg before preparation / **Schilling**	655
Dinner Mexicana, Tamale Pie: 1 pkg before preparation / **McCormick**	860
Dinner Mexicana, Tamale Pie: 1 pkg before preparation / **Schilling**	860
Hamburger Helper: 1/5 prepared dinner	
Beef Noodle / **Betty Crocker**	320
Beef Romanoff / **Betty Crocker**	340
Cheeseburger Macaroni / **Betty Crocker**	360
Chili Tomato / **Betty Crocker**	330
Hamburger Hash / **Betty Crocker**	300
Hamburger Pizza Dish / **Betty Crocker**	340
Hamburger Stew / **Betty Crocker**	290
Lasagne / **Betty Crocker**	330
Potato Stroganoff / **Betty Crocker**	330
Rice Oriental / **Betty Crocker** (6½ oz pkg)	300
Rice Oriental / **Betty Crocker** (8 oz pkg)	340
Spaghetti / **Betty Crocker**	330
Tuna Helper: 1/5 prepared dinner	
Dumplings and noodles / **Betty Crocker**	230
Noodles / **Betty Crocker**	280
Noodles w cheese sauce / **Betty Crocker**	230

Dips

CALORIES

(Ready to serve unless noted)

	CALORIES
Bacon and horseradish: 1 oz	
Borden	79
Kraft Ready	71
Kraft Teez	57
Lucerne	63
Bacon and smoke flavor: 1 oz / **Sealtest** Dip 'n Dressing	47
Barbecue: 1 oz / **Borden's** Western Bar BQ	48
Bean, chili / **Lucerne**	51
Bean, Jalapeno: 1 oz	
Fritos	36
Gebhardt	30
Granny Goose	37
Lucerne	36
Blue cheese: 1 oz	
Granny Goose Chip-Dip	108
Kraft Ready	69
Kraft Teez	51
Lucerne Bleu Tang	67
Sealtest Dip 'n Dressing	49
Casino Dip 'n Dressing: 1 oz / **Sealtest**	44
Chipped beef: 1 oz / **Sealtest** Dip 'n Dressing	46
Clam: 1 oz	
Kraft Ready	66
Kraft Teez	45
Lucerne	34
and lobster / **Borden**	60
Dill pickle: 1 oz / **Kraft** Ready	67
Garden Spice: 1 oz / **Borden**	66
Garlic: 1 oz / **Granny Goose** Chip-Dip	101
Garlic: 1 oz / **Kraft** Teez	47
Garlic: 1 oz / **Lucerne**	58
Green chili: 1 oz / **Borden**	55

CALORIES

Green Goddess: 1 oz / **Kraft** Teez	46
Green onion: 1 oz / **Granny Goose** Chip-Dip	105
Green onion, mix: ½ oz pkg / **Lawry's**	50
Guacamole: 1 oz / **Lucerne**	83
Guacamole, mix: ½ oz pkg / **Lawry's**	60
Hickory-smoke flavor: 1 oz / **Lucerne**	60
Onion: 1 oz unless noted	
Borden	48
Kraft Ready	68
French / **Kraft** Teez	43
French / **Lucerne**	58
French / **Sealtest** Dip 'n Dressing	47
and garlic / **Sealtest** Dip 'n Dressing	46
mix: ½ oz pkg / **Lawry's**	48
Tasty Tartar: 1 oz / **Borden**	48

E_{ggs}

	CALORIES
Chicken egg	
Raw, hard-cooked or poached	
Extra large	94
Large	82
Medium	72
Raw, white only	
Extra large	19
Large	17
Medium	15
1 cup	124
Raw, yolk only	
Extra large	66
Large	59
Medium	52
Fried	
Extra large	112
Large	99
Medium	86
Scrambled	
Extra large	126
Large	111
Medium	97
Duck, raw: 1 egg	134
Goose, raw: 1 egg	266
Turkey, raw: 1 egg	135

EGG MIXES AND SEASONINGS

Egg, imitation, frozen: ¼ cup / **Morningstar Farms** Scramblers	64

CALORIES

Egg, imitation, mix: ½ pkg / **Eggstra**	50
Egg, imitation, refrigerated: ¼ cup /	
No-Fat **Egg Beaters**	40
Omelet, prepared: 1 pkg / **Durkee** Puffy	604
Omelet, dry mix: 1 pkg / **Durkee** Puffy	112
Omelet, bacon, prepared: 1 pkg / **Durkee**	620
Omelet, bacon, dry mix: 1 pkg / **Durkee**	128
Omelet, cheese, prepared: 1 pkg / **Durkee**	617
Omelet, cheese, dry mix: 1 pkg / **Durkee**	125
Omelet, cheese: 1¼ oz pkg / **McCormick**	130
Omelet, cheese: 1¼ oz pkg / **Schilling**	130
Omelet, Western: 1 pkg prepared w	
water only / **Durkee**	170
Omelet, Western: 1 pkg prepared w eggs /	
Durkee	604
Omelet, Western, dry mix: 1 pkg / **Durkee**	110
Omelet, Western: 1¼ oz pkg / **McCormick**	115
Omelet, Western: 1¼ oz pkg / **Schilling**	115
Scrambled: 1 pkg / **Durkee**	124
Scrambled w bacon: 1 pkg / **Durkee**	181

Fish and Seafood

FRESH

	CALORIES
Abalone, raw: 3½ oz	98
Abalone, canned: 3½ oz	80
Bass, black sea, raw, whole: 1 lb	165
Bass, striped, raw: 4 oz	120
Bass, striped, oven fried: 1 oz	56
Bass, white, raw: 4 oz	110
Bluefish	
Baked or broiled: 1 fillet (3½″ x 3″ x ½″)	200
Baked or broiled w butter or margarine: 1 oz	180
Fried: 1 fillet (3½″ x 3″ x ½″)	310
Catfish, raw, meat only: 3½ oz	103
Caviar, sturgeon, granular: 1 tbsp	42
Caviar, sturgeon, pressed: 1 tbsp	54
Clams, hard or round, raw, meat only: 1 pint (1 lb)	363
Clams, 4 cherrystone or 5 little neck clams	56
Clams, soft, raw, meat only: 1 pint (1 lb)	345
Cod, raw: 4 oz	90
Cod, broiled: 4 oz	195
Crab, cooked, pieces: 1 cup	144
Crab, cooked, flaked: 1 cup	116
Crayfish, freshwater, raw, meat only: 3½ oz	72
Eel, raw: 4 oz	183
Flounder, raw, whole: 1 lb	120
Flounder, raw: 4 oz	90
Frog legs, raw, meat only: 3½ oz	73

CALORIES

Haddock, raw: 4 oz	90
Haddock, fried: 3½ oz	165
Halibut, raw: 4 oz	115
Halibut, steak, broiled (4″ x 3″ x ½″)	255
Lobster, northern, cooked pieces: 1 cup	138
Lobster, whole, steamed, meat only: 3½ oz	95
Mackerel, Atlantic, whole, raw: 1 lb	470
Mackerel, Atlantic, raw: 4 oz	220
Oysters, raw	
Eastern: 1 cup (13-19 Selects) or (27-44 Standards)	158
Pacific and Western: 1 cup (about 4-6 medium) or (6-9 small)	218
Cooked, fried: 4 Select (medium)	108
Perch, ocean, Atlantic (redfish), raw, meat only: 3½ oz	88
Perch, ocean, Pacific, raw, meat only: 3½ oz	95
Pike, northern, raw, meat only: 3½ oz	88
Pompano, raw, meat only: 4 oz	188
Rockfish, oven steamed: 4 oz	120
Roe, carp, cod, haddock, shad: 3½ oz	130
Salmon	
Fresh, raw Atlantic: 4 oz	245
Fresh, raw Chinook: 4 oz	251
Fresh, raw Pink: 4 oz	134
Broiled or baked w butter or margarine: 1 oz	52
Smoked: 1 oz	50
Shad, raw: 4 oz	192
Shad, baked w butter or margarine: 1 lb	912
Scallops, bay and sea, raw: 4 oz	92
Scallops, bay and sea, steamed: 4 oz	127
Shrimp, raw, peeled: 4 oz	103
Shrimp, french fried: 1 oz	64
Snails, raw: 1 oz	26
Sole, raw: 4 oz	90
Squid, raw, edible portion only: 3½ oz	84
Sturgeon, cooked, steamed: 1 oz	45
Sturgeon, smoked: 1 oz	42

CALORIES

Swordfish, raw: 4 oz	135
Swordfish, broiled w butter or margarine: 3½ oz	174
Turbot, raw: 4 oz	165
Turtle, green, raw, meat only: 3½ oz	89
Whitefish, raw: 4 oz	175
Whitefish, smoked: 4 oz	175

CANNED AND FROZEN

Clams
Chopped or minced, canned: 6 oz can, drained / **Doxsee**	84
Chopped or minced, canned: 8 oz can, drained / **Doxsee**	112
Chopped or minced, canned: 10½ oz can, drained / **Doxsee**	147
Chopped or minced, canned: ½ cup / **Snow's**	60
Fried, frozen: 5 oz / **Howard Johnson's**	395
Fried, frozen: 2½ oz / **Mrs. Paul's**	270
Cakes, frozen: 1 cake / **Mrs. Paul's** Thins	155
Deviled, frozen: 1 cake / **Mrs. Paul's**	180
Sticks, frozen: 1 stick / **Mrs. Paul's**	48
In cocktail sauce: 4 oz jar / **Sau-Sea**	99

Crab
Canned: 6½ oz can / **Gold Seal** Fancy	185
Canned: 7½ oz can / **Icy Point**	215
Canned: 7½ oz can / **Pillar Rock**	215
King, in cocktail sauce: 4 oz jar / **Sau-Sea**	107
King, frozen: 8 oz / **Ship Ahoy**	211
King, frozen: 6 oz / **Wakefield's**	158
Cakes, frozen: 1 cake / **Mrs. Paul's** Thins	160
Deviled, frozen: 1 cake / **Mrs. Paul's**	160
Deviled, frozen: 3½ oz / **Mrs. Paul's** Miniatures	220

Fish, frozen
Cakes: 1 cake / **Mrs. Paul's**	105
Cakes: 1 cake / **Mrs. Paul's** Beach Haven	110
Cakes: 1 cake / **Mrs. Paul's** Thins	160

Fillets, buttered: 1 fillet (2½ oz) /
  Mrs. Paul's   155
Fillets, fried: 1 fillet (2 oz) /
  Mrs. Paul's   110
Fillets, in light batter: 1 fillet /
  Mrs. Paul's   140
Fillets, in light batter, fried: 1 fillet /
  Mrs. Paul's Supreme   220
In light batter: 3 oz / Mrs. Paul's
  Miniatures   150
Sticks: 1 stick / Mrs. Paul's   37
Sticks, in light batter, fried: 1 stick /
  Mrs. Paul's   57
Flounder, fried, frozen: 1 fillet (2 oz) /
  Mrs. Paul's   110
Flounder w lemon butter, frozen: 4½ oz /
  Mrs. Paul's   150
Gefilte fish, canned or in jars:
  1 piece unless noted
  Manischewitz (4 piece, 12 oz jar)   53
  Manischewitz (8 piece, 24 oz jar)   53
  Manischewitz (24 piece, 4 lb jar)   48
  Manischewitz, sweet (4 piece, 12 oz jar)   65
  Manischewitz, sweet (8 piece, 24 oz jar)   65
  Manischewitz, sweet (24 piece, 4 lb jar)   59
  Mother's (4 piece, 12 oz jar)   41
  Mother's (4 piece, 1 lb jar)   55
  Mother's (5 piece, 27 oz jar)   74
  Mother's (6 piece, 15 oz jar), unsalted   34
  Mother's (6 piece, 1 lb jar)   37
  Mother's (6 piece, 24 oz jar)   55
  Mother's (8 piece, 24 oz jar)   41
  Mother's (8 piece, 2 lb jar)   55
  Mother's (12 piece, 2 lb jar)   37
  Rokeach (in liquid broth): 1 oz   14
  Rokeach Old Vienna (in jellied broth): 1 oz   19
  Fishlets, 24 oz jar / Manischewitz   8

Whitefish and pike, 4 piece, 12 oz jar / **Manischewitz**	49
Whitefish and pike, 8 piece, 24 oz jar / **Manischewitz**	49
Whitefish and pike, 24 piece, 4 lb jar / **Manischewitz**	44
Whitefish and pike, sweet, 4 piece, 12 oz jar / **Manischewitz**	64
Whitefish and pike, sweet, 8 piece, 24 oz jar / **Manischewitz**	64
Whitefish and pike, sweet, 24 piece, 4 lb jar / **Manischewitz**	58
Haddock, fried, frozen: 1 fillet (2 oz) / **Mrs. Paul's**	115
Herring, in jars	
Pickled: 6 oz jar, drained / **Vita** Bismark	238
Pickled: 8½ oz jar / **Vita** Cocktail	365
Pickled: 8¾ oz jar / **Vita** Lunch	372
Pickled: 8¾ oz jar, drained / **Vita** Matjes	220
Pickled: 8¾ oz jar, drained / **Vita** Party Snacks	345
Pickled: 8¾ oz jar, drained / **Vita** Tastee Bits	283
Pickled, in cream sauce, 8⅓ oz jar / **Vita**	407
Oysters wo shell, canned: ½ cup / **Bumblebee**	86
Perch, fried, frozen: 1 fillet (2 oz) / **Mrs. Paul's**	125
Salmon, canned	
Blueback: 3¾ oz can / **Icy Point**	181
Blueback: 7¾ oz can / **Icy Point**	376
Coho steak: 3¾ oz can / **Icy Point**	162
Pink: 7¾ oz / **Del Monte**	310
Red: 1 lb can / **Icy Point**	775
Red: 3¾ oz can / **Pillar Rock**	181
Red: 7¾ oz can / **Pillar Rock**	376
Red: 1 lb can / **Pillar Rock**	775
Red sockeye: ½ cup / **Bumblebee**	143
Red sockeye: 7¾ oz / **Del Monte**	340

	CALORIES
Sardines, in mustard sauce: 1 oz / **Underwood**	52
Sardines, in soya bean oil: 1 oz / **Underwood**	62
Sardines, in tomato sauce, canned:	
7½ oz / **Del Monte**	330
Sardines, in tomato sauce: 1 oz / **Underwood**	45
Scallops, fried, frozen: 3½ oz / **Mrs. Paul's**	210
Scallops, in light batter, fried, frozen: 3½ oz /	
Mrs. Paul's	200
Seafood, combination, fried, frozen: 9 oz /	
Mrs. Paul's Platter	510
Seafood croquettes, frozen: 1 cake / **Mrs. Paul's**	180
Shrimp	
Baby, solids and liquids: 4½ oz can /	
Bumblebee	90
Fancy, tiny: 4½ oz can, drained /	
Icy Point	148
Fancy, tiny: 4½ oz can, drained /	
Pillar Rock	148
Fried, frozen: 3 oz / **Mrs. Paul's**	170
Fried, frozen: 4 oz / **Sau-Sea**	
Shrimp Fries	240
Frozen, in bag, cooked: 2 oz / **Sau-Sea**	36
Cakes, frozen: 1 cake / **Mrs. Paul's**	150
Cakes, frozen: 1 cake / **Mrs. Paul's Thins**	155
Sticks, frozen: 1 stick / **Mrs. Paul's**	47
In cocktail sauce: 4 oz jar / **Sau-Sea**	
Shrimp Cocktail	107
Sole w lemon butter, frozen: 4½ oz /	
Mrs. Paul's	160
Tuna, canned	
In oil, drained:	
½ cup / **Bumblebee**	167
In water, undrained:	
1 cup / **Bumblebee**	300
Light, chunk, in oil, drained:	
6½ oz / **Del Monte**	450
Light, chunk, in oil:	
3¼ oz can / **Chicken of The Sea**	224
drained	192

CALORIES

Light, chunk, in oil:
6½ oz can / **Chicken of The Sea**	447
drained	384

Light, chunk in oil:
9¼ oz can / **Chicken of The Sea**	636
drained	543

Light, chunk, in oil:
12½ oz can / **Chicken of The Sea**	860
drained	738

Light, chunk, in oil:
5 oz can drained / **Gold Seal**	278

Light, chunk, in oil:
5 oz can drained / **Icy Point**	278

Light, chunk, in oil:
5 oz can drained / **Pillar Rock**	278

Light, chunk, in oil:
5 oz can drained / **Snow Mist**	278

Light, grated, in oil:
6¼ oz can / **Van Camp**	440
drained	415

Light, solid, in oil:
3½ oz can / **Chicken of The Sea**	220
drained	153

Light, solid, in oil:
7 oz can / **Chicken of The Sea**	440
drained	305

White, flake, in oil:
5 oz can drained / **Gold Seal**	278

White, solid, in oil:
5.1 oz can drained / **Gold Seal**	290

White, solid, in oil:
5.1 oz can drained / **Icy Point**	290

White, solid, in oil:
5.1 oz can drained / **Pillar Rock**	290

White, solid, in vegetable oil:
3½ oz can / **Chicken of The Sea**	254
drained	164

White, solid, in vegetable oil:
  6½ oz can / **Chicken of The Sea**   413
    drained   324
White, solid, in vegetable oil:
  7 oz can / **Chicken of The Sea**   507
    drained   328
White, solid, in vegetable oil:
  9¼ oz can / **Chicken of The Sea**   588
    drained   461
White, solid, in vegetable oil:
  12½ oz can / **Chicken of The Sea** 794
    drained   623
White, solid, in vegetable oil:
  13 oz can / **Chicken of The Sea**   942
    drained   609
White, solid, in water:
  7 oz can / **Chicken of The Sea**   230
    drained   216

FISH AND SEAFOOD ENTREES, FROZEN

Crepes, clam: 5½ oz / **Mrs. Paul's**   280
Crepes, crab: 5½ oz / **Mrs. Paul's**   240
Crepes, scallop: 5½ oz / **Mrs. Paul's**   220
Crepes, shrimp: 5½ oz / **Mrs. Paul's**   250
Croquette, shrimp w Newburg sauce:
  12 oz / **Howard Johnson's**   478
Fish Au Gratin: 5 oz / **Mrs. Paul's**   250
Fish Au Gratin: 4 oz / **Mrs. Paul's Party Pak**   200
Fish 'n' Chips: 1 entree / **Swanson "TV"**   290
Fish 'n' Chips, in light batter, fried: 7 oz /
  Mrs. Paul's   370
Fish Parmesan: 5 oz / **Mrs. Paul's**   220
Fish Parmesan: 4 oz / **Mrs. Paul's Party Pak**   150
Flounder w chopped broccoli, cauliflower, red
  peppers: 8½ oz / **Weight Watchers**   160
Haddock au Groton: 10 oz / **Howard Johnson's**   318
Haddock w stuffing and spinach: 8¾ oz /
  Weight Watchers   180

CALORIES

Perch, ocean w chopped broccoli: 8½ oz / **Weight Watchers**	190
Scallops w butter and cheese: 7 oz / **Mrs. Paul's**	260
Shrimp and Scallops Mariner: 1 pkg / **Stouffer's** 10¼ oz	400
Sole w peas, mushrooms, lobster sauce: 9½ oz / **Weight Watchers**	200
Tuna, creamed w peas: 5 oz / **Green Giant** Boil-in-Bag Toast Toppers	140
Turbot w peas, carrots: 8 oz / **Weight Watchers**	280

Flavorings, Sweet

CALORIES

1 tsp unless noted

Almond extract, pure / **Durkee**	13
Almond extract, pure / **Ehlers**	5
Anise extract, imitation / **Durkee**	16
Anise extract, pure / **Ehlers**	12
Banana extract, imitation / **Durkee**	15
Banana extract, imitation / **Ehlers**	7
Black walnut flavor, imitation / **Durkee**	4
Brandy extract, imitation / **Durkee**	15
Brandy extract, imitation / **Ehlers**	18
Cherry extract, imitation / **Ehlers**	8
Chocolate extract / **Durkee**	7
Coconut flavor, imitation / **Durkee**	8
Coconut extract, imitation / **Ehlers**	13
Lemon extract, imitation / **Durkee**	17
Lemon extract, pure / **Ehlers**	14
Maple extract, imitation / **Durkee**	6
Maple extract, imitation / **Ehlers**	9

CALORIES

	CALORIES
Mocha extract, imitation / **Durkee**	14
Orange extract, imitation / **Durkee**	16
Orange extract, pure / **Ehlers**	14
Peppermint extract, imitation / **Durkee**	15
Peppermint extract, pure / **Ehlers**	12
Pineapple extract, pure / **Ehlers**	13
Raspberry extract, imitation / **Ehlers**	10
Rum extract, imitation / **Durkee**	14
Rum extract, imitation / **Ehlers**	11
Strawberry extract, imitation / **Durkee**	12
Strawberry extract, imitation / **Ehlers**	13
Vanilla extract, imitation / **Durkee**	3
Vanilla extract, pure / **Durkee**	8

Flour and Meal

FLOUR

CALORIES

1 cup unless noted

	CALORIES
Biscuit mix / **Bisquick**	480
Buckwheat, dark, sifted	326
Buckwheat, light, sifted	340
Carob	252
Corn	431
Corn: 1 lb	1669
Lima bean, sifted	432
Peanut, defatted	223
Rye	
Light	314
Medium	308
Medium / **Pillsbury**	420

Dark	419
Wheat / **Pillsbury** Bohemian	400
Soybean	
Full fat	295
Low fat	313
Defatted	326
Tortilla, corn: ⅓ cup / **Quaker's** Masa Harina	137
Tortilla, wheat: ⅓ cup / **Quaker's** Masa Trigo	149
Wheat	
All purpose	499
Bread	500
Cake or pastry	430
Gluten	529
Self-rising	440
Whole wheat	400
Whole wheat / **Pillsbury**	400
White	
Ballard	400
Peavey Family High Altitude Hungarian	400
Peavey Family Occident	400
Peavey Family King Midas	400
Pillsbury All Purpose	400
Cake, self-rising / **Presto**	400
Cake / **Softasilk**	412
Self-rising: ¼ cup / **Aunt Jemima**	109
Self-rising / **Ballard**	380
Self-rising / **Pillsbury**	380
Unbleached / **Pillsbury**	400

MEAL

Almond, partially defatted: 1 oz	116
Corn	
White or yellow, whole ground	
unbolted, dry: 1 cup	433
White: 1 oz (2 tbsp and 2 tsp) / **Albers**	100
White: about 3 tbsp / **Aunt Jemima**	
Enriched	102
White: about 3 tbsp / **Quaker** Enriched	102

CALORIES

White, bolted, mix: 1/6 cup / **Aunt Jemima**	99
White, bolted, self-rising: 1/6 cup / **Aunt Jemima**	99
White, self-rising: 1/6 cup / **Aunt Jemima**	98
Yellow: 1 oz (2 tbsp and 2 tsp) / **Albers**	100
Yellow: about 3 tbsp / **Aunt Jemima** Enriched	102
Yellow: about 3 tbsp / **Quaker** Enriched	102
Crackermeal: 1 cup / **Sunshine**	400
Matzo meal: 1 cup / **Manischewitz**	438

Frostings

CALORIES

Ready to spread: 1 can unless noted

Cake and cookie decorator, all colors:

1 tbsp / **Pillsbury**	70
Butter pecan / **Betty Crocker**	2040
Cherry / **Betty Crocker**	2040
Chocolate / **Betty Crocker**	2040
Chocolate fudge / **Pillsbury**	1920
Chocolate nut / **Betty Crocker**	1920
Dark Dutch fudge / **Betty Crocker**	1920
Double Dutch / **Pillsbury**	1920
Lemon / **Betty Crocker** Sunkist	2040
Lemon / **Pillsbury**	1920
Milk chocolate / **Betty Crocker**	1920
Milk chocolate / **Pillsbury**	1920
Orange / **Betty Crocker**	2040
Sour cream, chocolate / **Betty Crocker**	2040
Sour cream, vanilla / **Pillsbury**	1920
Sour cream, white / **Betty Crocker**	1920

	CALORIES
Strawberry / **Pillsbury**	1920
Vanilla / **Betty Crocker**	2040
Vanilla / **Pillsbury**	2040

1 pkg: prepared

Banana / **Betty Crocker** Chiquita	1800
Butter Brickle / **Betty Crocker**	1800
Butter pecan / **Betty Crocker**	1800
Caramel / **Pillsbury Rich 'n Easy**	2040
Cherry / **Betty Crocker**	1800
Chocolate / **Betty Crocker** Lite	1200
Chocolate fudge / **Betty Crocker**	1920
Chocolate fudge / **Pillsbury Rich 'n Easy**	2040
Coconut almond / **Pillsbury**	2040
Coconut pecan / **Betty Crocker**	1320
Coconut pecan / **Pillsbury**	1800
Dark chocolate fudge / **Betty Crocker**	1800
Double Dutch / **Pillsbury Rich n' Easy**	2040
Lemon / **Betty Crocker** Sunkist	1800
Lemon / **Pillsbury Rich 'n Easy**	2040
Milk chocolate / **Betty Crocker**	1800
Milk chocolate / **Pillsbury Rich n' Easy**	2040
Sour cream, chocolate / **Betty Crocker**	1800
Sour cream, white / **Betty Crocker**	1800
Strawberry / **Pillsbury Rich 'n Easy**	2040
Vanilla / **Betty Crocker** Lite	1200
Vanilla / **Pillsbury Rich 'n Easy**	2040
White, creamy / **Betty Crocker**	1920
White, fluffy / **Betty Crocker** Lite	720
White, fluffy / **Pillsbury**	840

Fruit

FRESH

	CALORIES
Acerola cherries: 10 fruits	23
Apples	
w skin: 1 small (about 4 per lb)	61
w skin: 1 medium (about 3 per lb)	80
w skin: 1 large (about 2 per lb)	123
Peeled: 1 small (about 4 per lb)	53
Peeled: 1 medium (about 3 per lb)	70
Peeled: 1 large (about 2 per lb)	107
Apricots	
Raw, halves: 1 cup	79
Raw, halves: 1 lb	231
Raw, whole: 3 apricots	55
Raw, whole (12 per lb): 1 lb	217
Avocados	
California: ½ average	185
California, cubed: 1 cup	257
California, puree: 1 cup	393
Florida: ½ average	196
Florida, cubed: 1 cup	192
Florida, puree: 1 cup	294
Bananas	
1 small, 7¾ in	81
1 medium, 8¾ in	101
1 large, 9¾ in	116
Mashed: 1 cup	191
Red: 1 banana, 7¼ in	118
Red, sliced: 1 cup	135
Sliced: 1 cup	128
Dehydrated or flakes: 1 tbsp	21
Dehydrated or flakes: 1 cup	340
Blackberries (including dewberries, boysenberries, youngberries), raw: 1 cup	84
Blueberries, raw: 1 cup	90

CALORIES

Blueberries, raw: 1 lb	281
Cherries	
Raw, sour, red: 1 cup	60
Raw, sour, red: 1 lb	237
Raw, sweet: 1 cup	82
Raw, sweet: 1 lb	286
Cranberries, raw, chopped: 1 cup	51
Cranberries, raw, whole: 1 cup	44
Figs, raw, whole: 1 small	32
Figs, raw, whole: 1 medium	40
Figs, raw, whole: 1 large	52
Gooseberries, raw: 1 cup	59
Grapefruit: half, 3½-in diam	40
Grapefruit, sections: 1 cup	94
Grapes	
Concord, Delaware, Niagara, Catawba,	
Scuppernong: 10 grapes	18
Flame Tokay, Emperor: 10 grapes	38
Ribier: 10 grapes	45
Thompson Seedless, Malaga, Muscat:	
10 grapes	34
Lemons, wedge: 1 from large lemon	7
Lemons, whole fruit: 1 large	29
Limes, raw: 1 lime	19
Loganberries, raw: 1 cup	89
Loquats, raw: 10 fruits	59
Lychees, raw: 10 fruits	58
Mangoes, raw, whole: 1 fruit	152
Muskmelons	
Canteloupes, cubed, diced or balls: 1 cup	48
Canteloupes: half, 5-in diam	82
Casaba, cubed, diced or balls: 1 cup	46
Casaba, whole about 6 lbs: 1 melon	367
Honeydew, cubed, diced or balls: 1 cup	56
Honeydew, whole about 5¼ lbs: 1 melon	495
Nectarines, raw, 2½-in diam: 1 nectarine	88
Oranges	
California navels (winter): 1 small	45

	CALORIES
California navels (winter): 1 medium	71
California navels (winter): 1 large	87
California navels, sections: 1 cup	77
Valencias (summer): 1 small	50
Valencias (summer): 1 medium	62
Valencias (summer): 1 large	96
Valencias, sections: 1 cup	92
Florida: 1 small	57
Florida: 1 medium	71
Florida: 1 large	89
Florida, sections: 1 cup	87
Papaws, raw, whole: 1 papaw	83
Papayas, raw, cubed, ½-in pieces: 1 cup	55
Papayas, raw, whole, about 1 lb: 1 papaya	119

Peaches

Raw, pared, sliced: 1 cup	65
Raw, whole, peeled: 1 small (about 4 per lb)	38
Raw, whole, peeled: 1 large (about 2½ per lb)	58
Raw, whole, peeled: 1 lb	150

Pears

Raw, sliced or cubed: 1 cup	101
Raw, whole, Bartlett: 1 pear (about 2½ per lb)	100
Raw, whole, Boscs: 1 pear (about 3 per lb)	86
Raw, whole, D'Anjous: 1 pear (about 2 per lb)	122
Persimmons, raw, Japanese or kaki: 1 persimmon	129
Persimmons, raw, native: 1 persimmon	31
Pineapple, raw, diced pieces: 1 cup	81
Pineapple, raw, sliced: 1 slice, ¾-in thick	44

Plums

Raw, whole, Damson: 10 plums, 1-in diam	66
Raw, whole, Damson: 1 lb	272
Raw, Japanese and hybrid: 1 plum, 2⅛-in diam	32

Raw, Japanese and hybrid: 1 lb	299
Prune type, raw: 1 plum, 1½-in diam	21
Prune type, raw: 1 lb	320
Pomegranate: 1 pomegranate, 3⅜-in diam	97
Raspberries, raw, black: 1 cup	98
Raspberries, raw, red: 1 cup	70
Rhubarb, raw, diced: 1 cup	20
Rhubarb, cooked w sugar: 1 cup	381
Strawberries, raw, whole berries: 1 cup	55
Tangerines, raw, whole fruit: 1 large, 2½-in diam	46
Watermelon	
Raw: 1 lb	118
Raw, diced pieces: 1 cup	42
Raw, slice, 10-in diam by 1-in thick	111
Raw, wedge, 4 in x 8 in radius	111

CANNED AND FROZEN

Applesauce in cans or jars	
Del Monte / ½ cup	85
Mott's Natural Style / 8 oz	90
S and W Nutradiet / ½ cup	48
Stokely-Van Camp / 1 cup	180
Tillie Lewis / ½ cup	60
Town House / 8 oz	170
Unswt: ½ cup / S and W Nutradiet	48
Apricots: 1 cup unless noted	
Halves / Del Monte	200
Halves / Stokely-Van Camp	220
Halves / Tillie Lewis	120
Halves, in heavy syrup / Libby's	200
Halves, in heavy syrup / Town House	220
Halves, in light syrup / Scotch Buy	160
Halves, in light syrup / Town House	160
Whole / Del Monte	200
Whole, in heavy syrup / Town House	201
Swt: 4 halves / S and W Nutradiet	40

Unswt: 4 halves / **S and W Nutradiet**	38
Swt, whole: 2 whole / **S and W Nutradiet**	31
Blackberries, canned, swt: ½ cup / **S and W Nutradiet**	36
Blueberries, unswt, frozen: ½ cup / **Seabrook Farms**	45
Boysenberries, canned, swt: ½ cup / **S and W Nutradiet**	32
Cherries, canned: 1 cup unless noted	
Tillie Lewis	120
Dark, sweet / **Del Monte**	180
Dark, sweet / **S and W Nutradiet**	106
Dark, sweet, in heavy syrup / **Libby's**	200
Dark, sweet, pitted / **Del Monte**	190
Light, sweet / **Del Monte** Royal Anne	190
Light, sweet, in heavy syrup / **Libby's**	200
Light, sweet, unswt: 14 whole / **S and W Nutradiet** Royal Anne	47
Sour, pitted / **Stokely-Van Camp**	100
Cranberry orange, crushed: 2 oz / **Ocean Spray**	100
Cranberry orange relish: 2 oz / **Ocean Spray**	100
Cranberry sauce, jellied: 2 oz / **Ocean Spray**	90
Cranberry sauce, whole: 2 oz / **Ocean Spray**	90
Currants, canned: ½ cup / **Del Monte** Zante	190
Figs, whole, canned: 1 cup / **Del Monte**	210
Figs, whole, swt, canned: 6 whole / **S and W Nutradiet**	49
Figs, whole, unswt, canned: 6 whole / **S and W Nutradiet**	52
Fruit cocktail, canned: 1 cup	
Del Monte	170
Libby's Juice Pack	150
S and W Nutradiet	72
Stokely-Van Camp	190
Tillie Lewis	100
In heavy syrup / **Libby's**	170

CALORIES

In heavy syrup / **Town House**	170
Unswt / **S and W Nutradiet**	70
Fruit mixed, canned: 5 oz / **Del Monte**	100
Fruit mixed, frozen: 5 oz / **Birds Eye** Quick Thaw	130
Fruit salad, canned: 1 cup / **Del Monte** Tropical	200
Fruits for salad, canned: 1 cup	
Del Monte	170
Stokely-Van Camp	190
In heavy syrup / **Libby's**	180
Swt / **S and W Nutradiet**	70
Unswt / **S and W Nutradiet**	76
Grapefruit sections, canned: 1 cup / **Tillie Lewis**	90
Grapefruit sections, in juice, canned: 1 cup / **Del Monte**	90
Grapefruit sections, in syrup, canned: 1 cup / **Del Monte**	140
Grapefruit sections, unswt, canned: ½ cup / **S and W Nutradiet**	36
Oranges, Mandarin, canned: 5½ oz / **Del Monte**	100
Oranges, Mandarin, canned: ½ cup / **Tillie Lewis**	45
Oranges, Mandarin, swt, canned: ½ cup / **S and W Nutradiet**	27
Oranges, Mandarin, unswt, canned: ½ cup / **S and W Nutradiet**	27
Peaches, canned: 1 cup unless noted	
Stokely-Van Camp	190
Cling / **Del Monte**	170
Cling / **Tillie Lewis**	100
Cling, diced: 5 oz can / **Del Monte**	110
Cling, in heavy syrup / **Libby's**	170
Cling, in heavy syrup / **Town House**	190
Cling, in light syrup / **Highway**	140
Cling, in light syrup / **Scotch Buy**	140

Cling, slices / **Del Monte**	170
Cling, slices, in heavy syrup / **Town House**	190
Cling, slices, in light syrup / **Highway**	140
Cling, slices, in swt juice / **Libby's**	
Juice Pack	150
Cling, slices, swt / **S and W Nutradiet**	50
Cling, slices, unswt / **S and W Nutradiet**	48
Cling, unswt: 2 halves / **S and W Nutradiet**	28
Freestone, halves / **Del Monte**	170
Freestone, halves, in extra heavy syrup /	
Town House	260
Freestone, mixed pieces, in heavy	
syrup / **Highway**	200
Freestone, mixed pieces, in heavy	
syrup / **Scotch Buy**	200
Freestone, slices / **Del Monte**	170
Freestone, slices, in extra heavy syrup /	
Town House	260
Freestone, swt: ½ cup / **S and W Nutradiet**	24
Slices / **Stokely-Van Camp**	180
Spiced w pits: 7¼ oz / **Del Monte**	150
Peaches, frozen: 5 oz / **Birds Eye Quick Thaw**	130
Peaches, frozen, slices: ½ cup / **Seabrook Farms**	106
Pears, canned: 1 cup unless noted	
Bartlett / **Tillie Lewis**	100
Bartlett, halves / **Del Monte**	160
Bartlett, halves, in light syrup / **Highway**	160
Bartlett, halves, in light syrup / **Scotch Buy**	140
Bartlett, halves, in heavy syrup / **Libby's**	170
Bartlett, halves, in heavy syrup /	
Town House	190
Bartlett, slices / **Del Monte**	160
Bartlett, slices, in heavy syrup /	
Town House	190
Halves / **Stokely-Van Camp**	210
Halves, in swt juice / **Libby's**	
Juice Pack	150
Halves, swt: 2 halves / **S and W Nutradiet**	28

CALORIES

Quartered, swt / **S and W Nutradiet**	52
Quartered, unswt / **S and W Nutradiet**	54
Slices / **Stokely-Van Camp**	200
Pineapple, canned: 1 cup	
Tillie Lewis	140
Chunks, in juice / **Del Monte**	140
Chunks, in juice / **Dole**	128
Chunks, in juice, unswt / **Town House**	140
Chunks, in syrup / **Del Monte**	190
Chunks, in syrup / **Dole**	168
Chunks, in syrup / **Town House**	190
Chunks, swt / **S and W Nutradiet**	98
Crushed, in juice / **Del Monte**	140
Crushed, in juice, unswt / **Town House**	140
Crushed, in syrup / **Del Monte**	190
Crushed, in syrup / **Town House**	190
Slices, in juice / **Del Monte**	140
Slices, in juice, unswt / **Town House**	140
Slices, in syrup / **Del Monte**	190
Slices, in syrup / **Town House**	190
Slices, swt / **S and W Nutradiet**	112
Slices, unswt / **S and W Nutradiet**	178
Tidbits, in syrup / **Town House**	190
Tidbits, swt / **S and W Nutradiet**	98
Tidbits, unswt / **S and W Nutradiet**	138
Plums, canned: 1 cup	
Del Monte	190
Libby's	210
S and W Nutradiet	100
Stokely-Van Camp	240
Tillie Lewis	140
Prunes, stewed, canned: 1 cup / **Del Monte**	230
Raspberries, red, frozen: 5 oz / **Birds Eye** Quick Thaw	140
Strawberries	
Canned: 1 cup / **S and W Nutradiet**	40
Frozen: 5 oz / **Birds Eye** Quick Thaw	110
Halves, frozen: 5.3 oz / **Birds Eye**	170

	CALORIES
Slices, frozen: 5 oz / **Birds Eye**	180
Slices, frozen: ½ cup / **Seabrook Farms**	140
Whole, frozen: 4 oz / **Birds Eye**	70
Whole, frozen, unswt: ½ cup / **Seabrook Farms**	42

DRIED

Uncooked

Apples: 2 oz / **Del Monte**	140
Apples: 1 pkg / **Weight Watchers** Apple Snacks	50
Apricots: 2 oz / **Del Monte**	140
Currants: 1 cup / **Del Monte** Zanta	410
Dates, chopped: 1 cup / **Dromedary**	493
Dates, diced: 1 cup / **Bordo**	660
Dates, whole, pitted: 4 average / **Bordo**	76
Dates, whole, pitted: 1 cup / **Dromedary**	470
Figs: 1 large (2 in x 1 in)	60
Fruits and peels, glazed: 4 oz / **Liberty**	388
Fruits: 1 pkg / **Weight Watchers** Fruit Snacks	50
Peaches: 2 oz / **Del Monte**	140
Pears: 2 oz / **Del Monte**	150
Prunes, w pits: 2 oz / **Del Monte**	120
Prunes, w pits: 2 oz / **Del Monte** Moist-pak	120
Prunes, pitted: 2 oz/ **Del Monte**	140
Raisins, muscat: 3 oz / **Del Monte**	250
Raisins, seedless, golden: 3 oz / **Del Monte**	260
Raisins, seedless, Thompson: 3 oz / **Del Monte**	260

Fruit Drinks and Fruit-Flavored Beverages

	CALORIES
All flavors, mix, w sugar:	
1 env / **Ann Page Cheeri-Aid**	320
All flavors, mix, wo sugar:	
1 env / **Ann Page Cheeri-Aid**	32
All flavors, mix, prepared:	
8 fl oz / **Funny Face**	80
All flavors, mix, prepared, swt:	
8 fl oz / **Kool-Aid**	90
All flavors, mix, unswt:	
8 fl oz prepared w sugar / **Kool-Aid**	100
Apple, canned: 8 fl oz / **Ann Page**	120
Apple, canned: 6 fl oz / **Hi-C**	92
Apple-grape, canned: 6 fl oz / **Mott's "P.M."**	90
Berry, canned: 8 fl oz / **Cragmont** Wild Berry	120
Cherry	
Canned: 8 fl oz / **Ann Page**	120
Canned: 8 fl oz / **Cragmont**	120
Canned: 6 fl oz / **Hi-C**	93
Mix, prepared: 6 fl oz / **Hi-C**	76
Citrus cooler, canned: 8 fl oz / **Ann Page**	120
Citrus cooler, canned: 8 fl oz / **Cragmont**	120
Citrus cooler, canned: 6 fl oz / **Hi-C**	93
Cranberry juice cocktail	
Bottled: 8 fl oz / **Ann Page**	160
Bottled: 6 fl oz / **Ocean Spray**	110
Bottled: 6 fl oz / **Ocean Spray** Low Calorie	35
Canned: 4 fl oz / **Seneca**	79
Canned: 6 fl oz / **Town House**	110
Canned and bottled: 6 fl oz / **Welch's**	105
Cranberry-apple drink	
Bottled: 8 fl oz / **Ann Page**	180

CALORIES

Bottled: 6 fl oz / **Ocean Spray Cranapple**	130
Bottled: 6 fl oz / **Ocean Spray**	
Low Calorie **Cranapple**	30
Canned: 6 fl oz / **Town House**	132
Cranberry-apricot drink, bottled:	
6 fl oz / **Ocean Spray Cranicot**	110
Cranberry-grape drink, bottled:	
6 fl oz / **Ocean Spray Crangrape**	110
Cranberry-prune drink, bottled:	
6 fl oz / **Ocean Spray Cranprune**	120
Fruit, canned: 6 fl oz / **Mott's "A.M."**	
Fruit Drink	90
Fruit, mix, prepared:	
8 fl oz / **Hawaiian Punch** Red	100
Grape	
Bottled: 6 fl oz / **Sunshake**	90
Canned: 8 fl oz / **Ann Page**	120
Canned: 6 fl oz / **Hi-C**	89
Canned: 8 fl oz / **Cragmont**	130
Canned: 6 fl oz / **Welchade**	90
Canned: 6 fl oz / **Welchade** Red	90
Mix: 1 heaping tsp / **Ann Page**	
Instant Breakfast Drink	30
Mix, prepared: 6 fl oz / **Hi-C**	76
Mix, prepared: 4 fl oz / **Tang**	60
Refrigerated: 6 fl oz / **Welch's** Juice Drink	110
Grapefruit, bottled: 6 fl oz /	
Ann Page Ready-Made	80
Grapefruit, mix, prepared: 4 fl oz / **Tang**	50
Lemonade	
Frozen, reconstituted: 6 fl oz /	
Minute Maid	74
Mix, prepared: 8 fl oz / **Country Time**	90
Mix, prepared: 6 fl oz / **Hi-C**	76
Mix, prepared: 6 fl oz /	
Minute Maid Crystals	80
Mix, prepared: 6 fl oz / **Wyler's**	66

CALORIES

Pink, mix, prepared: 8 fl oz /
Country Time   90
Pink, mix, prepared: 6 fl oz /
Minute Maid Crystals   80
Lemon-limeade, frozen, reconstituted:
 6 fl oz / **Minute Maid**   75
Limeade, frozen, reconstituted:
 6 fl oz / **Minute Maid**   75
Orange
  Bottled: 6 fl oz / **A & P** Ready-Made   80
  Bottled: 6 fl oz / **Sunshake**   90
  Canned: 8 fl oz / **Ann Page**   120
  Canned: 8 fl oz / **Cragmont**   130
  Canned: 6 fl oz / **Hi-C**   92
  Canned: 6 fl oz / **Welchade**   100
  Frozen, reconstituted: 6 fl oz /
    Birds Eye Orange Plus   100
  Mix: 1 heaping tsp / **Ann Page**
    Instant Breakfast Drink   30
  Mix: 3 rounded tsp / **Town House**
    Instant Breakfast Drink   100
  Mix, prepared: 6 fl oz / **Hi-C**   76
  Mix, prepared: 4 fl oz / **Start**   60
  Mix, prepared: 4 fl oz / **Tang**   60
Orangeade, frozen, reconstituted:
 6 fl oz / **Minute Maid**   94
Orange-pineapple, canned: 8 fl oz / **Ann Page**   120
Orange-pineapple, canned: 6 fl oz / **Hi-C**   94
Peach, canned: 6 fl oz / **Hi-C**   90
Peach, mix, prepared: 6 fl oz / **Hi-C**   76
Pineapple-grapefruit, canned:
 6 fl oz / **Town House** Juice Drink   90
Pineapple-pink grapefruit, canned:
 6 fl oz / **Dole** Drink   91
Pineapple-orange, canned: 8 fl oz / **Cragmont**   130
Punch
    All flavors, canned: 8 fl oz /
     Hawaiian Punch   120

CALORIES

All flavors, frozen, reconstituted:
8 fl oz / **Hawaiian Punch**	120

All flavors, mix, prepared:
8 fl oz / **Hawaiian Punch** Shelf Concentrate	120
Florida punch, canned: 6 fl oz / **Hi-C**	95
Fruit, canned: 6 fl oz / **Welchade**	100
Tropical fruit, canned: 8 fl oz / **Ann Page**	120
Tropical, canned: 8 fl oz / **Cragmont**	130
Mix, prepared: 6 fl oz / **Hi-C**	76
Strawberry, canned: 6 fl oz / **Hi-C**	89
Tangerine, canned: 6 fl oz / **Hi-C**	90
Wild berry, canned: 8 fl oz / **Ann Page**	120
Wild berry, canned: 6 fl oz / **Hi-C**	88

Fruit Juices

FRESH

CALORIES

1 cup unless noted

Acerola cherry	56
Grapefruit	96
Lemon	61
Lemon: 1 tbsp	4
Lime: 1 tbsp	4
Orange	
California navels	120
Florida	106
Valcencias	117
Tangerine	106

BOTTLED, CANNED AND FROZEN

	CALORIES
6 fl oz unless noted	
Apple	
Bottled: 8 fl oz / **Ann Page**	120
Canned / **Mott's**	80
Canned / **Mott's** Natural Style	80
Canned / **Pillsbury**	90
Canned and bottled: 4 fl oz / **Seneca**	61
Canned from concentrate / **Welch's**	90
Apricot nectar	
Canned / **Del Monte**	100
Canned / **Libby's**	110
Canned: 4 fl oz / **Seneca**	77
Canned / **Town House**	110
Grape	
Bottled, canned and frozen concentrate: 4 fl oz / **Seneca**	74
Bottled / **Welch's**	120
Bottled, red / **Welch's**	120
Bottled, red / **Welch's** Sparkling	120
Bottled, white / **Welch's**	120
Bottled, white / **Welch's** Sparkling	120
Frozen, reconstituted / **Minute Maid**	99
Grapefruit	
Bottled / **Ocean Spray**	70
Canned: 4 fl oz / **Seneca**	54
Canned from concentrate / **Welch's**	75
Canned, swt / **Del Monte**	80
Canned, swt / **Libby's**	100
Canned, unswt / **Del Monte**	70
Canned, unswt / **Libby's**	75
Canned, unswt: 1 cup / **Treesweet**	100
Frozen, reconstituted / **Minute Maid**	75
Frozen, reconstituted: 1 cup / **Treesweet**	100
Grapefruit-orange, canned: 4 fl oz / **Seneca**	59
Lemon, bottled, reconstituted: 2 tbsp / **ReaLemon**	8

Lemon, canned, reconstituted:
  1 tbsp / **Town House**   3
Lemon, frozen, reconstituted / **Minute Maid**   40
Orange
    Canned: 4 fl oz / **Seneca**   59
    Canned from concentrate / **Welch's**   90
    Canned, swt / **Del Monte**   70
    Canned, swt / **Libby's**   100
    Canned, unswt / **Del Monte**   80
    Canned, unswt / **Libby's**   90
    Canned, unswt: 1 cup / **Treesweet**   120
    Frozen, reconstituted / **Bright and Early**   90
    Frozen, reconstituted / **Minute Maid**   90
    Frozen, reconstituted / **Snow Crop**   90
    Frozen, reconstituted: 1 cup / **Treesweet**   120
    Imitation, frozen, reconstituted /
      Birds Eye Awake   90
Orange-grapefruit
    Canned, swt / **Del Monte**   80
    Canned, unswt / **Libby's**   80
    Canned, unswt / **Del Monte**   80
    Frozen, reconstituted / **Minute Maid**   76
Peach nectar, canned / **Del Monte**   100
Peach nectar, canned / **Libby's**   90
Pear nectar, canned / **Del Monte**   110
Pear nectar, canned / **Libby's**   100
Pineapple
    Canned / **Del Monte**   100
    Canned / **Dole**   93
    Canned: 4 fl oz / **Seneca**   68
    Canned, unswt / **Town House**   100
    Frozen, reconstituted / **Minute Maid**   92
Pineapple-grapefruit, canned / **Del Monte**   90
Pineapple-orange, frozen, reconstituted /
  Minute Maid   94
Pineapple-pink grapefruit, canned / **Del Monte**   90
Prune
    Bottled / **Ann Page**   140

CALORIES

	CALORIES
Bottled / **RealPrune**	130
Canned / **Del Monte**	120
Canned / **Mott's**	140
Canned / **Mott's** Prune Nectar	100
Canned: 4 fl oz / **Seneca**	102
Canned or bottled / **Sunsweet**	123
Canned / **Welch's**	150
Canned w pulp / **Mott's**	120
Tangerine, frozen, reconstituted / **Minute Maid**	86

Gelatin

	CALORIES
All flavors, mix, prepared: ½ cup / **D-Zerta**	8
All flavors, mix, prepared:	
½ cup / **Estee** Low Calorie	40
All flavors, mix, prepared: ½ cup / **Jell-O**	80
All flavors, mix, prepared: ½ cup / **Royal**	80
All flavors, unswt, mix, prepared:	
½ cup / **Royal Sweet As You Please**	6
Orange-flavored, drinking: 1 env / **Knox** Gelatine	70
Unflavored: 1 pkg (¼ oz) / **Ann Page**	24
Unflavored: 1 env / **Knox** Gelatine	25

Gravies

¼ cup unless noted

	CALORIES
Au Jus	
Mix, prepared: 1 env / **Ann Page**	64
Mix, prepared / **Durkee**	8
Mix w roasting bag:	
1 pkg / **Durkee** Roastin' Bag	64
Mix, prepared / **French's**	8
Mix, prepared / **French's** Pan Rich	30
Mix, prepared: ½ cup / **McCormick**	8

CALORIES

Mix, prepared: ½ cup / **Schilling**	8
Beef, canned: 1/5 can / **Ann Page**	25
Beef, canned: 2 oz / **Franco-American**	30
Beef, canned: ½ cup / **Howard Johnson's**	51

Brown

Mix, prepared: 1 env / **Ann Page**	80
Mix, prepared / **Durkee**	15
Mix, prepared / **French's**	20
Mix, prepared / **French's** Pan Rich	60
Mix, prepared / **McCormick**	26
Mix, prepared / **McCormick** Lite	10
Mix, prepared / **Pillsbury**	15
Mix, prepared / **Schilling**	26
Mix, prepared / **Schilling** Lite	10
Mix, prepared: 1 fl oz / **Spatini** Family Style	10
Mix, prepared / **Weight Watchers**	8
Herb-flavored, mix, prepared / **McCormick**	21
Herb-flavored, mix, prepared / **Schilling**	21
w mushroom broth, canned:	
1 oz / **Dawn Fresh**	10
w mushrooms, mix, prepared / **Durkee**	15
w mushrooms, mix, prepared /	
Weight Watchers	12
w onions, canned: 2 oz /	
Franco-American	25
w onions, mix, prepared / **Durkee**	17
w onions, mix, prepared / **Weight Watchers**	13

Chicken

Canned: 2 oz / **Franco-American**	50
Mix, prepared: 1 env / **Ann Page**	120
Mix, prepared / **Durkee**	22
Mix, prepared / **Durkee** Creamy	39
Mix w roasting bag:	
1 pkg / **Durkee** Roastin' Bag	122
Mix w roasting bag:	
1 pkg / **Durkee** Roastin' Bag	
Italian Style	144
Mix, prepared / **French's**	25

CALORIES

Mix, prepared / **French's** Pan Rich	60
Mix, prepared / **McCormick**	21
Mix, prepared / **McCormick** Lite	10
Mix, prepared / **Pillsbury**	25
Mix, prepared / **Schilling**	21
Mix, prepared / **Schilling** Lite	10
Mix, prepared / **Weight Watchers**	10
Mix, creamy w roasting bag:	
1 pkg / **Durkee** Roastin' Bag	242
Chicken giblet, canned: 2 oz / **Franco-American**	35
Homestyle, mix, prepared / **Durkee**	18
Homestyle, mix, prepared / **French's**	25
Homestyle, mix, prepared / **Pillsbury**	15
Meatloaf, mix w roasting bag:	
1 pkg / **Durkee** Roastin' Bag	129
Mushroom	
Canned: 2 oz / **Franco-American**	35
Mix, prepared: 1 env / **Ann Page**	80
Mix, prepared / **French's**	20
Mix, prepared / **McCormick**	19
Mix, prepared / **Schilling**	19
Onion, mix, prepared: 1 env / **Ann Page**	120
Onion, mix, prepared / **Durkee**	21
Onion, mix, prepared / **French's**	25
Onion, mix, prepared / **French's** Pan Rich	50
Onion pot roast, mix w roasting bag:	
1 pkg / **Durkee** Roastin' Bag	124
Pork, mix, prepared / **Durkee**	18
Pork, mix w roasting bag: 1 pkg /	
Durkee Roastin' Bag	130
Pork, mix, prepared / **French's**	20
Pot roast stew, mix w roasting bag:	
1 pkg / **Durkee** Roastin' Bag	125
Sparerib sauce, mix w roasting bag:	
1 pkg / **Durkee** Roastin' Bag	162
Swiss steak, mix, prepared / **Durkee**	11
Swiss steak, mix w roasting bag:	
1 pkg / **Durkee** Roastin' Bag	115

CALORIES

Turkey giblet, canned:
  ½ cup / **Howard Johnson's**   55
Turkey, mix, prepared / **Durkee**   23
Turkey, mix, prepared / **French's**   25
Turkey, mix, prepared / **McCormick**   21
Turkey, mix, prepared / **Schilling**   21

Health Foods

CALORIES

Flour, Meal, Rice and Yeast

Flour, soy: ¼ cup / **Loma Linda**	115
Meal, almond: 2 tbsp / **Roberts**	114
Meal, coconut: 2 tbsp / **Roberts**	126
Meal, millet seed: 2 tbsp / **Roberts**	65
Meal, sesame, 2 tbsp / **Roberts**	111
Meal, sunflower: 2 tbsp / **Roberts**	106
Rice, brown: ¼ cup raw / **Datetree**	180
Rice, brown: ¼ cup raw / **Roberts**	180
Yeast, brewer's: 1 rounded tbsp / **Datetree**	49
Yeast, brewer's: 1 rounded tbsp / **Roberts**	49

Granola Bars

w cinnamon: 1 bar / **Nature Valley**	110
w coconut: 1 bar / **Nature Valley**	120
w oats and honey: 1 bar / **Nature Valley**	110
Peanut: 1 bar / **Nature Valley**	120

Seasonings and Gravy

Gravy, mix, brown:	
1/6 pkg / **Loma Linda** Gravy Quick	15
Seasoning, chicken: 1 tbsp / **Loma Linda**	8

Soy Milk

Soyagen, all purpose:	
1 cup prepared / **Loma Linda**	140

113

CALORIES

Soyagen, carob:
   1 cup prepared / **Loma Linda**   140
Soyalac, concentrated:
   6 fl oz prepared / **Loma Linda**   120
Soyalac, powder:
   6 fl oz prepared / **Loma Linda**   120
I-Soyalac, concentrated:
   6 fl oz prepared / **Loma Linda**   120

Soybeans and Legumes

Beans, brown, canned:
   ½ cup / **Loma Linda**   122
Beans, in tomato sauce, canned:
   ½ cup / **Loma Linda**   118
Garbanzo beans, canned:
   ½ cup / **Loma Linda**   145
Lentils, canned: ¾ cup / **Loma Linda**   91
Soy beans
   Boston style, canned:
     ½ cup / **Loma Linda**   141
   Cooking: ½ cup raw / **Datetree**   331
   Cooking: ½ cup raw / **Roberts**   331
   Dry roasted: 1 oz / **Soy Ahoy**   129
   Dry roasted: 1 oz / **Soy Town**   129
   Green, canned: ½ cup / **Loma Linda**   109
   Oil roasted: 1 oz / **Soy Ahoy**   145
   Oil roasted: 1 oz / **Soy Town**   145
   Roasted: ¼ cup / **Datetree**   118
   Roasted: ¼ cup / **Roberts**   118

Spreads and Sandwich Fillings

Almond butter: 1 tbsp / **Roberts**   96
Cashew butter: 1 tbsp / **Roberts**   90
Marmalade, orange: 1 tbsp / **Datetree**   50
Mayonnaise: 1 tbsp / **Datetree**   92
Peanut butter: 1 tbsp / **Datetree**   93
Peanut butter: 1 tbsp / **Roberts**   93

Preserves: 1 tbsp
    Blackberry / **Datetree**   55
    Grape / **Datetree**   50
    Red raspberry / **Datetree**   55
    Rose hip / **Datetree**   50
    Strawberry / **Datetree**   55
Sandwich filling:
    ½-in slice / **Loma Linda** Vegelona   154
Sandwich spread: 3 tbsp / **Loma Linda**   80
Sesame butter: 1 tbsp / **Roberts**   93
Soy bean cheese:
    ½-in slice / **Loma Linda** Vegechee   106

Sweets, Nuts and Snacks: Natural

Almonds, raw: ¼ cup / **Datetree**   191
Almonds, raw: ¼ cup / **Roberts**   191
Apricot chew: ¼ bar / **Datetree**   92
Apricot chew: ¼ bar / **Roberts**   92
Candy bridge mix: 1 piece / **Joan's Natural**   10
Cashews, raw: ¼ cup / **Datetree**   180
Cashews, raw: ¼ cup / **Roberts**   180
Coconut shreds: 2 tbsps / **Datetree**   119
Coconut shreds: 2 tbsps / **Roberts**   119
Date 'n' seed chew: ¼ bar / **Roberts**   92
Fruit 'n' nut bar:
    1 section of 4 oz bar / **Joan's Natural**   74
Fruit 'n' nut chew: ¼ bar / **Datetree**   92
Fruit 'n' nut chew: ¼ bar / **Roberts**   92
Honey-sesame bar:
    1 section of 4 oz bar / **Joan's Natural**   78
Milk bar:
    1 section of 4 oz bar / **Joan's Natural**   78
Peanut butter-carob bar:
    1 section of 4 oz bar / **Joan's Natural**   79
Peanut butter cups: 1 piece / **Joan's Natural**   40
Peanutettes: 1 peanut / **Joan's Natural**   7
Pistachio nuts, natural: ¼ cup / **Datetree**   149

Protein, bar:
　¼ bar / **Roberts Hi Protein Bar**　　92
Raisin nut mix: ½ cup / **Datetree**　　228
Raisin nut mix: ½ cup / **Roberts**　　228
Raisin 'n' peanut chew: ¼ bar / **Roberts**　　97
Raisins, coated: 1 raisin / **Joan's Natural**　　4
Rose hip chew: ¼ bar / **Datetree**　　97
Rose hip chew: ¼ bar / **Roberts**　　97
Seeds
　Millet: ¼ cup / **Datetree**　　144
　Millet: ¼ cup / **Roberts**　　144
　Pepitas: ¼ cup / **Datetree**　　177
　Pumpkin: ¼ cup / **Datetree**　　177
　Pumpkin: ¼ cup / **Roberts**　　177
　Sesame: ¼ cup / **Datetree**　　280
　Sesame: ¼ cup / **Roberts**　　280
　Squash, dry, hulled: 1 oz　　165
　Sunflower: 1 oz / **Frito Lay**　　181
　Sunflower: 1 oz / **Granny Goose**　　174
　Sunflower, dry roasted: 1 oz / **Planters**　　160
　Sunflower, unsalted: 1 oz / **Planters**　　170
　Sunflower, raw or roasted:
　　¼ cup / **Datetree**　　179
　Sunflower, raw or roasted:
　　¼ cup / **Roberts**　　179
　Sunflower, whole: 1 oz / **Granny Goose**　　159
Sesame carob chew: ¼ bar / **Datetree**　　97
Sesame carob chew: ¼ bar / **Roberts**　　97
Sesame 'n' almond bar: ¼ bar / **Roberts**　　97
Sesame 'n' cashew bar: ¼ bar / **Roberts**　　97
Sesame 'n' coconut bar: ¼ bar / **Roberts**　　97
Sesame 'n' fruit bar: ¼ bar / **Roberts**　　97
Sesame 'n' honey bar: ¼ bar / **Roberts**　　97

Sweeteners

Honey, tupelo: 1 tbsp / **Datetree**　　61
Honey, wildflower: 1 tbsp / **Datetree**　　61

Molasses, blackstrap: 1 tbsp / **Datetree**	43
Sugar, turbinado: 1 tsp / **Datetree**	15
Sugar, turbinado: 1 tsp / **Roberts**	15

Wheat and Wheat Germ

Bulgur, club wheat: 1 cup dry	628
Bulgur, hard red winter wheat: 1 cup dry	602
Bulgur, white wheat: 1 cup dry	553
Wheat, oven cooked: ½ cup / **Loma Linda**	263
Wheat germ: ¼ cup / **Kretschmer** Regular	106
Wheat germ:	
¼ cup / **Kretschmer** Sugar 'N Honey	107
Wheat germ, natural and toasted:	
2 tbsp / **Loma Linda**	80
Wheat germ, raw: 2 rounded tbsp / **Datetree**	58
Wheat germ, raw: ¼ cup / **Pillsbury**	115
Wheat germ, raw: 2 rounded tbsp / **Roberts**	58
Wheat germ, toasted: ¼ cup / **Pillsbury**	120

Vegetarian meat substitutes (gluten base unless noted)

Bologna: ½-in slice / **Loma Linda**	190
Burgers:	
1 burger / **Loma Linda** Sizzle Burgers	180
Chicken (4-in diameter):	
½-in slice / **Loma Linda**	180
Frankfurters:	
1 frank / **Loma Linda** Big Franks	110
Linketts: 1 link / **Loma Linda**	70
Little Links: 1 link / **Loma Linda**	45
Meatballs: 1 ball / **Loma Linda**	48
Nuteena (peanut-butter base):	
½-in slice / **Loma Linda**	210
Proteena (gluten-peanut-butter base):	
½-in slice / **Loma Linda**	160
Redi-Burger: ½-in slice / **Loma Linda**	150
Roast beef: ½-in slice / **Loma Linda**	200
Salami: ½-in slice / **Loma Linda**	210

CALORIES

Sausage: 1 link / **Loma Linda** Breakfast Links 47
Sausage:
    1 piece / **Loma Linda** Breakfast Sausage 140
Stew Pac: 2 oz / **Loma Linda** 70
Swiss Steak: 1 steak / **Loma Linda** 140
Tender Bits: 1 bit / **Loma Linda** 20
Tender Rounds: 1 round / **Loma Linda** 47
Turkey: ½-in slice / **Loma Linda** 190
Vegeburger: ½ cup / **Loma Linda** 120
Vegeburger, unsalted: ½ cup / **Loma Linda** 120
Vegelona: ½-in slice / **Loma Linda** 160

Ice Cream and Similar Frozen Products

	CALORIES
Frozen dessert:	
5 fl oz / **Weight Watchers** Dietary	100
Frozen dessert:	
6 fl oz / **Weight Watchers** Frosted Treat	120
Ice cream: ½ cup unless noted	
Black raspberry / **Breyers**	130
Black walnut / **Meadow Gold**	160
Butter almond / **Sealtest**	160
Butter almond, chocolate / **Breyers**	160
Butter brickle / **Sealtest**	150
Butter pecan / **Meadow Gold**	150
Butter pecan / **Sealtest**	160
Caramel pecan crunch / **Breyers**	160
Cherry nugget / **Sealtest**	140
Cherry-vanilla / **Breyers**	140
Cherry-vanilla / **Meadow Gold**	140
Cherry-vanilla / **Sealtest**	130
Chocolate / **Breyers**	161
Chocolate: 4 oz / **Howard Johnson's**	260
Chocolate / **Meadow Gold**	140
Chocolate / **Sealtest**	140
Chocolate / **Swift's**	130
Chocolate almond / **Breyers**	180
Chocolate almond / **Sealtest**	160
Chocolate chip / **Meadow Gold**	150
Chocolate chip / **Sealtest**	150

119

CALORIES

Chocolate Revel / Meadow Gold	140
Coconut / Sealtest	160
Coffee / Breyers	140
Coffee / Sealtest	140
Dutch chocolate almond / Breyers	180
Lemon / Sealtest	140
Maple walnut / Sealtest	160
Mint chocolate chip / Breyers	170
Peach / Meadow Gold	130
Peach / Sealtest	130
Pineapple / Sealtest	130
Southern pecan butterscotch / Breyers	160
Strawberry / Breyers	130
Strawberry: 4 oz / Howard Johnson's	220
Strawberry / Meadow Gold	140
Strawberry / Sealtest	131
Strawberry / Swift's	120
Vanilla / Breyers	150
Vanilla: 4 oz / Howard Johnson's	247
Vanilla / Meadow Gold	140
Vanilla / Meadow Gold Golden	140
Vanilla / Sealtest	140
Vanilla / Swift's	130
Vanilla, French / Sealtest	140
Vanilla-flavored cherry / Sealtest Royale	140
Vanilla-flavored red raspberry / Sealtest Royale	140
Vanilla fudge / Breyers	156
Ice milk: ½ cup	
Banana-strawberry twirl / Sealtest Light N' Lively	110
Chocolate / Sealtest Light N' Lively	100
Chocolate / Swift Light'n Easy	110
Coffee / Sealtest Light N' Lively	100
Fudge Twirl / Sealtest Light N' Lively	100
Neapolitan / Sealtest Light N' Lively	100
Peach / Sealtest Light N' Lively	100
Strawberry / Sealtest Light N' Lively	100

CALORIES

Strawberry / **Swift Light'n Easy**	100
Vanilla / **Sealtest Light N' Lively**	100
Vanilla / **Swift Light'n Easy**	110
Sherbet: ½ cup unless noted	
Lemon / **Sealtest**	130
Lemon-lime / **Sealtest**	130
Lime / **Meadow Gold**	120
Lime / **Sealtest**	130
Orange: 4 oz / **Howard Johnson's**	133
Orange / **Meadow Gold**	120
Orange / **Sealtest**	130
Pineapple / **Meadow Gold**	130
Pineapple / **Sealtest**	130
Rainbow / **Sealtest**	130
Red raspberry / **Sealtest**	130
Strawberry / **Sealtest**	130

ICE CREAM BARS

1 bar or piece

Almond, toasted / **Good Humor**	220
Banana: 2½ fl oz bar / **Fudgsicle**	102
Chocolate: 2½ fl oz bar / **Bi-Sicle**	112
Chocolate: 2½ fl oz bar / **Fudgsicle**	102
Chocolate eclair / **Good Humor**	220
Creamsicle / 2½ fl oz bar	78
Dreamsicle / 2½ fl oz bar	70
Drumstick, ice cream	181
Drumstick, ice milk	163
Ice Whammy, assorted flavors / **Good Humor**	50
Orange cream: 2 fl oz bar / **Sealtest**	70
Orange Treat: 3 fl oz bar / **Sealtest**	90
Popsicle, all fruit flavors / 3 fl oz	70
Sandwich / **Good Humor**	200
Strawberry Shortcake / **Good Humor**	200
Whammy Assorted Ice Cream / **Good Humor**	100
Whammy Chip Crunch / **Good Humor**	110
Vanilla, chocolate coated / **Good Humor**	170

Italian Foods

See also Pizza and Spaghetti

CALORIES

Cannelloni Florentine w veal, spinach, cheese and sauce, frozen: 13 oz / **Weight Watchers**	450
Eggplant Parmigiana, frozen: 4 oz / **Buitoni**	208
Eggplant Parmigiana, frozen: 13 oz / **Weight Watchers**	280
Lasagna	
Canned: 10 oz / **Hormel**	370
Canned: 7½ oz can / **Hormel Short Orders**	270
Frozen: 4 oz / **Buitoni** 26 oz	120
Frozen: 4 oz / **Buitoni** Family Size	168
Frozen: 7 oz / **Green Giant** Oven Bake Entrees	300
Frozen: 9 oz / **Green Giant** Boil-in-Bag Entrees	310
Frozen: 10½ oz / **Stouffer's**	385
Frozen: 1 entree / **Swanson** Hungry-Man	540
Frozen w cheese, veal and sauce: 13 oz / **Weight Watchers**	350
Frozen w meat sauce: 4 oz / **Buitoni** 14 oz	168
Mix, prepared: 1/5 pkg / **Golden Grain** Stir-n-Serv	140
Manicotti, frozen w sauce: 4 oz / **Buitoni**	176
Manicotti, frozen wo sauce: 4 oz / **Buitoni**	196
Ravioli	
Beef, in sauce, canned: 7½ oz / **Franco-American**	220
Beef, in sauce, canned: 7½ oz / **Franco-American** Raviolos	220
Cheese, canned: ½ can / **Buitoni**	204
Cheese, frozen: 4 oz / **Buitoni** 12 Count Round	272

CALORIES

Cheese, frozen: 4 oz / **Buitoni** 40 Count	316
Meat, canned: ½ can / **Buitoni**	224
Meat, frozen: 4 oz / **Buitoni** 40 Count	340
Meat, frozen: 4 oz / **Buitoni** Raviolettes	340
Ravioli Parmigiana, cheese, frozen:	
4 oz / **Buitoni**	152
Ravioli Parmigiana, meat, frozen:	
4 oz / **Buitoni**	192
Rotini in tomato sauce, canned:	
7½ oz / **Franco-American**	200
Rotini and meatballs, in tomato sauce, canned:	
7¼ oz / **Franco-American**	230
Sausage and peppers w rigati, frozen:	
4 oz / **Buitoni**	164
Shells w sauce, frozen: 4 oz / **Buitoni**	136
Shrimp Marinara w shells, frozen:	
4 oz / **Buitoni**	116
Spaghetti, in sauce w veal:	
1 entree / **Swanson "TV"** 8¼ oz	290
Veal Parmigiana	
Frozen: 5 oz / **Banquet** Cookin' Bag	287
Frozen: 7 oz / **Green Giant**	
Oven Bake Entrees	310
Frozen w spaghetti twists: 4 oz / **Buitoni**	160
Frozen w tomato sauce:	
32 oz / **Banquet** Buffet Supper	1563
Frozen w zucchini:	
9½ oz / **Weight Watchers**	230
Ziti, baked w sauce, frozen: 4 oz / **Buitoni**	136
Ziti w veal and sauce, frozen:	
13 oz / **Weight Watchers**	350

Jams, Jellies, Preserves, Butters, Marmalade

Butters
Apple: 1 tbsp / **Bama**	31
Apple, cider: 1 tsp / **Smucker's**	13
Apple, spiced: 1 tsp / **Smucker's**	13
Peach: 1 tsp / **Smucker's**	15

Jams
All flavors: 1 tsp / **Ann Page**	17
All flavors: 1 tsp / **Kraft**	16
All flavors: 1 tsp / **Smucker's**	18
All flavors, imitation:	
1 tsp / **Smucker's Slenderella** Low Calorie	8
Apricot: 1 tbsp / **Bama**	51
Apricot-pineapple, swt:	
1 tbsp / **Diet Delight**	21
Blackberry, swt: 1 tbsp / **Diet Delight**	21
Blackberry, swt: 1 tbsp / **S and W Nutradiet**	10
Peach: 1 tbsp / **Bama**	51
Pear: 1 tbsp / **Bama**	51
Plum: 1 tbsp / **Bama**	51
Raspberry, swt: 1 tbsp / **Diet Delight**	21
Raspberry, art swt: 1 tbsp / **S and W Nutradiet**	10
Strawberry, swt: 1 tbsp / **Diet Delight**	18
Strawberry, art swt:	
1 tbsp / **S and W Nutradiet**	12
Strawberry, imitation, art swt:	
1 tsp / **Smucker's**	1

CALORIES

Jellies
    All flavors: 1 tsp / **Ann Page** 17.5
    All flavors: 1 tbsp / **Bama** 51
    All flavors: 1 tsp / **Empress** 18
    All flavors: 1 tsp / **Kraft** 16
    All flavors except low calorie:
      1 tbsp / **Kraft** 47
    All flavors: 1 tsp / **Smucker's** 18
    All flavors, imitation: 1 tsp / **Smucker's**
      Slenderella Low Calorie 8
    Apple: 1 tbsp / **Kraft** Low Calorie 22
    Apple, swt: 1 tbsp / **Diet Delight** 22
    Apple, art swt: 1 tbsp / **S and W Nutradiet** 13
    Blackberry-apple: 1 tbsp / **Kraft**
      Low Calorie 22
    Blackberry, imitation: ⅜ oz / **Smucker's**
      Single Service 4
    Cherry, imitation: ⅜ oz / **Smucker's**
      Single Service 4
    Grape: 1 tsp / **Home Brands** 18
    Grape: 1 tbsp / **Kraft** Low Calorie 22
    Grape, swt: 1 tbsp / **Diet Delight** 21
    Grape, art swt: 1 tbsp / **S and W Nutradiet** 10
    Grape, imitation: 1 tsp / **Kraft** Low Calorie 6
    Grape, imitation, art swt: 1 tsp / **Smucker's** 1
    Grape, imitation, art swt: ⅜ oz /
      Smucker's Single Service 4
Marmalade
    All flavors: 1 tsp / **Ann Page** 18
    Orange: 1 tbsp / **Bama** 54
    Orange: 1 tbsp / **Kraft** 54
    Orange: 1 tbsp / **Kraft** Low Calorie 25
    Orange: 1 tsp / **Smucker's** 18
    Orange, art swt: 1 tbsp / **S and W Nutradiet** 11
    Orange, imitation: 1 tsp / **Smucker's**
      Slenderella Low Calorie 8
Preserves
    All flavors: 1 tsp / **Ann Page** 18

CALORIES

All flavors: 1 tsp / **Empress**   18
All flavors: 1 tsp / **Kraft**   16
All flavors: 1 tbsp / **Kraft** Regular   55
All flavors: 1 tsp / **Smucker's**   18
Apricot: 1 tbsp / **Bama**   51
Apricot-pineapple, art swt: 1 tbsp /
  S and W Nutradiet   10
Boysenberry, art swt: 1 tbsp / **S and W**
  Nutradiet   11
Cherry, art swt: 1 tbsp / **S and W Nutradiet**   11
Peach: 1 tbsp / **Bama**   51
Peach: 1 tbsp / **Kraft** Low Calorie   25
Pear: 1 tbsp / **Bama**   51
Plum: 1 tbsp / **Bama**   51
Raspberry, black: 1 tbsp / **Kraft**
  Low Calorie   25
Strawberry: 1 tsp / **Home Brands**   18
Strawberry, imitation: 1 tsp / **Kraft**
  Low Calorie   6
Spreads
  All fruit flavors: 1 tsp / **Smucker's**
    Low Sugar   8
  All fruit flavors: 1 tsp / **Tillie Lewis**   4

Liqueurs and Brandies

CALORIES

Brandies: 1 fl oz
Leroux Deluxe	67
Apricot / **Leroux**	92
Blackberry / **Leroux**	91
Blackberry / **Leroux Polish** type	92
Cherry / **Leroux**	91
Cherry / **Leroux** Kirschwasser	80
Coffee / **Leroux**	91
Ginger / **Leroux**	76
Peach / **Leroux**	93

Liqueurs: 1 fl oz
Anesone / **Leroux**	86
Anisette / **Leroux**	89
Apricot / **Leroux**	85
Aquavit / **Leroux**	75
Banana / **Leroux**	92
Blackberry / **Leroux**	78
Cherry / **Kijafa**	49
Cherry / **Leroux**	80
Cherry / **Leroux Cherry Karise**	71
Chocolate, cherry / **Cheri-Suisse**	90
Chocolate, minted / **Vandermint**	90
Chocolate, orange / **Sabra**	91
Claristine / **Leroux**	114
Coffee / **Pasha Turkish Coffee**	97
Creme de Cacao, brown / **Leroux**	101
Creme de Cacao, white / **Leroux**	98
Creme de Cafe / **Leroux**	104

CALORIES

Creme de Cassis / **Leroux**	88
Creme de Menthe, green / **Leroux**	110
Creme de Menthe, white / **Leroux**	101
Creme de Noya / **Leroux**	108
Curacao / **Leroux**	88
Gold-O-Mint / **Leroux**	110
Grenadine / **Leroux**	81
Kummel / **Leroux**	75
Lochan Ora Scotch	89
Maraschino / **Leroux**	88
Peach / **Leroux**	85
Peppermint Schnapps / **Leroux**	87
Raspberry / **Leroux**	74
Rock and Rye / **Leroux**	91
Rock and Rye–Irish Moss / **Leroux**	110
Sloe gin / **Leroux**	74
Strawberry / **Leroux**	74
Triple Sec / **Leroux**	102

Macaroni

plain, cooked to firm stage "al dente":
  1 cup   192
plain, cooked to tender stage:
  1 cup   155
and beef, in tomato sauce, canned:
  7½ oz / **Franco-American** Beefy Mac   220
and beef, frozen:
  32 oz / **Banquet** Buffet Supper   1000
and beef w tomato sauce, frozen:
  9 oz / **Green Giant** Boil-in-Bag Entrees   240
and beef w tomatoes, frozen:
  ½ pkg / **Stouffer's** 11½ oz   190
and cheese

	CALORIES
Canned: 7¼ oz / **Franco-American**	180
Canned: 7½ oz can / **Hormel Short Orders**	340
Frozen: 8 oz / **Banquet**	279
Frozen: 32 oz / **Banquet** Buffet Supper	1027
Frozen: 8 oz / **Banquet** Cookin' Bag	261
Frozen: 9 oz / **Green Giant** Boil-in-Bag Entrees	330
Frozen: 8 oz / **Green Giant** Oven Bake Entrees	290
Frozen: 10 oz / **Howard Johnson's**	541
Frozen: 19 oz / **Howard Johnson's**	1028
Frozen: 1 pkg / **Morton** Casserole	280
Frozen: ½ pkg / **Stouffer's** 12 oz	260
Frozen / **Swanson** 7 oz	230
Mix, dry: 1.8 oz / **Ann Page**	190

	CALORIES
Mix, prepared: ¼ pkg / **Betty Crocker**	310
Mix, prepared: 1 pouch / **Betty Crocker** Mug-O-Lunch	240
Mix, prepared: ¼ pkg / **Golden Grain** Macaroni and Cheddar	200
Mix, prepared: ¾ cup / **Kraft**	280
Mix, prepared: ½ cup / **Pennsylvania Dutch Brand**	160
and meatballs, in tomato sauce, canned: 7½ oz / **Franco-American** Meatball Mac	220

Mayonnaise

	CALORIES
1 tbsp	
Ann Page	100
Best	100
Hellmann's	100
Kraft Real	100
Mrs. Filbert's Real	100
Nu Made	100
Piedmont	100
Sultana	100
Flavored / **Durkee** Famous Sauce	69
Imitation	
Mrs. Filbert's	40
Piedmont	50
Weight Watchers	40
Miracle Whip / **Kraft**	70
w relish / **Mrs. Filbert's** Relish Spread	80

Meat

FRESH

Beaver, roasted: 3 oz	211
Beef, ground, lean (10% fat), raw: 4 oz	202
Beef, ground, regular (21% fat), raw: 4 oz	303
Beef, roast, oven-cooked, no liquid added:	
relatively fat, such as rib:	
3 oz lean and fat	375
1.8 oz lean only	125
relatively lean, such as heel of round:	
3 oz lean and fat	165
2.7 oz lean only	125
Brains, all varieties, raw: 4 oz	141
Hamburger (ground beef), broiled:	
3 lean oz	185
3 regular oz	245
Heart	
Beef, lean, cooked: 4 oz	212
Beef, lean, raw: 4 oz	122
Calf, cooked: 4 oz	235
Calf, raw: 4 oz	140
Lamb, cooked: 4 oz	294
Lamb, raw: 4 oz	183
Kidney, beef, cooked: 4 oz	285
Kidney, beef, raw: 4 oz	147
Kidney, lamb, raw: 4 oz	119
Lamb,* cooked:	
Chop, 4.8 oz thick w bone, broiled	400
4.0 oz lean and fat, broiled	400
2.6 oz lean only, broiled	140
Leg, roasted:	
3 oz lean and fat	235

* Outer layer of fat on cut removed to within approx ½ in of lean.

	CALORIES
2.5 oz lean only	130
Shoulder, roasted:	
3 oz lean and fat	285
2.3 oz lean only	130
Liver	
Beef, fried: 4 oz	259
Beef, raw: 4 oz	158
Calf, fried: 4 oz	295
Calf, raw: 4 oz	158
Lamb, broiled: 4 oz	295
Lamb, raw: 4 oz	154
Pork, fresh,* cooked:	
Chop, 3.5 oz thick w bone	260
2.3 oz lean and fat	260
1.7 lean only	130
Roast, oven-cooked, no liquid added:	
3 oz lean and fat	310
2.4 oz lean only	175
Cuts, simmered:	
3 oz lean and fat	320
2.2 oz lean only	135
Quail: 8 oz dressed, ready to cook	343
Rabbit, domesticated: 1 lb dressed, ready to cook	581
Rabbit, wild: 1 lb dressed, ready to cook	490
Steak, broiled	
relatively fat such as sirloin:	
3 oz lean and fat	330
2 oz lean only	115
relatively lean such as round:	
3 oz lean and fat	220
2.4 oz lean only	130
Sweetbreads, 4 oz cooked	
Beef	362
Calf	190
Lamb	198
Tongue, beef, cooked: 4 oz	276

* Outer layer of fat on cut removed to within approx ½ in of lean.

	CALORIES
Tongue, calf, cooked: 4 oz	181
Tongue, lamb, cooked: 4 oz	287
Veal, med fat, cooked, bone removed:	
Cutlet, 3 oz	185
Roast, 3 oz	230

CANNED, CURED, PROCESSED

Bacon, cooked	
Hormel Black Label / 1 slice	35
Hormel Range Brand / 1 slice	45
Hormel Red Label / 1 slice	37
Oscar Mayer / 1 slice	40
Swift Lazy Maple / 1 slice	40
Swift Premium / 1 slice	40
Wilson's Certified / 1 oz	169
Canadian: 1 slice / **Oscar Mayer**	40
Canadian: 1 oz / **Wilson's** Certified	42
Bacon bits, canned, cooked: 1 oz / **Wilson's**	140
Banquet loaf: 1 slice / **Eckrich** 8 oz pkg	75
Banquet loaf: 1 slice / **Eckrich** Beef Smorgas Pac	105
Bar-B-Q Loaf: 1 slice / **Oscar Mayer**	50
Beef, chopped: 1 slice / **Eckrich** Slender-Sliced	40
Beef, chopped, canned: 1 oz / **Wilson's** Certified Bif	91
Beef, corned, canned: 3 oz / **Dinty Moore**	190
Beef, corned, canned: 2.3 oz / **Libby's**	240
Beef, corned, canned: 1 oz / **Safeway**	35
Beef, corned brisket, cooked: 3½ oz / **Swift Premium** for Oven Roasting	270
Beef, corned brisket, canned: 1 oz / **Wilson's** Certified	45
Beef, corned, chopped: 1 slice / **Eckrich** Slender-Sliced	40
Beef, dried, chunked and formed: ¾ oz / **Swift Premium**	35
Beef, smoked, sliced: 1 oz / **Safeway**	35
Beef, smoked, sliced: 1 oz / **Safeway** Spicy	40
Beef roast, canned: 1 oz / **Wilson's** Certified	33

	CALORIES
Beef steaks, breaded, frozen: 4 oz / **Hormel**	370
Bologna	
Eckrich 12 oz pkg / 1 slice	95
Eckrich 16 oz pkg / 1 slice	95
Eckrich Smorgas Pac / 1 slice	90
Eckrich thick-sliced / 1 slice (12 oz pkg)	160
Eckrich thick-sliced / 1 slice (16 oz pkg)	170
Hormel / 1 oz	85
Swift Premium / 1 oz	95
Wilson's Certified / 1 oz	87
Beef: 1 slice / **Eckrich** 8 oz pkg	95
Beef: 1 slice / **Eckrich** 12 oz pkg	95
Beef: 1 slice / **Eckrich** Beef Smorgas Pac	70
Beef: 1 slice / **Oscar Mayer**	70
Coarse ground: 1 oz / **Hormel**	75
Fine ground: 1 oz / **Hormel**	80
Garlic: 1 slice / **Eckrich**	95
Ring: 2 oz / **Eckrich**	200
Ring, garlic: 1 slice / **Eckrich**	95
Ring, pickled: 2 oz / **Eckrich**	190
Braunschweiger: 1 oz / **Oscar Mayer**	100
Braunschweiger: 1 oz / **Wilson's Certified**	90
Breakfast strips: 1 strip / **Swift Sizzlean**	50
Frankfurters: 1 frank	
Eckrich 12 oz pkg	120
Eckrich Jumbo	190
Eckrich Skinless 16 oz pkg	150
Hormel Range Brand Wranglers	
Smoked Franks	180
Hormel Wieners 12 oz pkg	105
Hormel Wieners 16 oz pkg	140
Oscar Mayer Wieners	140
Wilson's Certified Skinless	139
Beef / **Eckrich**	150
Beef / **Eckrich** Jumbo	190
Beef / **Hormel** Wieners 12 oz pkg	105
Beef / **Hormel** Wieners 16 oz pkg	140
Beef / **Hormel Wranglers** Smoked Franks	160

Beef / **Oscar Mayer**	140
Beef / **Wilson's** Certified	136
Frozen, batter-wrapped / **Hormel Corn Dogs**	230
Frozen, batter-wrapped / **Hormel Tater Dogs**	190
Gourmet Loaf: 1 slice / **Eckrich**	40
Gourmet Loaf: 1 slice / **Eckrich** Beef Smorgas Pac	30
Ham, luncheon type	
Cooked: 1 slice / **Eckrich**	40
Cooked: 1 oz / **Hormel**	35
Cooked, sliced: 1 oz / **Safeway**	50
Cooked, smoked: 1 slice / **Oscar Mayer**	30
Chopped: 1 oz / **Hormel**	70
Chopped: 2 oz / **Hormel** 8 lb can	180
Chopped: 1 slice / **Oscar Mayer**	65
Chopped, smoked: 1 slice /	
Eckrich Slender-Sliced	40
Ham, whole, canned	
Oscar Mayer Jubilee / 4 oz	130
Swift Premium / 3½ oz	220
Swift Premium Hostess / 3½ oz	140
Wilson's Certified Boned and Rolled / 1 oz	56
Wilson's Certified Fully Cooked / 1 oz	48
Wilson's Certified Tender-Made / 1 oz	44
Ham, whole, plastic or other wrap	
Hormel Bone-In / 6 oz	310
Hormel Cure 81 / 6 oz	290
Hormel Curemaster / 6 oz	210
Swift Premium Hostess / 3½ oz	150
Smoked, aged:	
1 oz / **Wilson's** Certified Festival Ham	48
Ham slice, smoked: 4 oz / **Oscar Mayer** Jubilee	140
Ham steaks: 1 slice / **Oscar Mayer** Jubilee	70
Ham patties: 1 patty / **Hormel**	200
Ham patties:	
1 patty / **Swift** Premium Brown 'n Serve	250
Ham and cheese loaf: 1 slice / **Oscar Mayer**	75
Honey loaf: 1 slice / **Eckrich**	45
Honey loaf: 1 slice / **Eckrich** Smorgas Pac	45

CALORIES

Honey loaf: 1 slice / **Oscar Mayer**	40
Liver, beef, thin sliced:	
2.6 oz / **Swift's** Tru Tender	140
Liver cheese: 1 slice / **Oscar Mayer**	110
Luncheon meat: 1 slice / **Oscar Mayer**	100
Luncheon meat, spiced: 1 oz / **Hormel**	80
Old fashioned loaf: 1 slice / **Eckrich**	75
Old fashioned loaf: 1 slice / **Eckrich** Smorgas Pac	75
Old fashioned loaf: 1 slice / **Oscar Mayer**	65
Olive loaf: 1 slice / **Oscar Mayer**	65
Pastrami, chopped: 1 slice / **Eckrich** Slender-Sliced	47
Pastrami, sliced: 1 oz / **Safeway**	40
Pepperoni: 1 oz / **Swift**	150
Pepperoni, sliced: 1 oz / **Hormel**	140
Pickle loaf: 1 slice / **Eckrich** 8 oz pkg	85
Pickle loaf: 1 slice / **Eckrich** Smorgas Pac	85
Pickle loaf, beef: 1 slice / **Eckrich** Smorgas Pac	65
Pickle and pimento loaf: 1 slice / **Oscar Mayer**	65
Picnic, smoked: 1 oz / **Wilson's** Certified	70
Polish sausage:	
1 link / **Eckrich** Polska Kielbasa Skinless	190
Polish sausage, ring:	
2 oz / **Eckrich** Polska Kielbasa	200
Polish sausage ring: 3 oz / **Hormel** Kolbase	240
Polish sausage, smoked beef: 1 oz / **Frito-Lay**	73
Pork, chopped, canned: 1 oz / **Wilson's** Mor	87
Pork butt, cured smoked:	
1 oz / **Wilson's** Certified Smoked Tasty Meat	72
Pork loin, chipped, smoked:	
1 slice / **Eckrich** Slender-Sliced	47
Pork roast, canned: 1 oz / **Wilson's** Certified	440
Pork steaks, breaded, frozen: 3 oz / **Hormel**	220
Salami	
Hormel Dairy Hard / 1 oz	120
Hormel Di Lusso Genoa / 1 oz	130
Oscar Mayer Beef Cotto / 1 slice	50
Oscar Mayer for Beer / 1 slice	50
Oscar Mayer Cotto / 1 slice	50

Oscar Mayer Hard / 1 slice	37
Swift Premium Genoa / 1 oz	120
Swift Premium Hard / 1 oz	110
Sausage, beef, smoked: 2 oz / **Eckrich**	190
Sausage, pork bulk: 1 oz / **Wilson's** Certified	135
Sausage, pork, smoked: 3 oz / **Hormel** No-Link	290
Sausage links	
Hormel Brown 'n Serve / 1 sausage	78
Hormel Little Sizzlers / 1 sausage	67
Hormel Midget Links / 1 sausage	112
Oscar Mayer Little Friers / 1 link	65
Swift's The Original / 1 link	75
Swift Premium Bacon 'n Sausage / 1 link	70
Swift Premium Brown 'n Serve Kountry Kured / 1 link	85
Beef: 1 link / **Swift** Premium Brown 'n Serve	85
Sausage links, smoked	
Eckrich 16 oz pkg / 1 link	190
Eckrich Skinless / 1 link	115
Eckrich Smok-Y-Links / 1 link	75
Eckrich Skinless Smok-Y-Links / 1 link	85
Hormel Smokies / 1 sausage	92
Oscar Mayer / 1 link	140
Wilson's Certified Smokies / 1 oz	84
Beef: 1 link / **Eckrich** Smok-Y-Links	75
Sausage sticks	
Beef: 1¼ oz / **Slim Jim** Polish Sausage	108
Beef: ⅝ oz / **Cow-Boy Jo's**	81
Beef, smoked:	
¼ oz / **Cow-Boy Jo's** Smok-O-Roni	42
Beef, smoked: ½ oz / **Slim Jim**	83
Pickled: 1¼ oz / **Lowrey's** Hot Sausage	110
Pickled: ⅝ oz / **Lowrey's** Polish Sausage	50
Scrapple, in tube: 1 oz / **Oscar Mayer**	50
Scrapple, Philadelphia style, canned: 1 oz / **Oscar Mayer**	45
Spam: 3 oz / **Hormel**	260
Spam w cheese chunks: 3 oz / **Hormel**	260

	CALORIES
Spam, smoke-flavored: 3 oz / **Hormel**	260
Substitute, meat, BV in glass jars:	
1 oz / **Wilson's** Certified	43
Summer sausage:	
1 slice / **Oscar Mayer** Thuringer Cervelat	70
Summer sausage, beef: 1 slice / **Oscar Mayer**	70
Summer sausage, beef: 1 oz / **Swift** Premium	90
Thuringer: 1 oz / **Hormel Old Smokehouse**	100
Tripe, canned: 5 oz / **Libby's**	173
Veal steaks, frozen: 4 oz / **Hormel**	130
Veal steaks, breaded, frozen: 4 oz / **Hormel**	240
Vienna sausage, canned: 1 piece / **Hormel**	52
Vienna sausage, canned: 1 sausage / **Libby's**	84
Vienna sausage, canned, in barbecue sauce:	
1 sausage / **Libby's**	76

MEAT ENTREES, CANNED

Beef w barbecue sauce: 5 oz / **Morton House**	240
Beef, corned w cabbage: 8 oz / **Hormel**	150
Beef goulash: 7½ oz can / **Hormel Short Orders**	240
Beef, sliced w gravy: 6¼ oz can / **Morton House**	190
Beef stew	
Dinty Moore / 7½ oz	180
Dinty Moore Short Orders / 7½ oz	180
Libby's / 1 cup	78
Morton House / 8 oz	240
Swanson / 7½ oz	190
Hash, beef w potatoes:	
7½ oz can / **Dinty Moore Short Orders**	270
Hash	
Corned beef: 7½ oz / **Ann Page**	400
Corned beef: 7½ oz / **Mary Kitchen**	400
Corned beef: 3 oz / **Libby's**	156
Corned beef:	
7½ oz can / **Mary Kitchen Short Orders**	385
Roast beef: 7½ oz / **Mary Kitchen**	390
Roast beef:	
7½ oz can / **Mary Kitchen Short Orders**	355

Pork, sliced w gravy: 6¼ oz / **Morton House**	190
Salisbury steak w mushroom gravy:	
4 1/6 oz / **Morton House**	160
Sloppy Joe: 7½ oz can / **Hormel Short Orders**	365
Sloppy Joe, beef: ⅓ cup / **Libby's**	163
Sloppy Joe, pork: ⅓ cup / **Libby's**	139
Stew, meatball: 6¼ oz / **Morton House**	290
Stew, meatball: 1 cup / **Libby's**	121
Stew, Mulligan:	
7½ oz can / **Dinty Moore Short Orders**	240

MEAT ENTREES, FROZEN

Beef, chipped, creamed:	
5 oz / **Banquet** Cookin' Bag	124
Beef, chipped, creamed: 1 pkg / **Stouffer's** 5½ oz	235
Beef, sirloin, chopped w green beans, cauliflower	
and sauce: 9½ oz / **Weight Watchers**	560
Beef, sliced: 1 entree / **Swanson** Hungry-Man	330
Beef, sliced w barbecue sauce:	
5 oz / **Banquet** Cookin' Bag	126
Beef, sliced w gravy:	
32 oz / **Banquet** Buffet Supper	782
Beef, sliced w gravy: 5 oz / **Banquet** Cookin' Bag	116
Beef, sliced w gravy:	
5 oz / **Green Giant** Boil-in-Bag Toast Toppers	130
Beef, sliced w gravy and whipped potatoes:	
1 entree / **Swanson** "TV"	190
Beef stroganoff: 1 pkg / **Stouffer's** 9¾ oz	390
Green pepper steak: 1 pkg / **Stouffer's** 10½ oz	350
Meat loaf	
Banquet Buffet Supper / 32 oz	1445
Banquet Cookin' Bag / 5 oz	224
Banquet Man Pleaser / 19 oz	916
Morton Country Table / 1 entree	430
w tomato sauce and whipped potatoes:	
1 entree / **Swanson** "TV"	330
Meatballs w gravy and whipped potatoes:	
1 entree / **Swanson** "TV"	330

Noodles and beef: 32 oz / **Banquet** Buffet Supper	754
Salisbury steak	
Banquet Man Pleaser / 19 oz	873
Morton Country Table / 1 entree	490
Stouffer's 12 oz / ½ pkg	250
Swanson Hungry-Man / 1 entree	640
w crinkle-cut potatoes: 1 entree /	
Swanson "TV"	370
w gravy: 32 oz / **Banquet** Buffet Supper	1454
w gravy: 5 oz / **Banquet** Cookin' Bag	246
w gravy: 7 oz / **Green Giant** Oven Bake	
Entrees	290
w tomato sauce: 9 oz / **Green Giant**	
Boil-in-Bag Entrees	390
Sausage, cheese and tomato pies:	
7 oz / **Weight Watchers**	390
Sloppy Joe: 5 oz / **Banquet** Cookin' Bag	199
Sloppy Joe: 5 oz / **Green Giant** Boil-in-Bag	
Toast Toppers	160
Steak, beef, chopped w carrots, green peppers and	
mushroom sauce: 10 oz / **Weight Watchers**	390
Stew, beef: 32 oz / **Banquet** Buffet Supper	700
Stew, beef: 9 oz / **Green Giant** Boil-in-Bag	
Entrees	160
Stew, beef: 1 pkg / **Stouffer's** 10 oz	310
Stew, beef w biscuits: 7 oz / **Green Giant**	
Oven Bake Entrees	190
Stuffed cabbage w beef, in tomato sauce:	
7 oz / **Green Giant** Oven Bake Entrees	220
Stuffed green pepper w beef:	
7 oz / **Green Giant** Oven Bake Entrees	200

MEAT SUBSTITUTES

Breakfast links: 1 link / **Morningstar Farms**	62
Breakfast patties: 1 pattie / **Morningstar Farms**	111
Breakfast strips: 1 strip / **Morningstar Farms**	38

CALORIES

Grillers: 1 griller / **Morningstar Farms**	211
Luncheon slices: 1 slice / **Morningstar Farms**	25

Mexican Foods

CALORIES

Beans
    Pinto, in chili sauce, canned:

4 oz / **Old El Paso** Mexe Beans	124
Refried, canned: 4 oz / **Old El Paso**	108
Refried, canned:	
½ cup / **Ortega** Lightly Spicy	170
Refried, canned: ½ cup / **Ortega** True Bean	170
Burritos, beef, canned: 4 oz / **Hormel**	220
Chiles, diced, canned: 1 oz / **Ortega**	7
Chiles, in strips, canned: 1 oz / **Ortega**	7
Chiles, whole, canned: 1 oz / **Ortega**	7
Chili con carne, canned	
w beans: 8 oz / **A & P**	440
w beans: 7½ oz / **Hormel**	320
w beans: 7½ oz can / **Hormel Short Orders**	320
w beans: 1 cup / **Libby's**	178
w beans: 7½ oz / **Morton House**	340
w beans: 7¾ oz / **Swanson**	310
w beans, hot: 7½ oz can /	
Hormel Short Orders	320
w beans, low sodium: 7¾ oz / **Campbell**	310
wo beans: 7½ oz / **Hormel**	340
wo beans: 7½ oz can / **Hormel Short Orders**	340
wo beans: 1 cup / **Libby's**	130
wo beans: 7½ oz / **Morton House**	340
Chili Mac, canned:	
7½ oz can / **Hormel Short Orders**	220

Enchiladas
    Canned, beef w chili gravy:
        4 oz / **Old El Paso**   200
        Frozen: 1 dinner / **El Chico**   880
    Frozen, beef w cheese and chili gravy:
        32 oz / **Banquet** Buffet Supper   1118
    Frozen, beef and cheese w gravy:
        3 enchiladas / **El Chico**   710
    Frozen, beef w gravy:
        3 enchiladas / **El Chico**   710
    Frozen, beef w sauce:
        6 oz / **Banquet** Cookin' Bag   207
Mexican dinner, frozen: 1 dinner / **El Chico**   1080
Queso dinner, frozen: 1 dinner / **El Chico**   810
Pepper, hot, diced, canned: 1 oz / **Ortega**   8
Peppers, hot, whole, canned: 1 oz / **Ortega**   8
Salsa, green chile, canned: 1 oz / **Ortega**   7
Saltillo dinner, frozen: 1 dinner / **El Chico**   930
Tacos, beef, frozen: 3 tacos / **El Chico**   410
Tacos, prepared: 1 taco / **Ortega**   220
Taco shell: 1 shell / **Lawry's**   48
Taco shell: 1 shell / **Ortega**   50
Tamales
    Canned: 4 oz / **Old El Paso**   160
    Beef, canned: 1 tamale / **Hormel**   70
    Beef, canned:
        7½ oz can / **Hormel Short Orders**   320
        Beef, in jar: 2 tamales / **Swift Derby**   240
Tomatoes and hot green chiles, canned:
    1 oz / **Ortega**   7
Tostada dinner mix:
    1 complete pkg (shells, sauce, seasonings) /
    Lawry's Tostada Kit   1041
Tostada shells: 1 shell / **Lawry's**   48

Milk

CALORIES

Buttermilk: 8 fl oz (1 cup)
.1% fat / **Borden**	88
.2% fat / **Sealtest** Skim milk	71
.5% fat / **Borden**	90
.5% fat / **Meadow Gold**	105
.8% fat / **Golden Nugget**	92
.8% fat / **Light n' Lively**	95
1% fat / **Borden**	107
1.5% fat / **Borden**	110
1.4% fat / **Friendship**	120
1.5% fat / **Lucerne**	120
2% fat / **Borden**	122
2% fat / **Sealtest** Lowfat	114
3.5% fat / **Borden**	158
Condensed, swt: ¼ cup / **Borden** Dime Brand	252
Condensed, swt: ¼ cup / **Borden** Eagle Brand	250

Condensed, swt:
¼ cup / **Borden** Magnolia Brand	252

Dry, nonfat
¼ cup / **Carnation**	61
Reconstituted: 8 oz glass / **Borden**	82
Reconstituted: 8 oz glass / **Carnation**	81
Reconstituted: 8 oz glass / **Lucerne**	80
Reconstituted: 8 oz glass / **Sannalec**	82

Evaporated, canned: 8 fl oz (1 cup)
Carnation	348
Carnation Skimmed	192
Lucerne	345
Pet / ½ cup	170
Evaporated skim: ½ cup / **Pet**	100
Imitation milk: 8 fl oz / **Lucerne**	150

Skim or low-fat: 8 fl oz
0% fat / **Lucerne**	90
.1% fat / **Borden**	81

	CALORIES
.1% fat / **Sealtest**	79
.4% fat / **Sealtest** Diet Skim	103
.5% fat / **Meadow Gold**	87
1% fat / **Lucerne** 1-10	110
2% fat / **Lucerne** 2-10	130
2% fat / **Meadow Gold** Viva	137
Fortified, .1% fat / **Borden**	81
Fortified, .1% fat / **Gail Borden**	81
Fortified, 1% fat / **Light n' Lively** Lowfat	114
Fortified, 1.75% fat / **Borden** Lite Line	117
Fortified, 2% fat / **Borden** Hi-Protein	132
Fortified, 2% fat / **Sealtest** Vita-lure	137

Whole: 8 fl oz

3.25% fat / **Sealtest**	144
3.3% fat / **Meadow Gold**	166
3.5% fat / **Borden**	160
3.5% fat / **Lucerne**	160
3.5% fat / **Sealtest**	151
3.7% fat / **Borden** Cream Line	159
3.7% fat / **Sealtest**	157
3.8% fat / **Lucerne**	170
Fortified / **Sealtest** Multivitamin Milk	151

FLAVORED MILK BEVERAGES

All flavors, canned: 10 fl oz / **Carnation** Slender	225
All flavors, mix: 1 env / **Lucerne** Instant Breakfast	290
Cherry-vanilla, canned:	
8 fl oz / **Borden** Milk Shake	291
Chocolate, canned: 9½ fl oz / **Borden's** Dutch	232
Chocolate, dairy pack, 3.5% fat:	
8 fl oz / **Borden's** Dutch Chocolate Milk	210
Chocolate fudge, canned:	
8 fl oz / **Borden's** Frosted Shake	284
Chocolate mixes	
Carnation Instant Breakfast / 1 env	130
Carnation Slender / 1 env	110
Ovaltine / ¾ oz	80
PDQ / 3½ tsp	65

	CALORIES
Pillsbury Instant Breakfast / 1 pouch	290
Safeway / 2 tsp dry	90
Safeway (w 8 fl oz whole milk) / 2 tsp	215
Dutch, mix: 1 env / **Carnation** Slender	110
Malt, mix: 2 heaping tsp / **Borden**	77
Malt, mix:	
1 env / **Carnation** Instant Breakfast	130
Malt, mix: 1 env / **Carnation** Slender	110
Malt, mix, prepared:	
1 pouch / **Pillsbury** Instant Breakfast	290
Coffee	
Canned: 8 fl oz / **Borden's** Frosted Shake	286
Canned: 8 fl oz / **Borden's** Milk Shake	291
Mix: 1 env / **Carnation** Instant Breakfast	130
Mix: 1 env / **Carnation** Slender	110
Eggnog	
Dairy case, 4.7% fat: ½ cup / **Borden**	132
Dairy case, 6% fat: ½ cup / **Borden**	151
Dairy case, 8% fat: ½ cup / **Borden**	171
Mix: 1 env / **Carnation** Instant Breakfast	130
Mix: 2 heaping tbsp / **PDQ**	113
Malt-flavored	
Instant: 3 heaping tsp / **Carnation**	90
Mix: 2 heaping tsp / **Borden**	80
Mix: ¾ oz / **Ovaltine**	80
Chocolate, instant: 3 heaping tsp / **Carnation**	85
Mocha, canned: 8 fl oz / **Borden's** Milk Shake	291
Strawberry	
Canned: 8 fl oz / **Borden's** Frosted Shake	283
Canned: 8 fl oz / **Borden's** Milk Shake	291
Mix: 1 env / **Carnation** Instant Breakfast	130
Mix: 3½ tsp / **PDQ**	60
Mix, prepared:	
1 pouch / **Pillsbury** Instant Breakfast	290
Wild, mix: 1 env / **Carnation** Slender	110
Vanilla	
Canned: 8 fl oz / **Borden's** Frosted Shake	291
Mix: 1 env / **Carnation** Instant Breakfast	130

Mix, prepared:
    1 pouch / **Pillsbury** Instant Breakfast   290
French, mix: 1 env / **Carnation** Slender   110

Muffins: English and Sweet

CALORIES

1 muffin unless noted

	CALORIES
Apple cinnamon, mix, prepared / **Betty Crocker**	160
Apple cinnamon, refrigerator, to bake / **Pillsbury**	130
Banana nut, mix, prepared /	
Betty Crocker Chiquita	180
Blueberry	
Thomas' Toast-R-Cakes	110
Frozen / **Howard Johnson's** Toasties	121
Frozen / **Morton**	120
Frozen / **Morton** Rounds	110
Frozen / **Pepperidge Farm**	130
Mix, prepared / **Betty Crocker**	120
Bran / **Oroweat** Bran'nola	160
Bran / **Thomas'** Toast-R-Cakes	120
Corn	
Thomas'	190
Thomas' Toast-R-Cakes	120
Frozen / **Howard Johnson's** Toasties	112
Frozen / **Morton**	130
Frozen / **Morton** Rounds	130
Frozen / **Pepperidge Farm**	140
Frozen / **Thomas'** Toast-R-Cakes	120
Mix, prepared / **Betty Crocker**	160
Mix, prepared / **Flako**	140

CALORIES

    Refrigerator, to bake / **Pillsbury**   130
English
    Arnold   130
    Earth Grains / 2⅓ oz   160
    Home Pride   140
    Pepperidge Farm   130
    Thomas'   130
    Wonder   130
    Frozen / **Thomas'**   130
    Cinnamon-raisin / **Pepperidge Farm**   140
    Onion / **Thomas'**   130
    Sour dough / **Oroweat**   150
    Wheat / **Home Pride**   140
    Honeyberry wheat / **Oroweat**   160
    Honey butter / **Oroweat**   150
Orange, frozen / **Howard Johnson's** Toasties   113
Orange, mix, prepared / **Betty Crocker** Sunkist   160
Pineapple, mix, prepared / **Betty Crocker**   120
Raisin / **Oroweat**   160
Raisin / **Wonder** Rounds   150
Raisin bran, frozen / **Pepperidge Farm**   130
Sour dough / **Wonder**   130
Wild blueberry, mix, prepared / **Duncan Hines**   110

Noodles and Noodle Dishes

	CALORIES
Plain, cooked: 1 cup	200
Almondine, mix, prepared:	
¼ pkg / **Betty Crocker**	240
w beef, canned:	
7½ oz can / **Hormel Short Orders** Noodles 'n Beef	240
w beef sauce, mix, prepared:	
½ cup / **Pennsylvania Dutch Brand**	130
w beef-flavored sauce, mix, prepared:	
1 pouch / **Betty Crocker** Mug-O-Lunch	170
w butter sauce, mix, prepared:	
½ cup / **Pennsylvania Dutch Brand**	150
w cheese, mix, prepared:	
1/5 pkg / **Noodle-Roni** Parmesano	130
w cheese sauce, mix, prepared:	
½ cup / **Pennsylvania Dutch Brand**	150
w chicken, canned:	
7½ oz can / **Dinty Moore Short Orders**	215
w chicken sauce, mix, prepared:	
½ cup / **Pennsylvania Dutch Brand**	150
Romanoff, frozen:	
⅓ pkg / **Stouffer's**	170
Romanoff, mix, prepared:	
¼ pkg / **Betty Crocker**	230
Stroganoff, mix:	
2 oz / **Pennsylvania Dutch Brand**	210

CALORIES

Stroganoff, mix, prepared:

¼ pkg / **Betty Crocker**	230
w tuna, frozen:	
½ pkg / **Stouffer's** 11½ oz	200

Nuts

SALTED AND FLAVORED

CALORIES

1 oz unless noted (1 oz = 1/5 cup)

Almonds / **Granny Goose**	155
Almonds, dry roasted / **Planters**	170
Cashews	
Frito-Lay	168
Granny Goose	169
Planters	170
Planters Unsalted	160
Dry roasted, in jar / **A & P**	170
Dry roasted / **Planters**	160
Dry roasted / **Skippy**	165
Mixed	
Excel	190
Granny Goose	168
w peanuts / **Planters**	180
wo peanuts / **A & P** Fancy	190
wo peanuts / **Planters**	180
Unsalted / **Planters**	170
Dry roasted, in jar / **A & P**	180
Dry roasted / **Planters**	160
Dry roasted / **Skippy**	170
Peanuts	
A & P	180

Frito-Lay	172
Planters Old Fashioned	170
Unsalted / **Planters**	170
Cocktail halves / **Excel**	180
Cocktail / **Planters**	170
Dry roasted, in jar / **A & P**	180
Dry roasted / **Planters**	160
Dry roasted / **Skippy**	165
In shell: 1 oz edible portion / **A & P**	180
In shell:	
1 oz edible portion / **A & P** Raw Fancies	170
In shell: 1 oz edible portion / **Frito-Lay**	163
Spanish / **A & P**	180
Spanish / **Frito-Lay**	168
Spanish / **Granny Goose**	168
Spanish / **Planters**	170
Spanish, dry roasted / **Planters**	160
Virginia / **Granny Goose**	166
Virginia redskin / **Planters**	170
Pecans, pieces and chopped / **A & P**	200
Pecans / **Granny Goose**	203
Pecans, dry roasted / **Planters**	190
Pistachios: 1 oz of edible portion / **Frito-Lay**	175
Pistachios / **Granny Goose**	172
Pistachios, dry roasted / **Planters** Natural	170
Sesame Nut Mix / **Planters**	160
Soybeans, dry roasted / **Malt-O-Meal**	130
Soybeans, oil roasted / **Malt-O-Meal**	140
Soy nuts / **Planters**	130
Tavern / **Planters**	170

UNSALTED AND UNFLAVORED

Almonds

Dried, in shell: 10 nuts	60
Dried, in shell: 1 cup	187
Dried, shelled, chopped: 1 tbsp	48
Dried, shelled, chopped: 1 cup	777
Dried, shelled, slivered: 1 cup	688

CALORIES

Dried, shelled, whole: 1 cup	849
Roasted, in oil: 1 cup	984
Beechnuts, in shell: 1 lb	1572
Beechnuts, shelled: 1 lb	2576
Brazil nuts, in shell: 1 cup	383
Brazil nuts, shelled: 1 oz or 6-8 kernels	185
Brazil nuts, shelled: 1 cup	916
Butternuts, in shell: 1 lb	399
Butternuts, shelled: 1 lb	2853
Cashew nuts, roasted in oil: 1 cup	785
Cashew nuts, roasted in oil: 1 lb	2545
Chestnuts	
Fresh, in shell: 1 cup	189
Fresh, in shell: 1 lb	713
Fresh, shelled: 1 cup	310
Fresh, shelled: 1 lb	880
Filberts, in shell: 1 lb	1323
Filberts, shelled, chopped: 1 cup	729
Filberts, shelled, whole: 1 cup	856
Peanuts	
Roasted, in shell: 10 jumbo nuts	105
Roasted, in shell: 1 lb	1769
Roasted (Spanish and Virginia): 1 lb	2654
Roasted (Spanish and Virginia), chopped: 1 cup	842
Hickory nuts, shelled: 1 oz	201
Macadamia nuts, shelled: 1 oz	207
Pecans	
In shell: 10 large (64-77 per lb)	236
In shell: 10 extra large (56-63 per lb)	277
In shell: 10 oversize (55 or fewer per lb)	299
Chopped or pieces: 1 tbsp	52
Chopped or pieces: 1 cup	811
Halves: 10 large (451-550 per lb)	62
Halves: 10 jumbo (301-350 per lb)	96
Halves: 10 mammoth (250 or fewer per lb)	124
Pinenuts, Pignolias, shelled: 1 oz	156
Pinenuts, Piñon, shelled: 1 oz	180

Pistachio nuts, in shell: 1 lb	1347
Pistachio nuts, shelled: 1 lb	2694
Walnuts	
Black, in shell: 1 lb	627
Black, shelled, chopped or broken kernels: 1 tbsp	50
Black, shelled, chopped or broken kernels: 1 cup	785
Persian or English, in shell: 1 lb	1329
Persian or English, shelled, halves: 1 cup	651
Persian or English: 10 large nuts	322
Persian or English, chopped: 1 tbsp	52

Oils

1 tbsp unless noted

	CALORIES
Corn / **Mazola**	125
Corn: 2-second spray residue / **Mazla** No Stick	7
Corn / **Mrs. Tucker's** Salad Oil	130
Corn / **Nu Made**	120
Peanut / **Planters**	130
Popcorn / **Planters**	130
Safflower / **Nu Made**	120
Soybean / **Mrs. Tucker's** Salad Oil	130
Sunflower / **Sunlight**	120
Vegetable	
Crisco	120
Puritan	120
Swift Hi Lite	120
Swift Pour 'n Fry	120
Wesson	120
Vegetable-cottonseed / **Swift** Jewel	120
Vegetable-soybean / **Swift** Jewel	120

Olives

	CALORIES
Green	
10 small	33
10 large	45
10 giant	76
Ripe, black	
Ascolano: 10 extra large	61
Ascolano: 10 giant	89
Ascolano: 10 jumbo	105
Manzanillo: 10 small	38
Manzanillo: 10 medium	44
Manzanillo: 10 large	51
Manzanillo: 10 extra large	61
Mission: 10 small	54
Mission: 10 medium	63
Mission: 10 large	73
Mission: 10 extra large	87
Sevillano: 10 giant	64
Sevillano: 10 jumbo	76
Sevillano: 10 colossal	95
Sevillano: 10 supercolossal	114
Greek style: 10 medium	65
Greek style: 10 extra large	89

Pancakes, Waffles and Similar Breakfast Foods

Breakfast, frozen, French toast w sausages:
   1 entree / **Swanson** "TV" — 300

Breakfast, frozen, pancakes w sausages:
   1 entree / **Swanson** "TV" — ʃ 500

Breakfast, frozen, scrambled eggs w sausage and
   coffee cake: 1 entree / **Swanson** "TV" — 460

Breakfast bars, chocolate chip: 1 bar / **Carnation** — 210

Breakfast bars, chocolate crunch:
   1 bar / **Carnation** — 210

Breakfast bars, peanut butter crunch:
   1 bar / **Carnation** — 200

Breakfast squares: 1 bar / **General Mills** — 190

Crepes, mix, prepared:
   2 crepes 6-inch diam / **Aunt Jemima** — 110

French toast, frozen: 1 slice / **Aunt Jemima** — 85

French toast, frozen: 1 slice / **Downyflake** — 135

French toast w cinnamon, frozen:
   1 slice / **Aunt Jemima** Cinnamon Swirl — 105

Fritters, apple, frozen: 1 fritter / **Mrs. Paul's** — 120

Fritters, corn, frozen: 1 fritter / **Mrs. Paul's** — 130

Pancakes, frozen: 1 pancake / **Downyflake** — 80

Pancake batter, frozen:
   3 cakes 4-in diam / **Aunt Jemima** — 210

Pancake batter, frozen:
   3 cakes 4-in diam / **Aunt Jemima** Blueberry — 210

CALORIES

Pancake batter, frozen:
   3 cakes 4-in diam / **Aunt Jemima** Buttermilk   210
Pancake, mix, prepared
      Hungry Jack Complete / 3 cakes 4-in diam   220
      Hungry Jack Extra Lights / 3 cakes 4-in diam   180
      Tillie Lewis / 3 cakes 4-in diam   140
      Blueberry: 3 cakes 4-in diam / **Hungry Jack**   340
      Buttermilk: 3 cakes 4-in diam /
        Betty Crocker   270
      Buttermilk: 3 cakes 4-in diam /
        Betty Crocker Complete   210
      Buttermilk: 3 cakes 4-in diam / **Hungry Jack**   240
      Buttermilk: 3 cakes 4-in diam /
        Hungry Jack Complete   180
Pancake-waffle, mix, prepared
      Aunt Jemima Complete / 3 cakes 4-in diam   200
      Aunt Jemima Original / 3 cakes 4-in diam   220
      Log Cabin Complete / 3 cakes 4-in diam   180
      Log Cabin Regular / 3 cakes 4-in diam   180
      Buckwheat: 3 cakes 4-in diam /
        Aunt Jemima   200
      Buttermilk: 3 cakes 4-in diam /
        Aunt Jemima   300
      Buttermilk: 3 cakes 4-in diam /
        Aunt Jemima Complete   240
      Buttermilk: 3 cakes 4-in diam / **Log Cabin**   230
      Whole wheat: 3 cakes 4-in diam /
        Aunt Jemima   250
Waffles, frozen: 1 waffle
      Aunt Jemima Jumbo Original   90
      Downyflake   60
      Downyflake Hot 'n Buttery   65
      Downyflake Jumbo   85
      Eggo   120
      Blueberry / **Aunt Jemima** Jumbo   90
      Blueberry / **Downyflake**   90
      Blueberry / **Eggo**   130
      Bran / **Downyflake**   50

CALORIES

Bran / **Eggo**	170
Buttermilk / **Aunt Jemima** Jumbo	90
Buttermilk / **Downyflake**	85
Buttermilk / **Downyflake** Round	100
Strawberry / **Eggo**	130

Pastry

FROZEN

CALORIES

Donuts: 1 donut	
Morton Mini	120
Bavarian creme / **Morton**	180
Boston creme / **Morton**	210
Chocolate iced / **Morton**	150
Glazed / **Morton**	150
Jelly / **Morton**	180
Dumplings, apple: 1 dumpling / **Pepperidge Farm**	280
Pie tarts, frozen: 1 tart	
Apple / **Pepperidge Farm**	280
Blueberry / **Pepperidge Farm**	280
Cherry / **Pepperidge Farm**	280
Lemon / **Pepperidge Farm**	320
Raspberry / **Pepperidge Farm**	320
Strudel, apple: 3 oz / **Pepperidge Farm**	250
Turnovers: 1 turnover	
Apple, frozen / **Pepperidge Farm**	310
Apple, refrigerator / **Pillsbury**	180
Blueberry, frozen / **Pepperidge Farm**	320
Blueberry, refrigerator / **Pillsbury**	180
Cherry, frozen / **Pepperidge Farm**	340
Cherry, refrigerator / **Pillsbury**	190

CALORIES

Peach, frozen / **Pepperidge Farm**	320
Raspberry, frozen / **Pepperidge Farm**	340

TOASTER PASTRIES

1 portion

Cinnamon brown sugar, frosted / **Town House**	210
Pop-Tarts, all flavors / Kellogg's	210

Pickles and Relishes

CALORIES

Capers: 1 tbsp / **Crosse & Blackwell**	6
Cauliflower, sweet: 2 buds / **Smucker's**	47
Chow-Chow: 1 tbsp / **Crosse & Blackwell**	21
Onions, cocktail: 1 tbsp / **Crosse & Blackwell**	1
Peppers	
Chile: ¼ cup / **Del Monte**	11
Chile: 1 oz / **Ortega** Jalapenos	8
Chile, green: 1 oz / **Ortega**	5
Hot: 1 4-in / **Smucker's**	10
Mild, sweet, wax: ¼ cup / **Del Monte**	10
Pickled, hot: 1 oz / **Old El Paso**	
Chilies Jalapenos	9
Red, bell: 1 oz / **Ortega**	9
Pickles, dill	
Slices: 3 / **Heinz** Hamburger Dill Slices	1
Slices: 3 / **Smucker's** Hamburger Dill Slices	2
Spears: 1 piece / **Bond's** Fresh-Pack	2
Spears: 1 piece / **Bond's** Fresh-Pack Kosher	2
Sticks, candied: 1 4-in / **Smucker's**	40
Whole: 1 / **Bond's** Flavor Pack	1
Whole: 1 / **Bond's** Fresh-Pack Kosher	2

CALORIES

Whole: 1 large / **Del Monte**	7
Whole: 1 4-in / **Heinz** Genuine Dill	7
Whole: 1 3-in / **Heinz** Processed Dill	1
Whole: 1 large / **L & S**	15
Whole: 1 large / **L & S** Fresh-Pack Kosher	15
Whole: 1 3½-in / **Smucker's**	8
Whole: 2 2¾-in / **Smucker's**	
Fresh Pack Baby	7
Whole: 1 3½-in / **Smucker's** Kosher	8
Whole: 1 3½-in / **Smucker's**	
Kosher Fresh Pack	8
Pickles, mixed, hot: 4 pieces / **Smucker's**	5
Pickles, sour, whole: 1 large / **Del Monte**	10
Pickles, sweet	
Chips: 3 / **Smucker's** Fresh Pack	31
Chips: 3 / **Smucker's** Sweet Pickle Chips	31
Mixed: 3 pieces / **Heinz**	23
Pieces, mixed: 4 / **Smucker's**	48
Slices: 3 / **Bond's**	
Fresh-Pack Cucumber Slices	23
Slices: 3 / **Heinz** Cucumber Slices	20
Slices: 6 / **Lutz & Schramm**	
Fresh Cucumber Slices	29
Sticks: 1 4-in / **Smucker's** Fresh Pack	30
Whole: 1 pickle / **Bond's** Sweet Gherkins	19
Whole: 1 2-in / **Heinz** Sweet Gherkin	16
Whole: 1 med / **L & S** Sweet Pickles	11
Whole: 2 2½-in / **Smucker's**	35
Whole, candied: 2 2-in / **Smucker's** Midgets	29
Pimientos: 4 oz / **Dromedary**	32
Pimientos, canned: 4 oz / **Ortega**	28
Pimientos: ½ cup / **Stokely-Van Camp**	31
Relishes: 1 tbsp	
Barbecue / **Crosse & Blackwell**	22
Barbecue / **Heinz**	35
Corn / **Crosse & Blackwell**	15
Hamburger / **Crosse & Blackwell**	20
Hamburger / **Del Monte**	33

CALORIES

Hamburger / **Heinz**	15
Hot Dog / **Crosse & Blackwell**	22
Hot Dog / **Del Monte**	28
Hot Dog / **Heinz**	17
Hot Pepper / **Crosse & Blackwell**	22
India / **Crosse & Blackwell**	26
India / **Heinz**	17
Piccalilli / **Crosse & Blackwell**	26
Piccalilli / **Heinz** Green Tomato	23
Sweet / **Crosse & Blackwell**	26
Sweet / **Del Monte**	36
Sweet / **Heinz**	28
Sweet / **Lutz & Schramm**	14
Sweet / **Smucker's**	23
Watermelon rind / **Crosse & Blackwell**	38

Pies

FROZEN

CALORIES

1 whole pie

Apple

Banquet 20 oz	1440
Morton 24 oz	1740
Morton Mini 8 oz	590
Mrs. Smith's 8 in	1770
Mrs. Smith's (natural juice) 8 in	2880
Dutch / **Mrs. Smith's** 8 in	1860
Tart / **Mrs. Smith's** 8 in	1500

Banana cream

Banquet 14 oz	1032
Morton 16 oz	1020

CALORIES

Morton Mini 3½ oz	230
Mrs. Smith's 8 in	1290
Mrs. Smith's Light 13.8 oz	1320
Blueberry	
Banquet 20 oz	1520
Morton 24 oz	1680
Morton Mini 8 oz	580
Mrs. Smith's 8 in	1740
Mrs. Smith's (natural juice) 8 in	2040
Mrs. Smith's (natural juice) 9 in	2880
Boston cream / **Mrs. Smith's** 8 in	1980
Cherry	
Banquet 20 oz	1366
Morton 24 oz	1800
Morton Mini 8 oz	590
Mrs. Smith's 8 in	1860
Mrs. Smith's (natural juice) 8 in	2040
Mrs. Smith's (natural juice) 9 in	2880
Chocolate / **Mrs. Smith's** Light 13.8 oz	1500
Chocolate cream	
Banquet 14 oz	1064
Morton 16 oz	1200
Morton Mini 3½ oz	260
Mrs. Smith's 8 in	1470
Coconut / **Mrs. Smith's** Light 13.8 oz	1380
Coconut cream	
Banquet 14 oz	1044
Morton 16 oz	1140
Morton Mini 3½ oz	260
Mrs. Smith's 8 in	1380
Coconut custard / **Banquet** 20 oz	1219
Coconut custard / **Morton** Mini 6½ oz	370
Coconut custard / **Mrs. Smith's** 8 in	1590
Custard / **Banquet** 20 oz	1236
Egg custard / **Mrs. Smith's** 8 in	1470
Lemon / **Mrs. Smith's** 8 in	2040
Lemon cream	
Banquet 14 oz	1008

Morton 16 oz	1080
Morton Mini 3½ oz	240
Mrs. Smith's 8 in	1350
Lemon Krunch / Mrs. Smith's 8 in	2480
Lemon meringue / Mrs. Smith's 8 in	1560
Lemon yogurt / Mrs. Smith's 15.6 oz	1200
Mince / Morton 24 oz	1860
Mince / Morton Mini 8 oz	600
Mince / Mrs. Smith's 8 in	2010
Mincemeat / Banquet 20 oz	1514
Neopolitan cream / Morton 16 oz	1140
Neapolitan cream / Mrs. Smith's 8 in	1440

Peach

Banquet 20 oz	1315
Morton 24 oz	1680
Morton Mini 8 oz	560
Mrs. Smith's 8 in	1800
Mrs. Smith's (natural juice) 8 in	1980
Mrs. Smith's (natural juice) 9 in	2760
Pecan / Morton Mini 6½ oz	580
Pecan / Mrs. Smith's 8 in	2580
Pineapple / Mrs. Smith's 8 in	1800
Pineapple-cheese / Mrs. Smith's 8 in	1590

Pumpkin

Banquet 20 oz	1236
Morton 24 oz	1380
Morton Mini 8 oz	440
Mrs. Smith's 8 in	1440
Raisin / Mrs. Smith's 8 in	1890
Strawberry cream / Banquet 14 oz	1016
Strawberry cream / Morton 16 oz	1080
Strawberry cream / Mrs. Smith's 8 in	1320
Strawberry-rhubarb / Mrs. Smith's 8 in	1890
Strawberry-rhubarb / Mrs. Smith's (natural juice) 8 in	1920
Strawberry-rhubarb / Mrs. Smith's (natural juice) 9 in	2700
Strawberry yogurt / Mrs. Smith's 15.6 oz	1200

PIE MIXES

CALORIES

Prepared: 1 whole pie

Boston cream / **Betty Crocker**	2080
Chocolate creme / **Pillsbury** No Bake	2460
Lemon chiffon / **Pillsbury** No Bake	1980
Vanilla marble / **Pillsbury** No Bake	2340

PIE CRUSTS AND PASTRY SHELLS

Pastry sheets, frozen: 1 sheet / **Pepperidge Farm**	570
Pastry shells: 1 piece / **Stella D'Oro**	140
Patty shells, frozen: 1 shell / **Pepperidge Farm**	240
Pie crust, prepared	
Mix: double crust / **Betty Crocker**	1920
Mix: 1 whole crust / **Flako**	1560
Mix: double crust / **Pillsbury**	1740
Stick: 1 stick / **Betty Crocker**	960
Pie shells, deep, frozen: 1 shell / **Pepperidge Farm**	520
Pie shells, shallow bottom, frozen: 1 bottom / **Pepperidge Farm**	440
Pie shells, top, frozen: 1 top / **Pepperidge Farm**	760
Pot shells: 1 piece / **Stella D'Oro**	238
Tart shells, frozen: 1 shell / **Pepperidge Farm**	90

PIE FILLING

Apple: 21 oz can / **Wilderness**	660
Apple, French: 21 oz can / **Wilderness**	660
Apricot: 21 oz can / **Wilderness**	720
Banana cream, mix, prepared: whole 8-in pie / **Jell-O**	660
Blueberry: 21 oz can / **Wilderness**	660
Cherry: 21 oz can / **Wilderness**	660

CALORIES

Key Lime, mix, prepared: ½ cup / **Royal** Cooked	160
Lemon: 22 oz can / **Wilderness**	840
Lemon, mix, prepared: whole 8-in pie / **Jell-O**	1080
Lemon, mix, prepared: ½ cup / **Royal** Cooked	160
Mince: 22 oz can / **Wilderness**	840
Mincemeat: ⅓ cup / **None Such**	220
Peach: 21 oz can / **Wilderness**	660
Pumpkin, canned: 1 cup / **Stokely-Van Camp**	370
Pumpkin mix, canned: 1 cup / **Libby's**	210
Raisin: 22 oz can / **Wilderness**	720
Strawberry: 21 oz can / **Wilderness**	720

PIE AND PASTRY SNACKS

1 piece

Apple pastry / **Stella D'Oro** Dietetic	90
Apple pie / **Hostess**	400
Apple pie / **Tastykake** 4 oz	348
Apple pie, French / **Tastykake** 4 oz	405
Berry pie / **Hostess**	400
Blueberry pie / **Hostess**	390
Blueberry pie / **Tastykake** 4 oz	366
Cherry pie / **Hostess**	420
Cherry pie / **Tastykake** 4 oz	381
Fig pastry / **Stella D'Oro** Dietetic	95
Guava pastry / **Stella D'Oro**	127
Lemon pie / **Hostess**	420
Lemon pie / **Tastykake** 4 oz	370
Peach pie / **Hostess**	400
Peach pie / **Tastykake** 4 oz	349
Peach-apricot pastry / **Stella D'Oro**	97
Peach-apricot pastry / **Stella D'Oro** Dietetic	95
Pecan pie: 3 oz / **Frito-Lay**	353
Prune pastry / **Stella D'Oro** Dietetic	95

Pizza

CALORIES

1 whole pizza unless noted

Beef and cheese w enchilada seasoning, frozen / **El Chico** Mexican	1030
Beef and cheese w taco seasoning, frozen / **El Chico** Mexican	1000
Canadian bacon, frozen / **Totino's** Party	700
Cheese	
Frozen: 4 oz / **Buitoni**	276
Frozen / **Celeste** 7 oz	480
Frozen / **Celeste** 19 oz	1280
Frozen / **Celeste** Sicilian Style 20 oz	1400
Frozen / **Jeno's** 13 oz	840
Frozen / **Jeno's** Deluxe 20 oz	1470
Frozen / **La Pizzeria** 20 oz	1160
Frozen, thick crust / **La Pizzeria** 18.5 oz	1230
Frozen: ½ pkg / **Stouffer's**	330
Frozen / **Totino's** Crisp Party	880
Frozen / **Totino's** Party	880
Mix, prepared / **Jeno's**	840
w mushroom, frozen / **Celeste** 8 oz	460
w mushroom, frozen / **Celeste** 21 oz	1200
Chili and cheese, frozen / **El Chico** Mexican	1040
Combination	
Frozen / **Celeste** Deluxe 9 oz	600
Frozen / **Celeste** Deluxe 23½ oz	1480
Frozen / **Jeno's** Deluxe 23 oz	1680
Frozen / **La Pizzeria** 13.5 oz	840
Frozen / **La Pizzeria** 24½ oz	1520
Frozen: ½ pkg / **Stouffer's** Deluxe	400
Frozen / **Totino's** Classic	1680
Frozen, deep crust / **Totino's** Classic	1860
Hamburger, frozen / **Jeno's**	880

	CALORIES
Hamburger, frozen / **Totino's** Crisp Party	960
Hamburger, frozen / **Totino's** Party	920
Open face, frozen: 4 oz / **Buitoni**	256
Pepperoni	
Frozen / **Celeste** 7½ oz	540
Frozen / **Celeste** 20 oz	1440
Frozen / **Jeno's** 13 oz	900
Frozen / **La Pizzeria** 21 oz	1320
Frozen: ½ pkg / **Stouffer's**	400
Frozen, deep crust / **Totino's** Classic	1800
Frozen / **Totino's** Crisp Party	960
Frozen / **Totino's** Party	920
Mix, prepared / **Jeno's**	1020
w mushroom, frozen / **Totino's** Classic	1500
Pizza rolls, frozen	
Cheeseburger: 3 oz / **Jeno's**	270
Pepperoni and cheese: 3 oz / **Jeno's**	260
Sausage and cheese: 3 oz / **Jeno's**	260
Shrimp and cheese: 3 oz / **Jeno's**	220
Refried bean and cheese, frozen / **El Chico** Mexican	900
Regular, mix, prepared / **Jeno's**	840
Sausage	
Frozen / **Celeste** 8 oz	560
Frozen / **Celeste** 22 oz	1520
Frozen / **Jeno's** 13 oz	900
Frozen / **Jeno's** Deluxe 21 oz	1500
Frozen / **La Pizzeria** 13 oz	860
Frozen / **La Pizzeria** 23 oz	1520
Frozen, deep crust / **Totino's** Classic	1800
Frozen / **Totino's** Crisp Party	980
Frozen / **Totino's** Party	940
Mix, prepared / **Jeno's**	1060
w mushrooms, frozen / **Celeste** 9 oz	580
w mushrooms, frozen / **Celeste** 21 oz	1520
w mushrooms, frozen / **Totino's** Classic	1680

Popcorn

CALORIES

**Note: 1 oz candy-coated popcorn =
          a little over ¾ cup**

Plain, popped: 1 cup / **Pops-Rite**	40
Plain, popped: 1 cup / **Jolly Time**	54
Plain, popped: 1 cup / **TNT**	52
Butter flavor, read to eat: 1 cup / **Wise**	42
Caramel-coated: 1 oz / **Old London**	117
Caramel-coated: ½ cup / **Wise**	53
Caramel-coated w peanuts: 1 oz / **Wise Pixies**	103
Caramel Corn: 1 oz / **Granny Goose**	110
Cheese flavor, ready to eat: ½ cup / **Wise**	25
Cheese flavor, ready to eat: 1 oz / **Old London**	114
Cracker Jack: 1⅜ oz pkg	193
Cracker Jack: 6 oz pkg	750
Fiddle Faddle, almond: 1 oz	119
Fiddle Faddle, coconut: 1 oz	128
Fiddle Faddle, peanut: 1 oz	125
Krazy Korn: 1 oz	128
Poppycock: 1 oz	150
Screaming Yellow Zonkers: 1 oz	121

Pot Pies

CALORIES

Frozen: 1 whole pie

Beef

Banquet 8 oz	409
Morton 8 oz	320

	CALORIES
Stouffer's 10 oz	550
Swanson 8 oz	430
Swanson Hungry-Man 16 oz	770
Chicken	
Banquet 8 oz	427
Morton 8 oz	380
Stouffer's 10 oz	500
Swanson 8 oz	450
Swanson Hungry-Man 16 oz	780
Sirloin Burger / Swanson Hungry-Man 16 oz	800
Tuna	
Banquet 8 oz	434
Morton 8 oz	370
Turkey	
Banquet 8 oz	415
Morton 8 oz	390
Stouffer's 10 oz	460
Swanson 8 oz	450
Swanson Hungry-Man 16 oz	790

Poultry and Poultry Entrees

FRESH

	CALORIES
Chicken, cooked	
3 oz flesh only, broiled	115
3.3 oz breast (½), fried w bone	155
2.7 oz breast (½), fried, flesh and skin only	155
2.1 oz fried drumstick w bone	90
1.3 oz fried drumstick, flesh and skin only	90
Chicken, dark meat wo skin, roasted: 3½ oz	178
Chicken, light meat wo skin, roasted: 3½ oz	153

CALORIES

Duck, roasted wo skin: 3½ oz	201
Goose, domesticated, meat and skin, roasted: 3½ oz	441
Goose, domesticated, meat wo skin, roasted: 3½ oz	233
Turkey, dark meat, roasted: 3½ oz	203
Turkey, dark meat, roasted w skin: 3½ oz	221
Turkey, dark meat, roasted wo skin: 3½ oz	187
Turkey, light meat, roasted w skin: 3½ oz	197
Turkey, light meat, roasted wo skin: 3½ oz	157
Gizzard, chicken, cooked: 4 oz	167
Gizzard, goose, cooked: 4 oz	157
Heart, chicken, cooked: 4 oz	195
Heart, turkey, cooked: 4 oz	244
Liver, chicken, cooked: 4 oz	186
Liver, goose, raw: 4 oz	206
Liver, turkey, cooked: 4 oz	197

CANNED, FROZEN AND PROCESSED

Chicken a la King, canned: 5¼ oz / Swanson	190
Chicken a la King, frozen	
Banquet Cookin' Bag / 5 oz	138
Green Giant Boil-in-Bag Toast Toppers / 5 oz	170
Stouffer's 9½ oz / 1 pkg	330
Chicken, boned, canned: 3 oz / **Hormel** Tender Chunk	110
Chicken, boned, canned, white chunk: 2½ oz / **Swanson**	110
Chicken, boned, canned w broth: 2½ oz / **Swanson**	110
Chicken, chopped, pressed: 1 slice / **Eckrich** Slender Sliced	47
Chicken and biscuits, frozen: 7 oz / **Green Giant** Oven Bake Entrees	200
Chicken breast Parmigiana and spinach, frozen: 9 oz / **Weight Watchers**	200

Chicken, creamed, frozen: 1 pkg / **Stouffer's**
6½ oz   300
Chicken creole, frozen: 13 oz / **Weight Watchers**   250
Chicken croquette w sauce, frozen: 12 oz /
Howard Johnson's   505
Chicken divan, frozen: 1 pkg / **Stouffer's**
8½ oz   335
Chicken w dumplings, canned: 7½ oz / **Swanson**   230
Chicken w dumplings, frozen: 32 oz /
Banquet Buffet Supper   1209
Chicken, escalloped, frozen: ½ pkg / **Stouffer's**
11½ oz   250
Chicken, fried
    Frozen: 2 lb / **Banquet**   259
    Frozen: 6.4 oz / **Morton** 32 oz   440
    Frozen: 1 entree / **Morton** Country
      Table 12 oz   600
    Frozen, assorted pieces: 3.2 edible oz /
      Swanson   260
    Frozen, breast portions: 3.2 edible oz /
      Swanson   250
    Frozen, thighs and drumsticks: 3.2
      edible oz / **Swanson**   260
    Frozen, wing sections: 3.2 edible oz /
      Swanson Nibbles   290
Chicken livers w broccoli, frozen: 10½ oz /
Weight Watchers   220
Chicken Nibbles w french fries: 1 entree /
Swanson "TV" 6 oz   370
Chicken and noodles, frozen: 32 oz /
Banquet Buffet Supper   764
Chicken and noodles, frozen: 9 oz / **Green**
Giant Boil-in-Bag Entrees   250
Chicken, smoked, sliced: 1 oz / **Safeway**   50
Chicken stew, canned: 7½ oz / **Swanson**   180
Chicken stew w dumplings, canned: 1 cup /
Libby's   88

Chicken, white meat w peas, onions, frozen:	
9 oz / **Weight Watchers**	270
Turkey, boned, canned: 3 oz / **Hormel**	
Tender Chunk	90
Turkey, boned, canned w broth: 2½ oz /	
Swanson	110
Turkey slices	
Canned w gravy: 6¼ oz / **Morton House**	140
Frozen entree / **Morton** Country Table	
12¼ oz	390
Frozen entree / **Swanson** Hungry-Man	
13¼ oz	380
Frozen entree / **Swanson** "TV" 8¾ oz	260
Frozen w giblet gravy: 32 oz /	
Banquet Buffet Supper	564
Frozen w giblet gravy: 5 oz / **Banquet**	
Cookin' Bag	98
Frozen w gravy: 5 oz / **Green Giant**	
Boil-in-Bag Toast Toppers	100
Turkey tetrazzini, frozen: ½ pkg / **Stouffer's**	
12 oz	240
Turkey tetrazzini w mushrooms, red peppers,	
frozen: 13 oz / **Weight Watchers**	380
Turkey, roast, frozen, cooked	
Dark meat: 3½ oz / **Swift** Butterball	210
White meat: 3½ oz / **Swift** Butterball	170
White and dark meat w skin: 3½ oz /	
Swift Butterball	220
Roll, boneless white and dark meat: 3½	
oz / **Swift** Park Lane	140
Roll, boneless white and dark meat: 3½	
oz / **Swift** Premium Perfect Slice	120
Roll, white meat: 3½ oz / **Swift**	
Park Lane	140
Roll, white meat: 3½ oz / **Swift** Premium	
Perfect Slice	120

CALORIES

Turkey, smoked, chopped: 1 slice / **Eckrich**
  Slender Sliced | 47
Turkey, smoked, sliced: 1 oz / **Safeway** | 50

Pretzels

CALORIES

1 oz

Bavarian / **Granny Goose**	112
Mini / **Granny Goose**	110
Ring / **Granny Goose**	112
Stick	
Granny Goose	108
Pepperidge Farm Thin	100
Planters	110
Twists	
Granny Goose	109
Pepperidge Farm Tiny	100
Planters	110
Rold Gold	111

Pudding

CALORIES

½ cup unless noted

All flavors, mix, prepared / **Estee Low Calorie**	85
Banana	
Canned, ready to serve: 5 oz can /	
Del Monte	180

Canned: 8 oz can / **Sego**	250
Mix, prepared / **Ann Page**	170
Mix, prepared / **Jell-O** Instant	180
Mix, prepared / **Royal**	160
Mix, prepared / **Royal** Instant	180
Butter pecan, mix, prepared / **Jell-O** Instant	180

Butterscotch

Canned, ready to serve: 5 oz can / **Del Monte**	180
Canned: 8 oz can / **Sego**	250
Mix, prepared / **Ann Page**	190
Mix, prepared / **Ann Page** Instant	170
Mix, prepared / **Jell-O**	180
Mix, prepared / **Jell-O** Instant	180
Mix, prepared / **My-T-Fine**	143
Mix, prepared / **Royal**	160
Mix, prepared / **Royal** Instant	180
Mix, prepared w nonfat milk / **D-Zerta**	70
Mix, as packaged / **De-Zerta**	25

Chocolate

Canned, ready to serve / **Betty Crocker**	180
Canned, ready to serve: 5 oz can / **Del Monte**	190
Canned: 8 oz can / **Sego**	250
Mix, prepared / **Ann Page**	180
Mix, prepared / **Ann Page** Instant	190
Mix, prepared / **Jell-O**	170
Mix, prepared / **Jell-O** Instant	190
Mix, prepared / **My-T-Fine**	133
Mix, prepared / **Royal**	180
Mix, prepared / **Royal** Instant	190
Mix, prepared w nonfat milk / **De-Zerta**	70
Mix, as packaged / **D-Zerta**	20
Almond, mix, prepared / **My-T-Fine**	169
Fudge, canned, ready to serve / **Betty Crocker**	180
Fudge, canned, ready to serve: 5 oz can / **Del Monte**	190

CALORIES

Fudge, mix, prepared / **Jell-O**	170
Fudge, mix, prepared / **Jell-O** Instant	190
Fudge, mix, prepared / **My-T-Fine**	151
Milk, mix, prepared / **Jell-O**	170
Chocolate fudge: 8 oz can / **Sego**	250
Chocolate marshmellow: 8 oz can / **Sego**	250
Coconut	
Mix, prepared / **Royal** Instant	170
Cream, mix, prepared / **Ann Page**	190
Cream, mix, prepared / **Jell-O**	110
Cream, mix, prepared / **Jell-O** Instant	190
Toasted, mix, prepared / **Ann Page**	170
Coffee, mix, prepared / **Royal** Instant	180
Custard, mix, prepared / **Royal**	150
Custard, egg, mix, prepared / **Ann Page**	150
Custard, egg, mix, prepared / **Jell-O** Americana	170
Custard, rennet, all flavors, mix, prepared / **Junket**	120
Dark 'N Sweet, mix, prepared / **Royal**	180
Dark 'N Sweet, mix, prepared / **Royal** Instant	190
Flan, mix, prepared / **Royal**	150
Lemon	
Mix, prepared / **Ann Page**	150
Mix, prepared / **Ann Page** Instant	180
Mix, prepared / **Jell-O** Instant	180
Mix, prepared / **My-T-Fine**	164
Mix, prepared / **Royal** Instant	180
Pineapple cream, mix, prepared / **Jell-O** Instant	180
Pistachio, mix, prepared / **Ann Page** Instant	180
Pistachio, mix, prepared / **Jell-O** Instant	180
Pistachio nut, mix, prepared / **Royal** Instant	170
Plum pudding, canned, ready to serve / **R & R**	300
Rice, canned, ready to serve / **Betty Crocker**	150
Rice, mix, prepared / **Jell-O** Americana	180
Tapioca	
Minute Tapioca: 1 tbsp	40
Minute (Fluffy Pudding recipe)	150

CALORIES

Canned, ready to serve / **Betty Crocker**	150
Chocolate, mix, prepared / **Ann Page**	180
Chocolate, mix, prepared / **Jell-O** Americana	170
Chocolate, mix, prepared / **Royal**	180
Vanilla, mix, prepared / **Ann Page**	170
Vanilla, mix, prepared / **Jell-O** Americana	170
Vanilla, mix, prepared / **My-T-Fine**	130
Vanilla, mix, prepared / **Royal**	160

Vanilla

Canned, ready to serve / **Betty Crocker**	190
Canned, ready to serve: 5 oz can / **Del Monte**	190
Canned: 8 oz can / **Sego**	250
Mix, prepared / **Ann Page**	170
Mix, prepared / **Jell-O**	170
Mix, prepared / **Jell-O** Instant	180
Mix, prepared / **My-T-Fine**	133
Mix, prepared / **Royal**	160
Mix, prepared / **Royal** Instant	180
Mix, prepared w nonfat milk / **D-Zerta**	70
Mix, as packaged / **D-Zerta**	30
French, mix, prepared / **Jell-O**	180
French, mix, prepared / **Jell-O** Instant	180

Rice and Rice Dishes

	CALORIES
Brown, long grain, parboiled: ⅔ cup cooked	200
Brown and wild, seasoned, mix, prepared:	
½ cup / **Uncle Ben's**	126
White, instant: 1 cup	180
White, long grain: ⅔ cup cooked	225
White, parboiled: 1 cup, cooked	185
White and wild, frozen: 1 cup / **Green Giant**	
Boil-in-Bag	220
White and wild, w bean sprouts, pea pods	
and water chestnuts, frozen: 1 cup /	
Green Giant Boil-in-Bag Oriental	230
White and wild, w peas, celery, mushrooms	
and almonds, frozen: 1 cup /	
Green Giant Boil-in-Bag Medley	320
White, long grain and wild, mix, prepared:	
½ cup / **Uncle Ben's**	97
White, long grain and wild, mix, prepared:	
½ cup / **Uncle Ben's** Fast Cooking	95
Beef-flavored, mix, prepared	
1/6 pkg / **Ann Page** Rice 'n Easy	170
½ cup / **Minute** Rice Rib Roast	150
1/6 pkg / **Rice-A-Roni**	130
½ cup / **Uncle Ben's**	98
w bell peppers and parsley, frozen:	
1 cup / **Green Giant** Boil-in-Bag Verdi	270
w broccoli, in cheese sauce, frozen: 1 cup /	
Green Giant Boil-in-Bag	250
Chicken-flavored, mix, prepared	
1/6 pkg / **Ann Page** Rice 'n Easy	180

	CALORIES
1/5 pkg / **Rice-A-Roni**	160
½ cup / **Uncle Ben's**	103
Curried, mix, prepared: ½ cup / **Uncle Ben's**	99
Fried, mix, prepared: ½ cup / **Minute**	160
w green beans and almonds, frozen: 1 cup / **Green Giant** Boil-in-Bag Continental	230
w peas, mushrooms, frozen: 2.3 oz / **Bird's Eye** Combinations	100
w peas, mushrooms, frozen: 1 cup / **Green Giant** Boil-in-Bag Medley	200
Pilaf, mix, prepared: ½ cup / **Uncle Ben's**	101
Pilaf, w mushrooms and onions, frozen: 1 cup / **Green Giant** Boil-in-Bag	230
Poultry-flavored, mix, prepared: ½ cup / **Minute** Drumstick	170
Spanish	
Canned: 1 cup / **Libby's**	57
Mix, prepared: ½ cup / **Minute**	150
Mix, prepared: 1/6 pkg / **Rice-A-Roni**	120
Mix, prepared: ½ cup / **Uncle Ben's**	106

Rolls and Buns

	CALORIES
1 roll or bun unless noted	
Bagel, egg, 3-in diam	165
Bagel, water, 3-in diam	165
Buns for sandwiches	
Arnold Dutch Egg Buns	130
Arnold Francisco Sandwich Rolls	180
Arnold Soft Sandwich	110
w poppy seeds / **Arnold** Soft Sandwich	110

w sesame seeds / **Arnold** Soft Sandwich	110
w sesame seeds / **Pepperidge Farm**	120
Hamburger / **Arnold** 8's	110
Hamburger: 2 oz / **Colonial**	160
Hamburger: 2 oz / **Kilpatrick's**	160
Hamburger: 2 oz / **Manor**	160
Hamburger / **Mrs. Wright's** 12 oz pkg	130
Hamburger / **Mrs. Wright's** 16 oz pkg	110
Hamburger / **Pepperidge Farm**	110
Hamburger: 2 oz / **Rainbo**	160
Hamburger / **Wonder**	160
Hamburger w sesame seeds / **Mrs. Wright's**	140
Hot dog / **Arnold**	110
Hot dog: 2 oz / **Colonial**	160
Hot dog: 2 oz / **Kilpatrick's**	160
Hot dog / **Mrs. Wright's** 11 oz pkg	110
Hot dog / **Mrs. Wright's** 13½ oz pkg	110
Hot dog: 2 oz / **Manor**	160
Hot dog / **Pepperidge Farm**	120
Hot dog: 2 oz / **Rainbo**	160
Hot dog / **Wonder**	160

Dinner and soft rolls

Arnold Deli-Twist	110
Arnold Finger 24's	55
Arnold Francisco Variety	100
Arnold Party Finger 12's	55
Arnold Party Parkerhouse 12's	55
Arnold Party Rounds 12's	55
Arnold Party Tea 20's	35
Arnold 12's	60
Arnold 24's	60
Colonial	80
Home Pride	90
Kilpatrick's	80
Mrs. Wright's Buttermilk	100
Mrs. Wright's Cloverleaf	90
Mrs. Wright's Flaky Gem	90
Mrs. Wright's Twin	90

CALORIES

Manor	80
Pepperidge Farm Butter Crescent	130
Pepperidge Farm Dinner	65
Pepperidge Farm Finger	60
Pepperidge Farm Finger w poppy seeds	60
Pepperidge Farm Finger w sesame seeds	60
Pepperidge Farm Golden Twist	120
Pepperidge Farm Old-Fashioned	37
Pepperidge Farm Parkerhouse	60
Pepperidge Farm Party	35
Pepperidge Farm Party Pan	35
Rainbo Dinner	80
Wonder Buttermilk	85
Wonder Gem Style Dinner	85
Wonder Half & Half Dinner	85
Wonder Home Bake Dinner	85
Wonder Pan	105
Mix, prepared / **Pillsbury** Hot Roll Mix	95
Refrigerator / **Ballard** Crescent	95
Refrigerator / **Pillsbury** Butterflake	110
Refrigerator / **Pillsbury** Crescent	95

Hard rolls

Club / **Pepperidge Farm**	120
Deli / **Pepperidge Farm**	180
French / **Wonder**	85
French, four / **Pepperidge Farm**	230
French, large: ½ roll / **Pepperidge Farm**	190
French, nine / **Pepperidge Farm**	110
French, small: ½ roll / **Pepperidge Farm**	130
French sourdough / **Arnold** Francisco	100
French sourdough / **Arnold** Francisco Brown and Serve	90
Hearth / **Pepperidge Farm**	60
Italian: 2 oz / **Pepperidge Farm**	150
Kaiser: 2 oz / **Earth Grains**	140
Kaiser & Hoagie Rolls: 6 oz / **Wonder**	460
Onion: 2 oz / **Earth Grains**	170
Sandwich / **Pepperidge Farm**	140

Sesame Crisp / **Pepperidge Farm**	70
Popovers, mix, prepared: 1 popover / **Flako**	170

SWEET ROLLS

1 roll unless noted

Caramel, refrigerated / **Pillsbury** Danish	160
Cinnamon, refrigerated / **Ballard**	100
Cinnamon w icing, refrigerated /	
Hungry Jack Butter Tastin	145
Cinnamon w icing, refrigerated / **Pillsbury**	115
Cinnamon-nut: 3 oz / **Rainbo**	330
Cinnamon-raisin, refrigerated / **Merico**	180
Cinnamon-raisin, refrigerated / **Pillsbury** Danish	150
Danish, apple: 2 oz / **Earth Grains**	230
Danish Bear Claws: 2 oz / **Earth Grains**	250
Danish, cinnamon: 2 oz / **Earth Grains** Pastry	220
Danish, cherry: 2 oz / **Earth Grains** Pastry	170
Danish, fruit, refrigerated / **Merico**	180
Danish Horns: 2 oz / **Earth Grains**	260
Honey Buns / **Hostess**	580
Honey Buns: 3 oz / **Rainbo**	380
Honey Buns, frozen / **Morton**	230
Honey Buns, frozen / **Morton** Mini	100
Orange, refrigerated / **Pillsbury** Danish	130

Salad Dressings

Bottled unless noted: 1 tbsp unless noted

Ann Page Salad Dressing	70
Mrs. Filbert's Salad Dressing	65
Nu Made Salad Dressing	80
Piedmont Salad Dressing	70
Sultana Salad Dressing	50
Avocado / **Kraft**	70
Bacon, mix: ¾ oz pkg / **Lawry's**	69
Blue cheese	
Ann Page Low Calorie	18
Kraft Chunky	70
Kraft Low Calorie	14
Kraft Low Calorie Chunky	30
Lawry's	57
Nu Made	75
Roka	60
Seven Seas Real	70
Tillie Lewis / 1 tsp	4
Wish-Bone Chunky	80
Mix: ¾ oz pkg / **Lawry's**	79
Mix, prepared / **Weight Watchers**	10
Caesar	
Kraft Golden	70
Lawry's	70
Nu Made	75
Pfeiffer	70
Pfeiffer Low-Cal	10
Seven Seas	70
Wish-Bone	80
Mix: ¾ oz pkg / **Lawry's**	71

CALORIES

Canadian bacon-flavored / **Lawry's**	72
Chef Style / **Ann Page** Low Calorie	20
Chef Style / **Kraft** Low Calorie	18
Coleslaw dressing / **Kraft**	70
Coleslaw dressing / **Kraft** Low Calorie	30
Cucumber, creamy / **Kraft**	80
Cucumber, creamy / **Kraft** Low Calorie	30
French	
Casino	70
Kraft	60
Kraft Casino Garlic	70
Kraft Catalina	60
Kraft Herb and Garlic	90
Kraft Low Calorie	25
Kraft Miracle	70
Lawry's	54
Lawry's San Francisco French	53
Lawry's Sherry French	55
Nu Made Low Calorie	20
Nu Made Savory	65
Nu Made Zesty	65
Pfeiffer	55
Pfeiffer Low-Cal	18
Seven Seas Creamy	60
Seven Seas Family Style	60
Seven Seas Low Calorie	30
Wish-Bone Deluxe	50
Wish-Bone Garlic French	70
Wish-Bone Low Calorie	25
Wish-Bone Sweet 'n Spicy	70
Mix: 4/5 oz pkg / **Lawry's** Old Fashioned	72
Mix, prepared / **Weight Watchers**	4
French Style / **Ann Page** Low Calorie	25
French Style / **Kraft** Low Calorie	25
French Style: 1 tsp / **Tillie Lewis**	4
Garlic, creamy / **Kraft**	50
Garlic, creamy / **Wish-Bone**	80

CALORIES

Green Goddess
Kraft	80
Lawry's	59
Nu Made	80
Seven Seas	60
Wish-Bone	70
Mix: ¾ oz pkg / **Lawry's**	69

Green onion / **Kraft**	80
Hawaiian / **Lawry's**	77
Herbs and spices / **Seven Seas**	60

Italian
Ann Page Low Calorie	14
Kraft	80
Kraft Golden Blend	70
Kraft Low Calorie	6
Lawry's	79
Nu Made	90
Nu Made Low Calorie	16
Pfeiffer Chef	60
Pfeiffer Low-Cal	10
Seven Seas	70
Seven Seas Family Style	60
Seven Seas Low Calorie	35
Seven Seas Viva	70
Tillie Lewis / 1 tsp	2
Wish-Bone	80
Wish-Bone Low Calorie	20
Cheese / **Lawry's**	60
Creamy / **Kraft**	50
Creamy / **Seven Seas** Creamy	70
Creamy / **Weight Watchers**	50
Mix, prepared / **Good Seasons** Low Calorie	8
Mix: 3/5 oz pkg / **Lawry's**	44
Mix, prepared / **Weight Watchers**	2
Mix, cheese: ¾ oz pkg / **Lawry's**	69
Mix, creamy, prepared / **Weight Watchers**	4

Lemon garlic, mix: ⅞ oz pkg / **Lawry's**	64

	CALORIES
May Lo Naise / **Tillie Lewis**	25
Oil and vinegar	
Kraft	70
Lawry's	55
Nu Made	60
Red wine / **Seven Seas** Viva	70
Onion / **Wish-Bone** California	80
Red wine: 1 oz / **Pfeiffer** Low-Cal	20
Russian	
Kraft Low Calorie	30
Nu Made	55
Pfeiffer	65
Pfeiffer Low-Cal	15
Seven Seas Creamy	80
Tillie Lewis / 1 tsp	4
Weight Watchers	50
Wish-Bone	60
Wish-Bone Low Calorie	25
Creamy / **Kraft**	60
w honey / **Kraft**	60
Mix, prepared / **Weight Watchers**	4
Salad Secret / **Kraft**	60
Sour Treat: 1 oz / **Friendship**	49
Spin Blend / **Hellmann's**	55
Thousand Island	
Ann Page Low Calorie	25
Kraft	60
Kraft Low Calorie	30
Lawry's	69
Nu Made	30
Nu Made Low Calorie	30
Pfeiffer	65
Pfeiffer Low-Cal	15
Seven Seas	50
Tillie Lewis / 1 tsp	6
Weight Watchers	50
Wish-Bone	70
Wish-Bone Low Calorie	25

CALORIES

Mix: ⅞ oz pkg / **Lawry's**	78
Mix, prepared / **Weight Watchers**	12
Whipped / **Tillie Lewis**	25
Yogonaise / **Henri's**	60
Yogowhip / **Henri's**	60
Yogurt	
Blue cheese / **Henri's**	35
Creamy garlic / **Henri's**	35
Cucumber and onion / **Henri's**	35
French / **Henri's**	40
Italian / **Henri's**	35
Thousand Island / **Henri's**	30

Sauces

CALORIES

A la King, mix, prepared: ½ cup / **Durkee**	66
Barbecue, bottled or canned: 1 tbsp	
Chris' and Pitt's	15
French's	14
Open Pit	26
Hickory smoke flavor / **French's** Smoky	14
Hickory smoke flavor / **Open Pit**	27
Hot / **French's**	14
Hot / **Open Pit** Hot 'n Spicy	27
w onions / **Open Pit**	27
Cheese, mix, prepared: ½ cup / **Durkee**	169
Cheese, mix, prepared: ¼ cup / **French's**	80
Cheese, mix, prepared: ¼ cup / **McCormick**	78
Cheese, mix, prepared: ¼ cup / **Schilling**	78
Enchilada	
Canned: 4 oz / **Old El Paso** Hot	36
Canned: 4 oz / **Old El Paso** Mild	40

Mix: 1⅝ oz pkg / **Lawry's**	144
Mix: 1½ oz pkg / **McCormick**	115
Mix: 1½ oz pkg / **Schilling**	115
Hollandaise, mix, prepared: ¾ cup / **Durkee**	173
Hollandaise, mix, prepared: 3 tbsp / **French's**	45
Hollandaise, mix, prepared: ½ cup / **McCormick**	170
Hollandaise, mix, prepared: ½ cup / **Schilling**	170
Horseradish sauce: 1 tbsp / **Kraft**	50
Italian, canned: 2 fl oz / **Contadina** Cookbook	43
Italian, red, in jar: 5 oz / **Ragu**	45
Lasagna, mix: 1⅝ oz pkg / **Lawry's**	86
Lemon-butter-flavored, mix, prepared:	
1 tbsp / **Weight Watchers**	8
Mushroom steak, canned: 1 oz / **Dawn Fresh**	9
Pizza, canned: 4 oz / **Buitoni**	92
Pizza, in jar: 5 oz / **Ragu**	120
Sour cream, mix, prepared: ⅔ cup / **Durkee**	214
Sour cream, mix, prepared: 2½ tbsp / **French's**	40
Sour cream, mix, prepared: ¼ cup / **McCormick**	73
Sour cream, mix, prepared: ¼ cup / **Schilling**	73
Spaghetti	
Canned: 4 oz / **Ann Page**	70
Canned: 4 oz / **Buitoni**	92
Canned: ½ cup / **Town House**	80
In jar: 5 oz / **Ragu** Extra Thick	120
In jar: 5 oz / **Ragu** Plain	105
Mix, prepared: 1 env / **Ann Page**	120
Mix, prepared: ½ cup / **Durkee**	45
Mix, prepared: ⅝ cup / **French's**	
Italian Style	100
Mix: 1½ oz pkg / **Lawry's**	147
Mix, prepared: ½ cup / **McCormick**	53
Mix, prepared: ½ cup / **Schilling**	53
Mix, prepared: 4 fl oz / **Spatini**	160
Clam, canned: 5 oz / **Ragu**	110
Clam, red, canned: 4 oz / **Buitoni**	108
Clam, white, canned: 4 oz / **Buitoni**	144
Marinara, canned: 4 oz / **Ann Page**	70

CALORIES

Marinara, canned: 4 oz / **Buitoni**	88
Marinara, in jar: 5 oz / **Ragu**	120
Meat flavor, canned: 4 oz / **Ann Page**	80
Meat flavor, canned: 4 oz / **Buitoni**	120
Meat flavor, canned: ½ cup / **Town House**	80
Meat flavor, in jar: 5 oz / **Ragu**	115
Meat flavor, in jar: 5 oz / **Ragu** Extra Thick	130
w meatball seasonings, mix:	
3¼ oz pkg / **Lawry's**	316
w mushrooms, canned: 4 oz / **Ann Page**	70
w mushrooms, canned: 4 oz / **Buitoni**	88
w mushrooms, canned: ½ cup /	
Town House	90
w mushrooms, in jar: 5 oz / **Ragu**	105
w mushrooms, in jar: 5 oz / **Ragu**	
Extra Thick	110
w mushrooms, mix, prepared:	
1 env / **Ann Page**	120
w mushrooms, mix, prepared: ⅔	
cup / **Durkee**	52
w mushrooms, mix, prepared: ⅝	
cup / **French's**	100
Pepperoni flavor, in jar: 5 oz / **Ragu**	120
Stroganoff	
Mix, prepared: 1 cup / **Durkee**	820
Mix, prepared: ⅓ cup / **French's**	110
Mix: 1½ oz pkg / **Lawry's**	118
Mix, prepared: ½ cup / **McCormick**	115
Mix, prepared: ½ cup / **Schilling**	115
Sweet and sour, canned: 2 fl oz /	
Contadina Cookbook	79
Sweet and sour, canned: 1 cup / **La Choy**	524
Sweet and sour, mix, prepared: 1 cup / **Durkee**	230
Sweet and sour, mix, prepared: ½ cup / **French's**	55
Swiss steak, canned: 2 fl oz / **Contadina** Cookbook	24
Teriyaki, mix, prepared: 2 tbsp / **French's**	35
Tomato, canned	
Contadina / 1 cup	90

	CALORIES
Del Monte / 1 cup	80
Hunt's / 4 oz	35
Hunt's Prima Salsa Regular / 4 oz	110
Hunt's Special / 4 oz	40
Stokely-Van Camp / 1 cup	70
Town House Spanish Style / 8 oz	80
w bits: 4 oz / **Hunt's**	35
w cheese: 4 oz / **Hunt's**	70
w herbs: 4 oz / **Hunt's**	80
Meat-flavored: 4 oz / **Hunt's** Prima Salsa	120
w mushrooms: 1 cup / **Del Monte**	100
w mushrooms: 4 oz / **Hunt's**	40
w mushrooms: 4 oz / **Hunt's** Prima Salsa	110
w onion: 1 cup / **Del Monte**	100
w onions: 4 oz / **Hunt's**	45
w tidbits: 1 cup / **Del Monte**	80
Tuna casserole, mix, prepared: ½ cup / **McCormick**	128
Tuna casserole, mix, prepared: ½ cup / **Schilling**	128
White, mix, prepared: ½ cup / **Durkee**	119
Wine, burgundy, mix: 1 oz / **Lawry's**	98
Wine, sherry, mix: 1 oz / **Lawry's**	94
Wine, white, mix: 1 oz / **Lawry's**	113

Seasonings

	CALORIES
1 tsp unless noted	
Accent	9
Bacon, imitation, crumbled: 1 tbsp	
Ann Page	25
Baco's	40

CALORIES

Durkee Bacon Bits   8
French's Bacon Crumbles   6
Lawry's Baconion   40
McCormick Bacon Bits   30
McCormick Bacon Chips   35
Schilling Bacon Bits   30
Schilling Bacon Chips   35
Barbecue / **French's**   6
Chili powder / **Lawry's**   9
Garlic concentrate: 1 tbsp / **Lawry's**   88
Herb blend / **Lawry's**   9
Lemon pepper marinade / **Lawry's**   7
Meat tenderizer / **French's**   2
Meat tenderizer, seasoned / **French's**   2
Pepper, lemon-flavored / **French's** Lemon and
   Pepper Seasoning   6
Pepper, seasoned / **French's**   8
Pepper, seasoned / **Lawry's**   8
Pizza / **French's**   4
Salad / **Durkee**   4
Salad / **French's** Salad Lift   6
Salad w cheese / **Durkee**   10
Salt
   Butter flavor, imitation / **French's**   8
   Celery / **French's**   2
   Garlic / **French's**   4
   Garlic-flavored / **Lawry's**   5
   Garlic, parslied / **French's**   6
   Hickory smoke / **French's**   2
   Onion / **French's**   6
   Onion-flavored / **Lawry's**   4
   Seasoned / **French's**   2
   Seasoned / **Lawry's**   1
Seafood / **French's**   2
Stock base, chicken-flavored / **French's**   8
Stock base, beef-flavored / **French's**   8
Sugar, cinnamon-flavored / **French's**   16

SEASONING MIXES

	CALORIES
Beef	
Lawry's Beef Olé / 1¼ oz pkg	126
Lawry's Marinade / 1 1/16 oz pkg	69
Stew, mix, prepared: 1 cup / **Durkee**	379
Stew, dry mix: 1 pkg / **Durkee**	99
Stew: 1 env / **French's**	150
Stew: 1⅔ oz pkg / **Lawry's**	131
Stew: 1½ oz pkg / **McCormick**	90
Stew: 1½ oz pkg / **Schilling**	90
Burger: ⅓ oz / **Lipton** Make-A-Better-Burger	30
Burger, onion: ⅓ oz / **Lipton** Make-A-Better-Burger	30
Chili: 1 env / **Ann Page**	120
Chili: 1 env / **French's** Chili-O	150
Chili con carne	
Mix, prepared: 1 cup / **Durkee**	465
Mix dry: 1 pkg / **Durkee**	148
Lawry's / 1⅝ oz pkg	137
McCormick / 1¼ oz pkg	225
Schilling / 1¼ oz pkg	225
Chop suey, prepared: 1 cup / **Durkee**	318
Chop suey, dry mix: 1 pkg / **Durkee**	128
Enchilada, prepared: 1 cup / **Durkee**	57
Enchilada, dry mix: 1 pkg / **Durkee**	89
Enchilada: 1 env / **French's**	120
Fried rice, prepared: 1 cup / **Durkee**	215
Fried rice, dry mix: 1 pkg / **Durkee**	62
Goulash: 1⅝ pkg / **Lawry's**	127
Ground beef	
Mix, prepared: 1 cup / **Durkee**	653
Mix, dry: 1 pkg / **Durkee**	91
French's Hamburger Seasoning / 1 env	100
w onions: 1 env / **Ann Page**	100
w onions, prepared: 1 cup / **Durkee**	659
w onions, dry mix: 1 pkg / **Durkee**	102
w onions: 1 env / **French's**	100

CALORIES

Hamburger, prepared: 1 cup / **Durkee**	603
Hamburger, dry mix: 1 pkg / **Durkee**	110
Meatball: 1 env / **French's**	140
Meatball, Italian, prepared: 1 cup / **Durkee**	619
Meatball, Italian, dry mix: 1 pkg / **Durkee**	22
Meatball, Italian w cheese, prepared: 1 cup / **Durkee**	650
Meatball, Italian w cheese, dry mix: 1 pkg / **Durkee**	85
Meatloaf	
Contadina / 1 env	363
French's / 1 env	160
Lawry's / 3½ oz pkg	333
McCormick / 1½ oz pkg	120
Schilling / 1½ oz pkg	120
Meat marinade, prepared: ½ cup / **Durkee**	47
Meat marinade: 1 env / **French's**	80
Sloppy Joe	
Ann Page / 1 env	128
Durkee / 1 cup prepared	581
Durkee / dry mix: 1 pkg	118
French's / 1 env	128
Lawry's / 1½ oz pkg	139
McCormick / 1 5/16 oz pkg	170
Schilling / 1 5/16 oz pkg	170
Pizza flavor, prepared: 1 cup / **Durkee**	597
Pizza flavor, dry mix: 1 pkg / **Durkee**	99
Spanish rice, prepared: 1 cup / **Durkee**	274
Spanish rice, dry mix: 1 pkg / **Durkee**	129
Spanish rice: 1½ oz pkg / **Lawry's**	125
Swiss steak: 1 oz pkg / **McCormick**	45
Swiss steak: 1 oz pkg / **Schilling**	45
Taco	
Mix, prepared: 1 cup / **Durkee**	642
Mix, dry: 1 pkg / **Durkee**	67
French's / 1 env	150
McCormick / 1¼ oz pkg	65
Schilling / 1¼ oz pkg	65

Shortening

	CALORIES
Solid	
Lard: 1 cup	1850
1 tbsp	115
Vegetable: 1 tbsp / **Crisco**	110
Vegetable: 1 tbsp / **Fluffo**	110
Vegetable: 1 tbsp / **Mrs. Tucker's**	120
Vegetable: 1 tbsp / **Snowdrift**	110

Soft Drinks

	CALORIES
8 fl oz unless noted	
All flavors: 6 fl oz / **Weight Watchers** Dietary Carbonated Beverages	1
Birch beer / **Canada Dry**	110
Bitter Lemon / **Canada Dry**	100
Bitter lemon / **Schweppes**	112
Black cherry	
Canada Dry Low Calorie	2
No-Cal	0
Shasta	104
Shasta Diet	0
Tab	2
Black raspberry / **No-Cal**	2
Bubble Up	97
Bubble Up Sugar Free	1
Cactus Cooler / **Canada Dry**	120

CALORIES

Chocolate / **Canada Dry** Low Calorie	2
Chocolate / **No-Cal**	2
Chocolate / **Shasta** Diet	0
Chocolate mint / **No-Cal**	2
Club soda / **Canada Dry**	0
Club soda / **Schweppes**	0
Club soda / **Shasta**	0
Coffee / **No-Cal**	2
Cola	
Canada Dry Low Calorie	2
Coca-Cola	96
Diet-Rite	1
Jamaica cola / **Canada Dry**	110
No-Cal	0
Pepsi-Cola	104
Pepsi-Cola, Diet	1
Pepsi Light	47
Royal Crown	104
Shasta	90
Shasta Diet	0
Tab	1
Collins mixer / **Shasta**	78
Cream / **No-Cal**	0
Cream / **Shasta**	100
Cream / **Shasta** Diet	0
Dr. Nehi	98
Dr. Pepper	98
Dr. Pepper Sugar Free	1
Fresca	2
Ginger ale	
Canada Dry	90
Canada Dry Golden	100
Canada Dry Low Calorie	2
Fanta	84
Nehi	91
No-Cal	0
Schweppes	88
Shasta	78

	CALORIES
Shasta Diet	0
Tab	3
Ginger beer / **Schweppes**	96
Grape	
Canada Dry	130
Canada Dry Low Calorie	2
Crush	120
Fanta	114
Nehi	116
No-Cal	0
Patio	128
Schweppes	129
Shasta	114
Shasta Diet	0
Tab	2
Grapefruit / **Shasta**	103
Grapefruit / **Shasta** Diet	2
Half and Half / **Canada Dry**	110
Hi Spot / **Canada Dry**	100
Kick	118
Lemon / **Canada Dry** Low Calorie	2
Lemon-lime / **Shasta**	93
Lemon-lime / **Shasta** Diet	0
Lemon-lime / **TAB**	3
Lime / **Canada Dry**	130
Mello Yello	115
Mr. PiBB	93
Mr. PiBB wo sugar	1
Mountain Dew	118
Orange	
Canada Dry Low Calorie	2
Canada Dry Sunripe	130
Crush	114
Fanta	117
Nehi	124
No-Cal	0
Patio	128

	CALORIES
Schweppes Sparkling	118
Shasta	114
Shasta Diet	0
Tab	1
Pineapple / **Canada Dry**	110
Purple Passion / **Canada Dry**	120
Raspberry / **Canada Dry** Low Calorie	2
Red creme / **Schweppes**	115
Red Pop / **No-Cal**	0
Root beer	
A & W	114
A & W Sugar Free	11
Berks County	116
Canada Dry Barrelhead	110
Canada Dry Barrelhead Low Calorie	2
Canada Dry Low Calorie	2
Canada Dry Rooti	110
Dad's	105
Diet **Dad's**	1
Fanta	103
Hires	100
Hires Sugar Free	1
No-Cal	0
Patio	110
Schweppes	105
Shasta	100
Shasta Diet	0
Tab	1
7 Up	97
7 Up Diet	2
Shape-Up / **No Cal**	0
Sprite	95
Sprite wo sugar	3
Strawberry	
Canada Dry California	120
Canada Dry Low Calorie	2
Crush	114

Nehi	116
Shasta	94
Shasta Diet	0
Tab	2
Sun-Drop	118
Sun-Drop Sugar Free	1
Teem	93
TNT / No-Cal	0
Tahitian Treat / **Canada Dry**	130
Tiki	100
Tiki Diet	0
Tonic water	
Canada Dry	90
Canada Dry Low Calorie	2
No-Cal	0
Schweppes	88
Shasta	66
Upper 10	101
Vanilla cream / **Canada Dry**	130
Vanilla Cream / **Canada Dry** Low Calorie	2
Wild cherry / **Canada Dry**	130
Wink / **Canada Dry**	120
Wink / **Canada Dry** Low Calorie	2

Soups

CALORIES

Alphabet vegetable, mix, prepared: 6 fl oz / **Lipton** Cup-A-Soup	40
Asparagus, cream of, condensed, prepared: 10 oz / **Campbell**	100
Bean, canned	
Condensed, prepared: 8 oz / **Manischewitz**	111

Condensed, prepared: 1 cup / **Wyler's**	96
Semi-condensed, prepared: 1 can / **Campbell** Soup for One	210
w bacon, condensed, prepared: 1 cup / **Ann Page**	140
w bacon, condensed, prepared: 10 oz / **Campbell**	190
w bacon, condensed, prepared: 1 cup / **Town House**	157
Black, condensed, prepared: 10 oz / **Campbell**	130
Black, ready to serve: ½ can / **Crosse & Blackwell**	80
w ham, ready to serve: ½ can / **Campbell** Chunky 9½ oz	260
w ham, ready to serve, individual service size: 1 can / **Campbell** Chunky 10¾ oz	300
w hot dogs, condensed, prepared: 10 oz / **Campbell**	210
Lima, condensed, prepared: 8 oz / **Manischewitz**	93

Beef

Condensed, prepared: 10 oz / **Campbell**	100
Ready to serve: ½ can / **Campbell** Chunky 9½ oz	190
Ready to serve, individual service size: 1 can / **Campbell** Chunky 10¾ oz	220
Flavor, mix, prepared: 8 oz / **Lipton** Lite-Lunch	200
Barley, mix, prepared: 6 oz serving / **Wyler's**	54
Cabbage, condensed, prepared: 8 oz / **Manischewitz**	62
Low sodium, ready to serve, individual service size: 1 can / **Campbell** Chunky 7¼ oz	170
Mushroom, mix, prepared: 8 fl oz / **Lipton**	45
Noodle, condensed, prepared: 10 oz / **Campbell**	90

Noodle, condensed, prepared: 8 oz /
Manischewitz   83
Noodle, condensed, prepared: 1 cup /
Town House   74
Noodle, mix, prepared: 1 env / **Souptime**   30
Noodle, mix, prepared: 6 oz serving / **Wyler's**   37
Vegetable, condensed, prepared: 8 oz /
Manischewitz   59

Bouillon
Beef: 1 cube / **Herb-Ox**   6
Beef: 1 cube / **Maggi**   6
Beef: 1 cube / **Wyler's**   7
Beef-flavored: 1 cube / **Wyler's**   6
Beef-flavored, powder: 1 tsp / **Wyler's Instant**   10
Beef, powder: 1 tsp / **Wyler's Instant**   7
Chicken: 1 cube / **Herb-Ox**   6
Chicken: 1 cube / **Maggi**   7
Chicken-flavored: 1 cube / **Wyler's**   8
Chicken-flavored, powder: 1 tps / **Wyler's**
Instant   8
Chicken, powder: 1 tsp / **Wyler's Instant**   6
Onion: 1 cube / **Herb-Ox**   10
Onion: 1 cube / **Wyler's**   5
Vegetable: 1 cube / **Herb-Ox**   6
Vegetable: 1 cube / **Wyler's**   6
Vegetable-flavored, powder: 1 tsp /**Wyler's**
Instant   6

Broth
Beef: 1 packet / **Herb-Ox**   8
Beef: 1 tsp / **Herb-Ox** Instant   7
Beef, canned: 6¾ oz / **Swanson**   20
Beef, condensed, prepared: 10 oz / **Campbell**   35
Beef, mix: 1 packet / **Weight Watchers**   10
Chicken: 1 packet / **Herb-Ox**   12
Chicken: 1 tsp / **Herb-Ox** Instant   6
Chicken, canned: 6¾ oz / **Swanson**   25
Chicken, condensed, prepared: 10 oz /
Campbell   50

Chicken, mix, prepared: 6 fl oz / **Lipton** Cup-A-Broth	25
Chicken, mix: 1 packet / **Weight Watchers**	10
Onion: 1 packet / **Herb-Ox**	14
Onion, mix: 1 packet / **Weight Watchers**	10
Vegetable: 1 packet / **Herb-Ox**	12
Vegetable: 1 tsp / **Herb-Ox** Instant	6
Celery, cream of, condensed, prepared: 1 cup / **Ann Page**	60
Celery, cream of, condensed, prepared: 10 oz / **Campbell**	110
Celery, cream of, condensed, prepared: 1 cup / **Town House**	101
Cheddar cheese, condensed, prepared: 10 oz / **Campbell**	180
Chickarina, canned, ready to serve: 8 fl oz / **Progresso**	100
Chicken	
Canned, ready to serve: ½ can / **Campbell** Chunky 9½ oz	200
Canned, ready to serve, individual service size: 1 can / **Campbell** Chunky 10¾ oz	230
Flavor, mix, prepared: 8 oz / **Lipton** Lite-Lunch	220
Alphabet, condensed, prepared: 10 oz / **Campbell**	110
Barley, condensed, prepared: 8 oz / **Manischewitz**	83
Cream of, condensed, prepared: 1 cup / **Ann Page**	90
Cream of, condensed, prepared: 10 oz / **Campbell**	140
Cream of, condensed, prepared: 1 cup / **Town House**	93
Cream of, mix, prepared: 6 fl oz / **Lipton** Cup-A-Soup	80
Cream of, mix, prepared: 1 env / **Souptime**	100

w dumplings, condensed, prepared: 10 oz / **Campbell**	120
Gumbo, condensed, prepared: 10 oz / **Campbell**	70
Kasha, condensed, prepared: 8 oz / **Manischewitz**	41
Low sodium, ready to serve: 1 can / **Campbell** Chunky 7½ oz	170
Noodle, condensed, prepared: 1 cup / **Ann Page**	70
Noodle, condensed, prepared: 1 cup / **A & P "O" Style**	67
Noodle, condensed, prepared: 10 oz / **Campbell**	90
Noodle, condensed, prepared: 10 oz / **Campbell** Noodle-O's	90
Noodle, condensed, prepared: 8 oz / **Manischewitz**	46
Noodle, condensed, prepared: 1 cup / **Town House**	75
Noodle, condensed, prepared: 1 cup / **Town House** Star Noodle	66
Noodle, semi-condensed, prepared: 1 cup / **Campbell** Soup for One 11⅝ oz	120
Noodle, mix, prepared: 6 fl oz / **Lipton** Cup-A-Soup	45
Noodle, mix, prepared: 8 fl oz / **Lipton** Noodle	70
Noodle, mix, prepared: 8 fl oz / **Lipton** Ripple Noodle	80
Noodle, mix, prepared: 1 env / **Souptime**	30
Noodle, mix, prepared: 6 oz serving / **Wyler's**	33
Rice, canned, ready to serve: ½ can / **Campbell** Chunky 9½ oz	160
Rice, condensed, prepared: 1 cup / **Ann Page**	50

CALORIES

Rice, condensed, prepared: 10 oz /
  Campbell   80
Rice, condensed, prepared: 8 oz /
  Manischewitz   47
Rice, condensed, prepared: 1 cup /
  Town House   61
Rice, mix, prepared: 8 fl oz / **Lipton**   60
Rice, mix, prepared: 6 fl oz / **Lipton**
  Cup-A-Soup   50
Rice, mix, prepared: 6 oz serving / **Wyler's**   37
w stars, condensed, prepared: 1 cup /
  Ann Page   60
w stars, condensed, prepared: 10 oz /
  Campbell   80
Vegetable, canned, ready to serve: ½ can /
  Campbell Chunky 9½ oz   190
Vegetable, condensed, prepared: 1 cup /
  Ann Page   80
Vegetable, condensed, prepared: 10 oz /
  Campbell   90
Vegetable, condensed, prepared: 8 oz /
  Manischewitz   55
Vegetable, condensed, prepared: 1 cup /
  Town House   85
Vegetable, mix, prepared: 6 fl oz /
  Lipton Cup-A-Soup   40
Vegetable, mix, prepared: 6 oz serving /
  Wyler's   28
Chili beef
  Condensed, prepared: 10 oz / **Campbell**   190
  Condensed, prepared: 1 cup / **Town House**   161
  Ready to serve: ½ can / **Campbell**
    Chunky 9¾ oz   260
  Ready to serve, individual service size:
    1 can / **Campbell** Chunky 11 oz   300
Chowder
  Clam, prepared: 1 cup / **Howard**
    Johnson's   176

CALORIES

Clam, ready to serve: 8 fl oz / **Progresso**	100
Clam, Manhattan, ready to serve: ½ can / **Campbell** Chunky 9½ oz	160
Clam, Manhattan, condensed, prepared: 10 oz / **Campbell**	100
Clam, Manhattan, condensed, prepared: 1 cup / **Snow's**	58
Clam, Manhattan, condensed, prepared: 7 oz / **Snow's**	130
Clam, Manhattan, ready to serve: ½ can / **Crosse & Blackwell**	50
Clam, New England, condensed prepared: 10 oz / **Campbell**	100
Clam, New England, condensed, made w milk: 10 oz / **Campbell**	200
Clam, New England, condensed, prepared: 7 oz / **Snow's**	130
Clam, New England, condensed, prepared: 1 cup / **Snow's**	147
Clam, New England, semi-condensed, prepared: 1 can / **Campbell** Soup for One 11⅝ oz	125
Clam, New England, ready to serve: ½ can / **Crosse & Blackwell**	90
Corn, condensed, prepared: 1 cup / **Snow's**	154
Fish, condensed, prepared: 1 cup / **Snow's**	134
Seafood, New England, condensed, prepared: 1 cup / **Snow's**	147
Consommé, beef, condensed, prepared: 10 oz / **Campbell**	45
Consommé Madrilene, clear, ready to serve: ½ can / **Crosse & Blackwell**	25
Consommé Madrilene, red, ready to serve: ½ can / **Crosse & Blackwell**	25
Crab, ready to serve: ½ can / **Crosse & Blackwell**	50
Escarole, in chicken broth, ready to serve: 1 cup / **Progresso**	25

Gazpacho, ready to serve: ½ can / **Crosse & Blackwell**	30
Lentil, condensed, prepared: 8 oz / **Manischewitz**	166
Lentil, ready to serve: 1 cup / **Progresso**	150
Lentil w ham, ready to serve: ½ can / **Crosse & Blackwell**	80
Meatball Alphabet, condensed, prepared: 10 oz / **Campbell**	140

Minestrone

Condensed, prepared: 1 cup / **Ann Page**	80
Condensed, prepared: 10 oz / **Campbell**	110
Condensed, prepared: 1 can / **Town House**	200
Ready to serve: ½ can / **Campbell** Chunky 9½ oz	160
Ready to serve: ½ can / **Crosse & Blackwell**	90

Mushroom

Condensed, prepared: 10 oz / **Campbell**	110
Mix, prepared: 1 env / **Souptime**	80
Mix, prepared: 6 oz serving / **Wyler's**	113
Barley, condensed, prepared: 8 oz / **Manischewitz**	72
Bisque, ready to serve: ½ can / **Crosse & Blackwell**	90
Cream of, condensed, prepared: 1 cup / **Ann Page**	120
Cream of, condensed, prepared: 10 oz / **Campbell**	150
Cream of, condensed, prepared: 1 cup / **Town House**	124
Cream of, semi-condensed, prepared: 1 can / **Campbell** Soup for One 11¼ oz	160
Cream of, mix, prepared: 6 fl oz / **Lipton** Cup-A-Soup	80
Cream of, low sodium, ready to serve, individual service size: 1 can / **Campbell** 7¼ oz	140

Noodle
    Mix, prepared: 6 fl oz / **Lipton**
        Cup-A-Soup Giggle   40
    Mix, prepared: 6 fl oz / **Lipton**
        Cup-A-Soup Ring   50
    Mix, prepared: 8 fl oz / **Lipton**
        Giggle Noodle   80
    Mix, prepared: 8 fl oz / **Lipton**
        Ring-O-Noodle   50
    w beef flavor, mix, prepared: 6 fl oz /
        Lipton Cup-A-Soup   35
    w chicken, condensed, prepared: 10 oz /
        Campbell Curley   100
    w chicken broth, mix: 1/5 env / **Ann Page**   45
    w chicken broth, mix, prepared: 8 fl oz /
        Lipton Noodle   60
    w ground beef, condensed, prepared: 10 oz /
        Campbell   110
Onion
    Condensed, prepared: 10 oz / **Campbell**   80
    Mix: 1/5 env / **Ann Page**   25
    Mix, prepared: 8 fl oz / **Lipton**   40
    Mix, prepared: 8 fl oz / **Lipton** Beefy   30
    Mix, prepared: 6 fl oz / **Lipton** Cup-A-Soup   30
    Mix, prepared: 6 oz serving / **Wyler's**   28
    Cream of, condensed, prepared: 10 oz /
        Campbell   180
    French, condensed, prepared: 1 can /
        Town House   180
    French, mix, prepared: 1 env / **Souptime**   20
    Mushroom, mix, prepared: 8 fl oz / **Lipton**   35
Oriental style, mix, prepared: 8 oz / **Lipton**
    Lite-Lunch   210
Oyster stew, condensed, prepared: 10 oz /
    Campbell   70
Oyster stew, condensed, prepared w milk:
    10 oz / **Campbell**   170

Pea, green
    Condensed, prepared: 10 oz / **Campbell**   180
    Mix, prepared: 8 fl oz / **Lipton**   130
    Mix, prepared: 6 fl oz / **Lipton** Cup-A-Soup   120
    Mix, prepared: 1 env / **Souptime**   70
    Low sodium, ready to serve, individual
        service size: 1 can / **Campbell** 7½ oz   150
Pea, split
    Condensed, prepared: 8 oz / **Manischewitz**   133
    w ham, condensed, prepared: 1 cup /
        Ann Page   180
    w ham, condensed, prepared: 1 cup /
        Town House   153
    w ham, ready to serve: ½ can / **Campbell**
        Chunky 9½ oz   220
    w ham and bacon, condensed, prepared:
        10 oz / **Campbell**   210
Pepper Pot, condensed, prepared: 10 oz /
    Campbell   130
Potato, cream of, condensed, prepared: 10 oz /
    Campbell   90
Potato, cream of, condensed, prepared w
    milk: 10 oz / **Campbell**   140
Potato, cream of, condensed, prepared:
    1 can / **Town House**   220
Potato w leeks, mix, prepared: 6 oz serving /
    Wyler's   116
Scotch broth, condensed, prepared: 10 oz /
    Campbell   100
Shrimp, cream of, condensed, prepared: 10 oz /
    Campbell   110
Shrimp, cream of, condensed, prepared w milk:
    10 oz / **Campbell**   210
Shrimp, cream, ready to serve: ½ can /
    Crosse & Blackwell   90
Sirloin burger, ready to serve: ½ can /
    Campbell Chunky 9½ oz   210

Sirloin burger, ready to serve, individual service size: 1 can / **Campbell** Chunky 10¾ oz	230
Steak & potato, ready to serve: ½ can / **Campbell** Chunky 9½ oz	190
Stockpot, vegetable, mix, prepared: 8 oz /**Lipton** Lite-Lunch	220
Stockpot, vegetable-beef, condensed, prepared: 10 oz / **Campbell**	120

Tomato

Condensed, prepared: 1 cup / **Ann Page**	80
Condensed, prepared: 10 oz / **Campbell**	110
Condensed, prepared w milk: 10 oz / **Campbell**	210
Condensed, prepared: 8 oz / **Manischewitz**	60
Condensed, prepared: 1 cup / **Town House**	87
Mix, prepared: 6 fl oz / **Lipton** Cup-A-Soup	70
Mix, prepared: 1 env / **Souptime**	70
Ready to serve: 8 fl oz / **Progresso**	110
Beef, condensed, prepared: 10 oz / **Campbell** Noodle-O's	160
Bisque, condensed, prepared: 10 oz / **Campbell**	140
Low sodium, ready to serve, individual service size: 1 can / **Campbell** 7¼ oz	130
Rice, condensed, prepared: 1 cup / **Ann Page**	90
Rice, condensed, prepared: 10 oz / **Campbell** Old Fashioned	130
Rice, condensed, prepared: 8 oz / **Manischewitz**	78
Rice, condensed, prepared: 1 can / **Town House**	280
Royale, semi-condensed, prepared: 1 can / **Campbell** Soup for One	180

Turkey

Ready to serve: ½ can / **Campbell** Chunky 9¼ oz	160

Noodle, condensed, prepared: 1 cup / **Ann Page**	70
Noodle, condensed, prepared: 10 oz / **Campbell**	80
Noodle, condensed, prepared: 1 cup / **Town House**	83
Noodle, low sodium, ready to serve, individual service size: 1 can / **Campbell** 7¼ oz	60
Vegetable, condensed, prepared: 1 cup / **Ann Page**	60
Vegetable, condensed, prepared: 10 oz / **Campbell**	90
Vegetable	
Canned, ready to serve: ½ can / **Campbell** Chunky 9½ oz	140
Canned, ready to serve, individual service size: 1 can / **Campbell** Chunky 10¾ oz	150
Condensed, prepared: 1 cup / **Ann Page** Vegetarian	70
Condensed, prepared: 10 oz / **Campbell**	100
Condensed, prepared: 10 oz / **Campbell** Old Fashioned	90
Condensed, prepared: 10 oz / **Campbell** Vegetarian	90
Condensed, prepared: 8 oz / **Manischewitz**	63
Condensed, prepared: 1 cup / **Town House** Vegetarian	83
Semi-condensed, prepared: 1 can / **Campbell** Old World Soup for One	125
Mix, prepared: 8 fl oz / **Lipton** Country	70
Mix, prepared: 8 fl oz / **Lipton** Italian	100
Mix, prepared: 6 oz serving / **Wyler's**	56
Beef, condensed, prepared: 1 cup / **Ann Page**	80
Beef, condensed, prepared: 10 oz / **Campbell**	90
Beef, condensed, prepared: 1 cup / **Town House**	66
Beef, mix, prepared: 8 fl oz / **Lipton**	60

	CALORIES
Beef, mix, prepared: 6 fl oz / **Lipton** Cup-A-Soup	60
Beef, ready to serve: ½ can / **Campbell** Chunky 9½ oz	160
Beef, low sodium, ready to serve: 1 can / **Campbell** 7¼ oz	80
Beef w shells, mix, prepared: 8 fl oz / **Lipton**	100
w beef stock, condensed, prepared: 1 cup / **Ann Page**	70
w beef stock, condensed, prepared: 1 cup / **Town House**	83
Cream of, mix, prepared: 1 env / **Souptime**	80
Low sodium, ready to serve, individual service size: 1 can / **Campbell** 7¼ oz	90
w noodles, condensed, prepared: 10 oz / **Campbell** Noodle-O's	90
Spring, mix, prepared: 6 fl oz / **Lipton** Cup-A-Soup	45
Vichyssoise, ready to serve: ½ can / **Crosse & Blackwell**	70

Spaghetti and Spaghetti Dishes

CALORIES

	CALORIES
Spaghetti, plain, enriched, cooked firm, "al dente": 1 cup	192
Spaghetti, plain, enriched, cooked, tender stage: 1 cup	155
Spaghetti, in tomato sauce, canned **Buitoni** Twists / ½ can	160

CALORIES

w beef: 7½ oz can / **Hormel Short Orders**	280
w cheese: 7⅜ oz / **Franco-American**	170
w cheese sauce: 7⅜ oz / **Franco-American** "SpaghettiOs"	160
w frankfurters: 7⅜ oz / **Franco-American** "SpaghettiOs"	210
w meat sauce: 7¾ oz / **Franco-American**	220
w meatballs: ½ can / **Buitoni**	228
w meatballs: ½ can / **Buitoni** Twists	228
w meatballs: 7¼ oz / **Franco-American**	210
w little meatballs: 7⅜ oz / **Franco-American** "SpaghettiOs"	210
w meatballs: 7½ oz can / **Hormel Short Orders**	205
w meatballs: 1 cup / **Libby's**	84
Spaghetti w sauce, frozen	
Banquet / 3 oz	311
Morton Casserole / 1 pkg	220
Stouffer's / 1 pkg (14 oz)	445
w meatballs: 32 oz / **Banquet** Buffet Supper	1127
w meatballs: 9 oz / **Green Giant** Boil-in-Bag Entrees	280
Spaghetti and sauce, mixes	
Prepared: 1 pouch / **Betty Crocker** Mug-O-Lunch	170
Prepared: 1 cup / **Kraft** American Style	260
Prepared: 1 cup / **Kraft** Tangy Italian Style	260

Spreads

CALORIES

1 oz = about ¼ cup

Anchovy paste: 1 tbsp / **Crosse & Blackwell**	20
Chicken, canned: 1 oz / **Swanson**	70
Chicken: 1 oz / **Underwood**	63

CALORIES

Chicken salad: 1½ oz / **Carnation** Spreadables	94
Corned beef: 1 oz / **Underwood**	55
Ham	
Deviled: 1 oz / **Hormel**	70
Deviled, canned: 1½ tbsp / **Libby's**	300
Deviled: 1 oz / **Underwood**	97
Salad: 1½ oz / **Carnation** Spreadables	78
Liverwurst: 1 oz / **Underwood**	92
Peanut butter: 1 tbsp unless noted	
Ann Page Krunchy	105
Ann Page Smooth	105
Ann Page Regular Grand	105
Home Brands Natural	100
Home Brands Real	100
Kitchen King Crunchy	95
Kitchen King Smooth	95
Peter Pan Crunchy	95
Peter Pan, low sodium	95
Peter Pan Smooth	95
Planters Creamy	95
Planters Crunchy	95
Skippy Creamy Smooth	95
Skippy Old Fashioned Super Chunk	95
Skippy Super Chunk	95
Smucker's Crunchy	95
Smucker's Natural	100
Smucker's Smooth	90
Sultana Krunchy	105
and jelly: 1 oz / **Smucker's** Goober Grape	125
Potted meat: 1½ tbsp / **Libby's**	208
Roast Beef: 1 oz / **Underwood**	58
Sandwich spread: 1 tbsp unless noted	
Best Foods Spred	60
Hellmann's	60
Kraft	50
Mrs. Filbert's	50
Nu Made	60
Oscar Mayer / 1 oz	65

CALORIES

Spam, deviled: 1 oz / **Hormel**   80
Tuna salad: 1½ oz / **Carnation** Spreadables   81
Turkey salad: 1½ oz / **Carnation** Spreadables   86

Sugar and Sweeteners

CALORIES

Honey, strained or extracted: 1 tbsp	64
Honey, strained or extracted: 1 cup	1031
Sugar	
Brown, not packed: 1 cup	541
Brown, packed: 1 cup	821
Maple: 1 oz	99
Powdered, unsifted: 1 cup	462
Powdered, unsifted: 1 tbsp	31
Powdered, sifted: 1 cup	385
White, granulated: 1 cup	770
White, granulated: 1 tbsp	46
White, granulated: 1 tsp	15
Sugar substitute, granulated: 1 packet / **Weight Watchers** Sweet'ner	4
Sweetener, artificial: 1 tsp / **Sprinkle Sweet**	2
Sweetener, artificial: ⅛ tsp / **Sweet 10**	0

Syrups

CALORIES

1 tbsp

Pancake, waffle
    Aunt Jemima 53
    Cary's Diet 10
    Diet Delight 15
    Golden Griddle 50
    Karo 60
    Karo Imitation Maple 55
    Log Cabin Buttered 52
    Log Cabin Country Kitchen 51
    Log Cabin Maple-Honey 54
    Mrs. Butterworth's 53
    S & W Nutradiet 12
    Tillie Lewis 14
Corn, dark / **Karo** 60
Corn, light / **Karo** 60
Maple, pure / **Cary's** 60
Maple blend / **Log Cabin** 46
Molasses, cane, dark (third extraction) 45
Molasses, cane, light (first extraction) 50
Sorghum 55

T ea

Bags, or loose tea prepared: 1 cup	1
Iced tea	
Canned: 8 fl oz / **No-Cal**	0
Instant: 1 level tsp / **Nestea**	less than 1
Instant, lemon-flavored: 8 fl oz / **Nestea**	2
Instant, lemon-flavored: 1 tsp dry mix /	
A & P Our Own Low Calorie	4
Instant, lemon-flavored, w sugar: 1 env	
A & P Our Own	480
Instant, w sugar and lemon: 6 fl oz / **Nestea**	70

Toppings

1 tbsp unless noted

Black cherry: 1 tsp / **No-Cal**	0
Black raspberry: 1 tsp / **No-Cal**	0
Butterscotch / **Kraft**	60
Butterscotch / **Smucker's**	70
Caramel / **Smucker's**	70
Caramel, chocolate-flavored / **Kraft**	50
Cherry / **Smucker's**	65

CALORIES

Chocolate
Bosco	50
Hershey's	45
Kraft	50
No-Cal / 1 tsp	2
Smucker's	65
Tillie Lewis	16
Fudge / **Hershey's**	45
Fudge / **Kraft**	70
Fudge / **Smucker's**	65
Fudge, chocolate-mint / **Smucker's**	70
Fudge, Swiss milk chocolate / **Smucker's**	70
Coffee: 1 tsp / **No-Cal**	2
Cola: 1 tsp / **No-Cal**	0
Grape: 1 tsp / **No-Cal**	¼
Marshmallow / **Kraft**	35
Peanut butter caramel / **Smucker's**	75
Pecans in syrup / **Smucker's**	65
Pineapple / **Kraft**	50
Pineapple / **Smucker's**	65
Strawberry / **Kraft**	45
Strawberry: 1 tsp / **No-Cal**	0
Strawberry / **Smucker's**	60
Walnut / **Kraft**	90
Walnuts in syrup / **Smucker's**	65
Whipped, non-dairy, frozen / **Cool Whip**	14
Whipped, mix, prepared / **D-Zerta**	8
Whipped, mix, prepared / **Dream Whip**	10

Vegetables

FRESH

	CALORIES
Amaranth, raw, leaves: 1 lb	163
Artichokes (calorie range from 8 for freshly harvested artichokes to 44 for stored artichokes), cooked, bud or globe: 1 small	
Artichokes (calorie range from 10 for freshly harvested artichokes to 53 for stored artichokes), cooked, bud or globe: 1 medium	
Artichokes (calorie range from 12 for freshly harvested artichokes to 67 for stored artichokes), cooked, bud or globe: 1 large	
Asparagus	
Raw: 1 lb	118
Raw, cut (1½–2 in): 1 cup	35
Cooked, cut (1½–2 in), drained: 1 cup	29
Spears, cooked, drained: 1 small	8
Spears, cooked, drained: 1 medium	12
Spears, cooked, drained: 1 large	20
Bamboo shoots, raw, 1-in pieces: 1 lb	122
Barley, pearled, light: 1 cup	698
Barley, pearled, Pot or Scotch: 1 cup	696
Beans	
Great Northern, cooked, drained: 1 cup	212
Lima, immature (green), raw: 1 cup	191
Lima, immature (green), cooked, drained: 1 cup	189

	CALORIES
Lima, mature, cooked, drained: 1 cup	262
Mung, mature, dry, raw: 1 cup	714
Mung, mature, dry, raw: 1 lb	1542
Mung, sprouted seeds, raw: 1 cup	37
Mung, sprouted seeds, cooked, drained: 1 cup	35
Pea (navy), cooked, drained: 1 cup	224
Pinto, dry, raw: 1 cup	663
Pinto or calico or red Mexican, dry, raw: 1 lb	1583
Red, dry, cooked: ½ cup	118
Red, dry, raw: ½ cup	343
Red, kidney, cooked, drained: 1 cup	218
Snap, green, raw, cut: 1 cup	35
Snap, green, cooked, drained: 1 cup	31
Snap, yellow or wax, raw, cut: 1 cup	30
Snap, yellow or wax, cooked, drained: 1 cup	28
White, dry, raw: 1 lb	1542
Beets, common, red, raw, peeled, diced: 1 cup	58
Beets, common, red, peeled, cooked, drained, whole (2-in diam): 2 beets	32
Beets, common, red, peeled, cooked, drained, diced or sliced: 1 cup	54
Beets greens, common, edible leaves and stems, raw: 1 lb	109
Beet greens, common, edible leaves and stems, cooked, drained: 1 cup	26
Broadbeans, raw, immature seeds: 1 lb	476
Broadbeans, raw, mature seeds, dry: 1 lb	1533
Broccoli	
Stalks, raw: 1 lb	145
Cooked, drained: 1 small stalk	36
Cooked, drained: 1 medium stalk	47
Cooked, drained: 1 large stalk	73
Cooked, drained, ½-in pieces: 1 cup	40
Cooked, drained, whole or cut: 1 lb	118

CALORIES

Brussels sprouts, cooked: ½ cup	28
Brussels sprouts, raw: 9 med	45
Cabbage	
Raw: 1 lb	109
Raw, ground: 1 cup	36
Raw, shredded coarsely or sliced: 1 cup	17
Raw, shredded finely or chopped: 1 cup	22
Chinese, raw: 1 lb	109
Chinese, raw, 1-in pieces: 1 cup	11
Red, raw: 1 lb	141
Red, raw, shredded coarsely or sliced: 1 cup	22
Red, raw, shredded finely or chopped: 1 cup	28
Savoy, raw: 1 lb	109
Savoy, raw, shredded coarsely or sliced: 1 cup	17
Spoon, raw, 1-in pieces: 1 cup	11
Spoon, cooked, drained, 1-in pieces: 1 cup	24
Carrots	
Raw: 1 carrot(2⅞ oz)	30
Raw: 1 lb	191
Raw, grated or shredded: 1 cup	46
Raw, strips: 1 oz or 6-8 strips	12
Cooked, drained, diced: 1 cup	45
Cooked, drained, sliced crosswise: 1 cup	48
Cauliflower	
Raw: 1 head (1.9 lb)	232
Raw, flowerbuds, whole: 1 cup	27
Raw, flowerbuds, sliced: 1 cup	23
Raw, flowerbuds, chopped: 1 cup	31
Cooked, drained: 1 cup	28
Celeriac, raw: 4 to 6 roots	40
Celery	
Raw: 1 lb	77
Raw, large outer stalk (8-in long, 1½-in wide): 1 stalk	7
Raw, small inner stalk (5-in long, ¾-in wide): 3 stalks	9

CALORIES

Raw, chopped or diced: 1 cup	20
Cooked, diced: 1 cup	21
Chard, Swiss, raw: 1 lb	113
Chard, Swiss, cooked, drained, leaves: 1 cup	32
Chayote, raw: ½ med squash	28
Chickpeas or garbanzos, mature seeds, dry, raw: 1 cup	720
Chickpeas or garbanzos, mature seeds, dry, raw: 1 lb	1633
Chicory, Witloof, raw: 1 head (5-7 in long)	8
Chicory, Witloof, raw: 1 lb	68
Chicory, Witloof, raw, chopped, ½-in pieces: 1 cup	14
Chives, raw, chopped: 1 tbsp	1
Collards	
Raw, leaves w stems: 1 lb	181
Raw, leaves wo stems: 1 lb	204
Cooked, drained, leaves w stems: 1 cup	42
Cooked, drained, leaves wo stems: 1 cup	63
Corn, sweet, raw, white and yellow, husked: 1 lb	240
Corn, sweet, white and yellow, cooked, drained, kernels only: 1 cup	137
Corn, sweet, white and yellow, cooked, drained, on cob: 1 ear (5 x 1¾ in)	70
Cowpeas (including blackeye peas)	
Immature, raw: 1 cup blackeye peas	184
Immature, cooked, drained: 1 cup blackeye peas	178
Mature seeds, dry, cooked, drained: 1 cup	190
Young pods w seeds, raw: 1 lb	200
Young pods w seeds, cooked, drained: 1 lb	154
Cress, garden, raw, trimmed: 5 to 8 sprigs	3
Cress, garden, raw, trimmed: ½ lb	72
Cucumbers	
Raw, unpeeled, whole: 1 small	25
Raw, unpeeled, whole: 1 large	45
Raw, unpeeled, sliced: 1 cup	16

CALORIES

Raw, peeled, whole: 1 small	22
Raw, peeled, whole: 1 large	39
Dandelion greens, raw: 1 lb	204
Dandelion greens, cooked, drained: 1 cup	35
Dock or sorrel, raw: ½ lb	45
Eggplant, cooked, drained, diced: 1 cup	38
Endive, raw: 1 lb	91
Endive, raw, small pieces: 1 cup	10
Fennel leaves, raw, trimmed: ½ lb	59
Garlic, cloves, raw: 1 clove	4
Hyacinth-beans, raw, young pods, ½-in pieces: 1 cup	32
Hyacinth-beans, raw, mature, dry: 1 lb	1533
Kale, leaves wo stems, raw: 1 lb	240
Kale, cooked, drained: 1 cup	43
Kohlrabi, raw, diced: 1 cup	41
Kohlrabi, cooked, drained: 1 cup	40
Leeks, raw: 3 (5-in long)	52
Lentils, mature seeds, dry, whole, raw: 1 cup	646
Lentils, mature seeds, cooked, drained: 1 cup	212
Lettuce	
Butternut (Boston types and Bibb): 1 head	23
Butternut (Boston types and Bibb), chopped or shredded: 1 cup	8
Cos or romaine: 1 lb	82
Cos or romaine, chopped or shredded: 1 cup	10
Crisphead (including Iceberg): 1 wedge (¼ head)	18
Crisphead (including Iceberg): 1 head	70
Crisphead (including Iceberg), chopped or shredded: 1 cup	7
Looseleaf varieties, chopped or shredded: 1 cup	10
Mushrooms: 1 lb	127
Mushrooms, sliced, chopped or diced: 1 cup	20
Mustard greens, raw: 1 lb	141
Mustard greens, cooked, drained: 1 cup	32

CALORIES

Mustard spinach, raw: 1 lb	100
Mustard spinach, cooked, drained: 1 cup	29
New Zealand spinach, raw: 1 lb	86
New Zealand spinach, cooked, drained: 1 cup	23
Okra, crosscut slices, cooked, drained: 1 cup	46
Onions	
Raw: 1 lb	172
Raw, chopped: 1 cup	65
Raw, chopped or minced: 1 tbsp	4
Raw, sliced: 1 cup	44
Cooked, drained, whole or sliced: 1 cup	61
Young green: 2 medium or 6 small	14
Young green, chopped: 1 tbsp	2
Young green, chopped or sliced: 1 cup	36
Parsley, raw: 10 sprigs (2½-in long)	4
Parsley, raw, chopped: 1 tbsp	2
Parsnips, raw: 1 lb	293
Parsnips, cooked, drained: 1 large parsnip	106
Parsnips, cooked, drained, diced: 1 cup	102
Peas	
Green, immature, raw: 1 cup	122
Green, immature, raw: 1 lb	381
Cooked, drained: 1 cup	114
Mature, dry, split, cooked: 1 cup	230
Peppers, chili, green, raw: ½ lb	62
Peppers, chili, red w seeds: ½ lb	203
Peppers, chili, red wo seeds: ½ lb	108
Peppers, hot, red, wo seeds, dried: 1 tbsp	50
Peppers, sweet	
Green, raw, whole: 1 small (about 5 per lb)	16
Green, raw, whole: 1 large	
(about 2¼ per lb)	36
Green, chopped or diced: 1 cup	33
Green, cooked, drained: 1 large	29
Red, raw, whole: 1 small (about 5 per lb)	23
Red, raw, whole: 1 large	
(about 2¼ per lb)	51

CALORIES

Red, chopped or diced: 1 cup	47
Pokeberry (poke), shoots, cooked, drained:	
1 cup	33
Potatoes	
Baked in skin: 1 potato (2⅓ x 4¾ in)	145
Boiled in skin: 1 potato (2⅓ x 4¾ in)	173
Boiled in skin: 1 potato, round, 2½-in diam	104
Boiled in skin, diced or sliced: 1 cup	101
Peeled, boiled: 1 potato (2⅓ x 4¾ in)	146
Peeled, boiled: 1 potato, round, 2½-in diam	88
Peeled, boiled, diced or sliced: 1 cup	101
French fried: 10 strips, 2–3½-in long	137
Fried from raw: 1 cup	456
Mashed w milk and butter or margarine:	
1 cup	197
Pumpkin, pulp: 8 oz	42
Purslane leaves and stems, raw: ½ lb	48
Radishes, raw, whole: 10 medium	8
Radishes, raw, whole: 10 large	14
Radishes, raw, sliced: 1 cup	20
Rutabagas, raw, cubed: 1 cup	64
Rutabagas, cooked, drained, cubed or sliced:	
1 cup	60
Shallot bulbs, raw, chopped: 1 tbsp	7
Soybeans	
Mature seeds, dry, cooked: 1 cup	234
Sprouted seeds, raw: 1 cup	48
Sprouted seeds, cooked, drained: 1 cup	48
Curd (tofu): 1 piece (2½ x 2¾ x 1 in)	86
Spinach, raw: 1 lb	118
Spinach, raw, chopped: 1 cup	14
Spinach, leaves, cooked, drained: 1 cup	41
Squash	
Acorn, baked: ½ squash	97
Acorn, baked, mashed: 1 cup	113
Butternut, baked, mashed: 1 cup	139
Butternut, boiled, mashed: 1 cup	100

CALORIES

Crookneck and straightneck, yellow, raw, sliced: 1 cup	26
Crookneck and straightneck, yellow, raw: 1 lb	91
Crookneck and straightneck, yellow, cooked, sliced: 1 cup	27
Crookneck and straightneck, yellow, cooked, mashed: 1 cup	36
Hubbard, baked, mashed: 1 cup	103
Hubbard, boiled, mashed: 1 cup	74
Hubbard, boiled, diced: 1 cup	71
Scallop varieties, white and pale green, raw, sliced: 1 cup	27
Scallop varieties, white and pale green, raw: 1 lb	95
Summer, all varieties, cooked, sliced: 1 cup	25
Summer, all varieties, cooked, cubed or diced: 1 cup	29
Summer, all varieties, cooked, mashed: 1 cup	34
Winter, all varieties, cooked, baked, mashed: 1 cup	129
Winter, all varieties, cooked, boiled, mashed: 1 cup	93
Zucchini and Cocozelle, green, raw, sliced: 1 cup	22
Zucchini and Cocozelle, green, raw: 1 lb	77
Zucchini and Cocozelle, green, cooked, sliced: 1 cup	22
Zucchini and Cocozelle, green, cooked, mashed: 1 cup	29
Sweet potatoes, baked in skin: 1 potato (5 x 2 in)	161
Sweet potatoes, boiled in skin: 1 potato (5 x 2 in)	172
Sweet potatoes, mashed: 1 cup	291
Tomatoes, raw: 1 small (3½ oz)	20
Tomatoes, raw: 1 large (4¾ oz)	27
Tomatoes, boiled: 1 cup	63

CALORIES

Turnips, raw: 1 cup	39
Turnips, cooked, drained, cubed: 1 cup	36
Turnips, mashed: 1 cup	53
Turnip greens, raw: 1 lb	127
Turnip greens, cooked, drained: 1 cup	29
Water chestnut, peeled: 4 chestnuts	20
Watercress, raw, whole: 1 cup	7
Watercress, raw, finely chopped: 1 cup	24

CANNED AND FROZEN

Artichoke hearts, frozen: 3 oz (5 or 6 hearts) / **Birds Eye**	20
Asparagus, canned: 1 cup unless noted	
Cut / **Green Giant**	40
Cut / **Kounty Kist**	40
Cut / **Lindy**	40
Cut / **Stokely-Van Camp**	45
Spears / **Green Giant**	40
Spears / **Le Sueur**	40
Spears: 5 whole / **S and W Nutradiet**	16
Spears / **Town House**	35
Spears and tips / **Del Monte**	35
Spears, tipped / **Del Monte**	35
Whole / **Stokely-Van Camp**	50
White / **Del Monte**	35
Asparagus, frozen	
Cut: 3.3 oz (about ½ cup / **Birds Eye**	25
Cut, in butter sauce: 1 cup / **Green Giant**	90
Cuts and tips: ½ cup / **Seabrook Farms**	23
Cuts and tips, in Hollandaise sauce: ½ cup / **Seabrook Farms**	84
Spears: 3.3 oz (about ½ cup) / **Birds Eye**	25
Spears: 5 spears / **Seabrook Farms**	19

Spears, jumbo: 3.3 oz (about ½ cup) / **Birds Eye**	25
Beans, baked: 1 cup	
Howard Johnson's	340
Pea / **B & M**	336
Red kidney / **B & M**	336
Yellow eye / **B & M**	360
Beans, baked style	
w bacon: 7½ oz can / **Hormel Short Orders**	340
In barbecue sauce: 8 oz / **Campbell**	280
In chili gravy: 8 oz / **Ann Page**	230
w frankfurters: 7½ oz can / **Hormel Short Orders** Beans 'n Wieners	310
w frankfurters, in tomato and molasses sauce: 8 oz / **Campbell** Beans & Franks	370
w ham: 7½ oz can / **Hormel Short Orders**	385
In molasses and brown sugar sauce: 8 oz / **Campbell Old Fashioned**	290
w pork and molasses: 8 oz / **Ann Page** Boston Style	290
w pork, in molasses sauce: 1 cup / **Libby's**	270
w pork and tomato sauce: 8 oz / **Ann Page**	240
w pork, in tomato sauce: 8 oz / **Campbell**	260
w pork, in tomato sauce: 1 cup / **Libby's**	280
In tomato sauce: 8 oz / **Ann Page** Vegetarian	230
In tomato sauce: 1 cup / **Libby's** Vegetarian	260
In tomato sauce: 8 oz / **Morton House**	270
Beans, black turtle, canned: 1 cup / **Progresso**	205
Beans, fava, canned: 1 cup / **Progresso**	180
Beans, garbanzo, canned: 8 oz / **Old El Paso**	184
Beans, green, canned: 1 cup unless noted	
Cut / **Del Monte**	40
Cut / **Green Giant**	30
Cut / **Kounty Kist**	40
Cut / **Libby's** Blue Lake	40
Cut / **Lindy**	40

	CALORIES
Cut: ½ cup / S and W Nutradiet	16
Cut / Stokely-Van Camp	40
French / Del Monte	40
French / Green Giant	30
French / Kounty Kist	40
French / Libby's Blue Lake	35
French / Lindy	40
Italian / Del Monte	60
Seasoned / Del Monte	40
Sliced / Stokely-Van Camp	40
Whole / Del Monte	35
Whole / Green Giant	30
Whole / Kounty Kist	40
Whole / Libby's Blue Lake	35
Whole / Lindy	40
Whole / Stokely-Van Camp	40
Whole, tiny / Del Monte	40
Beans, green, frozen	
Cut: 3 oz (about ½ cup) / Birds Eye	25
Cut: 1 cup / Kounty Kist Poly Bag	30
Cut: ½ cup / Seabrook Farms	21
Cut, in butter sauce: 1 cup / Green Giant	70
Cut, in mushroom sauce: ½ cup / Seabrook Farms	100
French: 3 oz (about ½ cup) / Birds Eye	30
French: ½ cup / Seabrook Farms	23
French, in butter sauce: 1 cup / Green Giant	70
French w sliced mushrooms: 3 oz (about ½ cup) / Birds Eye Combinations	30
French w toasted almonds: 3 oz (about ½ cup) / Birds Eye Combinations	50
Italian: 3 oz (about ½ cup) / Birds Eye	30
w onions and bacon bits: 1 cup / Green Giant	80
and pearl onions: 3 oz (about ½ cup) / Birds Eye Combinations	30
and spaetzle w sauce: 3.3 oz (about ½ cup) / Birds Eye International	50
Whole: 3 oz (about ½ cup) / Birds Eye	25

CALORIES

Beans, kidney, red: 8 oz / **Ann Page**	220
Beans, kidney, red, canned: 1 cup / **Progresso**	185
Beans, kidney, white, canned: 1 cup / **Progresso** Cannellini	190
Beans, lima	
Baby, canned: 8oz / **Sultana**	200
Baby, frozen: 3.3 oz (about ½ cup) / **Birds Eye**	120
Baby, frozen: 1 cup / **Green Giant** Poly Bag	150
Baby, frozen: 1 cup **Kounty Kist** Poly Bag	190
Baby, frozen: ½ cup / **Seabrook Farms**	95
Baby, in butter sauce, frozen: 1 cup / **Green Giant**	220
Canned: 1 cup / **Del Monte**	150
Canned: 1 cup / **Libby's**	160
Canned: 1 cup / **Stokely-Van Camp**	180
Canned, seasoned: 1 cup / **Del Monte**	160
Fordhook, frozen: 3.3 oz (about ½ cup) / **Birds Eye**	100
Fordhook, frozen: ½ cup / **Seabrook Farms**	85
Tiny, frozen: 3.3 oz (about ½ cup) / **Birds Eye**	120
Beans, pinto, canned: 1 cup / **Progresso**	165
Beans, red, canned: 8 oz / **Ann Page**	220
Beans, Roman, canned: 1 cup / **Progresso**	210
Bean, salad, canned: 1 cup / **Green Giant** 3 Bean	190
Beans, Shellie, canned, 1 cup / **Stokely-Van Camp**	80
Beans, wax or yellow: 1 cup unless noted	
Cut, canned / **Del Monte**	35
Cut, canned / **Libby's**	40
Cut, canned / **Stokely-Van Camp**	45
Cut, frozen: 3 oz (about ½ cup) / **Birds Eye**	30
Cut, frozen: ½ cup / **Seabrook Farms**	20
French cut, canned / **Del Monte**	35
Sliced, canned / **Stokely-Van Camp**	40
Beets, canned: 1 cup unless noted	
Cut / **Del Monte**	70

CALORIES

Cut / Libby's	70
Cut / Stokely-Van Camp	90
Diced / Libby's	70
Diced / Stokely-Van Camp	70
Harvard / Stokely-Van Camp	160
Harvard, diced / Libby's	160
Pickled, crinkle cut / Del Monte	150
Pickled, sliced / Libby's	150
Pickled, sliced / Stokely-Van Camp	190
Pickled, sliced / Town House	140
Pickled, whole / Libby's	150
Pickled, whole / Stokely-Van Camp	200
Shoestring / Libby's	50
Sliced / Del Monte	70
Sliced / Libby's	70
Sliced: ½ cup / S and W Nutradiet	28
Sliced / Stokely-Van Camp	80
Whole / Del Monte	70
Whole / Libby's	70
Whole / Stokely-Van Camp	90
Broccoli, frozen	
Au gratin: ½ pkg / Stouffer's	170
w cauliflower and carrots, in cheese sauce: 1 cup / Green Giant	140
w cheese sauce: 3.3 oz (about ½ cup)/ Birds Eye Combinations	110
In cheese sauce: 1 cup / Green Giant	130
In cheese sauce: 1 cup / Green Giant Bake n' Serve	260
Chopped: 3.3 oz (about ½ cup) / Birds Eye	25
Chopped: ½ cup / Seabrook Farms	23
Cut: 1 cup / Green Giant Poly Bag	30
Cut: 1 cup / Kounty Kist Poly Bag	30
Spears: 3.3 oz (about ½ cup) / Birds Eye	25
Spears: ⅓ pkg / Seabrook Farms	21
Spears, baby: 3.3 oz (about ½ cup) / Birds Eye	25
Spears, in butter sauce: 1 cup / Green Giant	90

CALORIES

Brussels sprouts, frozen

Birds Eye / 3.3 oz (about ½ cup)	30
Green Giant Poly Bag / 1 cup	50
Kounty Kist Poly Bag / 1 cup	50
Seabrook Farms / ½ cup	38
Baby: 3.3 oz (about ½ cup) / **Birds Eye**	35
In butter sauce: 1 cup / **Green Giant**	110
Halves, in cheese sauce: 1 cup / **Green Giant**	170
Butterbeans, canned: 8 oz / **Sultana**	170
Butterbeans, frozen: ½ cup / **Seabrook Farms**	102
Butterbeans, baby, frozen: 3.3 oz (about ½ cup) / **Birds Eye**	130
Butterbeans, speckled, frozen: 1 cup / **Green Giant** Boil-in-Bag Southern Recipe	280
Butterbeans w ham, canned: 1 cup / **Libby's**	100

Carrots: 1 cup unless noted

Cut, canned: ½ cup / **S & W Nutradiet**	22
Diced, canned / **Del Monte**	60
Diced, canned / **Libby's**	40
Diced, canned / **Stokely-Van Camp**	60
Sliced, canned / **Del Monte**	60
Sliced, canned / **Libby's**	40
Sliced, canned / **Stokely-Van Camp**	50
w brown sugar glaze, frozen: 3.3 oz (about ½ cup) / **Birds Eye** Combinations	80
In butter sauce, frozen / **Green Giant** Nuggets	100

Cauliflower, frozen

Birds Eye / 3.3 oz (about ½ cup)	25
Green Giant Poly Bag / 1 cup	25
Kounty Kist Poly Bag / 1 cup	25
Seabrook Farms / ½ cup	17
w cheese sauce: 3.3 oz (about ½ cup) / **Birds Eye** Combinations	110
In cheese sauce: 1 cup / **Green Giant**	130
In cheese sauce: 1 cup / **Green Giant** Bake n' Serve	220

CALORIES

Chick-peas, canned: 1 cup / **Progresso**	195
Collard greens, chopped, frozen: 3.3 oz (about ½ cup) / **Birds Eye**	30
Collard greens, frozen: ½ cup / **Seabrook Farms**	22
Corn, golden, canned: 1 cup unless noted	
Cream style / **Del Monte**	210
Cream style / **Green Giant**	210
Cream style / **Kounty Kist**	230
Cream style / **Libby's**	170
Cream style / **Lindy**	230
Cream style: ½ cup / **S and W Nutradiet**	84
Cream style / **Stokely-Van Camp**	210
Liquid pack / **Del Monte** Family Style	170
Liquid pack / **Green Giant**	160
Liquid pack / **Kounty Kist**	180
Liquid pack / **Le Sueur**	170
Liquid pack / **Libby's**	160
Liquid pack / **Lindy**	180
Liquid pack: ½ cup / **S and W Nutradiet**	52
Liquid pack / **Stokely-Van Camp**	180
Vacuum pack / **Del Monte**	200
Vacuum pack / **Green Giant** Niblets	150
Vacuum pack / **Kounty Kist**	160
Vacuum pack / **Lindy**	160
Vacuum pack / **Stokely-Van Camp**	240
w peppers / **Del Monte** Corn 'n Peppers	190
w peppers / **Green Giant Mexicorn**	150
Corn, golden, frozen	
In butter sauce: 1 cup / **Green Giant** Niblets	190
On cob: 1 ear / **Birds Eye**	130
On cob: 1 ear / **Birds Eye** Little Ears	70
On cob: 1 ear / **Green Giant**	160
On cob: 1 ear / **Green Giant** Nibbler	90
Cream style: 1 cup / **Green Giant**	180
w peppers, in butter sauce: 1 cup / **Green Giant** Mexican	190
Souffle: ⅓ pkg / **Stouffer's**	155

Whole kernel: 3.3 oz (about ½ cup) / **Birds Eye**	70
Whole kernel: 1 cup / **Green Giant** Poly Bag	130
Whole kernel: 1 cup / **Kounty Kist** Poly Bag	140
Whole kernel: 3 oz / **Ore-Ida**	100
Whole kernel: ½ cup / **Seabrook Farms**	70
Corn, white: 1 cup	
Canned / **Stokely-Van Camp**	240
Cream style, canned / **Del Monte**	190
Cream style, canned / **Stokely-Van Camp**	220
Whole kernel, canned / **Del Monte**	150
Whole kernel, vacuum pack, canned / **Green Giant**	150
Whole kernel, frozen / **Green Giant** Poly Bag	130
Whole kernel, frozen / **Kounty Kist** Poly Bag	140
Whole kernel, in butter sauce, frozen / **Green Giant**	190
Eggplant Parmesan, frozen: 5½ oz / **Mrs. Paul's**	250
Eggplant slices, fried, frozen: 3 oz / **Mrs. Paul's**	230
Eggplant sticks, fried, frozen: 3½ oz / **Mrs. Paul's**	260
Green peppers, stuffed, frozen: 1 pkg / **Stouffer's**	225
Green peppers, stuffed, frozen: 13 oz / **Weight Watchers**	320
Kale, chopped, frozen: 3.3 oz (about ½ cup) / **Birds Eye**	30
Kale, chopped, frozen: ½ cup / **Seabrook Farms**	30
Kale, leaf, frozen: ½ cup / **Seabrook Farms**	30
Mixed, canned: 1 cup	
Del Monte	80
Libby's Garden Vegetables	80
Stokely-Van Camp	80
Town House	90
Mixed, frozen	
Birds Eye / 3.3 oz (about ½ cup)	60
Green Giant Poly Bag / 1 cup	90
Kounty Kist Poly Bag / 1 cup	90

CALORIES

Seabrook Farms / ½ cup	50
California blend: 1 cup / **Kounty Kist** Poly Bag	30
Cantonese style: 3.3 oz (about ½ cup) / **Birds Eye** Stir-Fry	50
Chinese: 1 pkg / **La Choy**	72
Chinese style: 1 cup / **Green Giant** Boil-in-Bag Oriental Combination	130
Chinese style w sauce: 3.3 oz (about ½ cup) / **Birds Eye** International	20
Chinese style w seasonings: 3.3 oz (about ½ cup) / **Birds Eye** Stir-Fry	35
Danish style w sauce: 3.3 oz (about ½ cup) / **Birds Eye** International	30
Hawaiian style: 1 cup / **Green Giant** Boil-in-Bag Oriental Combination	200
Hawaiian style w sauce: 3.3 oz (about ½ cup) / **Birds Eye** International	40
Italian style w sauce: 3.3 oz (about ½ cup) / **Birds Eye** International	45
Japanese: 1 pkg / **La Choy**	72
Japanese style: 1 cup / **Green Giant** Boil-in-Bag Oriental Combination	130
Japanese style w sauce: 3.3 oz (about ½ cup) / **Birds Eye** International	40
Japanese style w seasonings: 3.3 oz (about ½ cup) / **Birds Eye** Stir-Fry	30
Jubilee: 3.3 oz (about ½ cup) / **Birds Eye** Combinations	120
Mandarin style w seasonings: 3.3 oz (about ½ cup) / **Birds Eye** Stir-Fry	30
New England style: 3.3 oz (about ½ cup) / **Birds Eye** Americana Recipe	60
New Orleans creole style: 3.3 oz (about ½ cup) / **Birds Eye** Americana Recipe	70
Parisian style w sauce: 3.3 oz (about ½ cup) / **Birds Eye** International	30

CALORIES

Pennsylvania Dutch style: 3.3 oz (about ½ cup) / **Birds Eye** Americana Recipe   40

San Francisco style: 3.3 oz (about ½ cup) / **Birds Eye** Americana Recipe   45

Wisconsin country style: 3.3 oz (about ½ cup) / **Birds Eye** Americana Recipe   40

In butter sauce: 1 cup / **Green Giant**   130

In onion sauce: 2.6 oz / **Birds Eye**   100

Mushrooms

    Canned: 4 oz / **Dole**   19

    Pieces and stems, canned: 1 oz / **Green Giant**   7

    Sliced, canned: 1 oz / **Green Giant**   7

    Whole, canned: 1 oz / **Green Giant**   7

    In butter sauce, frozen: 2 oz / **Green Giant**   30

Mustard greens, chopped, frozen: 3.3 oz (about ½ cup) / **Birds Eye**   18

Mustard greens, chopped, frozen: ½ cup / **Seabrook Farms**   21

Mustard greens, leaf, frozen: ½ cup / **Seabrook Farms**   21

Okra

    Cut, frozen: 3.3 oz (about ½ cup) / **Birds Eye**   25

    Cut, frozen: ½ cup / **Seabrook Farms**   26

    Gumbo, frozen: 1 cup / **Green Giant** Boil-in-Bag Southern Recipe   220

    Whole, frozen: 3.3 oz (about ½ cup) / **Birds Eye**   35

    Whole, frozen: ½ cup / **Seabrook Farms**   26

Onions, boiled, canned: 4 oz / **O & C**   32

Onions, in cream sauce, canned: ½ cup / **O & C**   90

Onions, frozen

    Chopped: 1 oz / **Birds Eye**   8

    Chopped: 2 oz / **Ore-Ida**   20

    Small, whole: 3.3 oz (about ½ cup) / **Birds Eye**   40

In cheese flavor sauce: 1 cup / **Green Giant**	140
In cream sauce: 3 oz (about ½ cup) / **Birds Eye**	100
In cream sauce: ½ cup / **Seabrook Farms**	116
Onion rings, fried, canned: 1 oz / **O & C**	178
Onion rings, fried, frozen: 2½ oz / **Mrs. Paul's**	150
Onion rings, fried, frozen: 2 oz / **Ore-Ida** Onion Ringers	160
Peas, black-eye	
Canned: 1 cup / **Progresso**	165
Canned w pork: 8 oz / **Sultana**	220
Frozen: 3.3 oz (about ½ cup) / **Birds Eye**	120
Frozen: 1 cup / **Green Giant** Boil-in-Bag Southern Recipe	280
Frozen: ½ cup / **Seabrook Farms**	100
Peas, green, canned: 1 cup unless noted	
Early / **April Showers**	120
Early / **Del Monte**	110
Early / **Kounty Kist**	140
Early / **Lindy**	140
Early / **Minnesota Valley**	110
Early / **Stokely-Van Camp**	130
Early, small / **Le Sueur**	110
Early w onions / **Green Giant**	120
Seasoned / **Del Monte**	120
Sweet / **Green Giant**	110
Sweet / **Kounty Kist**	130
Sweet / **Le Sueur**	100
Sweet / **Libby's**	120
Sweet / **Lindy**	130
Sweet: ½ cup / **S and W Nutradiet**	35
Sweet / **Stokely-Van Camp**	130
Sweet, small / **Green Giant** Sweetlets	100
Sweet, tiny / **Del Monte**	100
Sweet w onions / **Green Giant**	110

CALORIES

and carrots / **Del Monte**	100
and carrots / **Libby's**	100
and carrots: ½ cup / **S and W Nutradiet**	32
and carrots / **Stokely-Van Camp**	120
Peas, green, frozen	
Early: 3.3 oz (about ½ cup) / **Birds Eye**	70
Early: 1 cup / **Kounty Kist** Poly Bag	120
Early: 1 cup / **Green Giant** Poly Bag	100
Early: ½ cup / **Seabrook Farms**	74
Early, in butter sauce: 1 cup / **Le Sueur**	150
Sweet: 1 cup / **Green Giant** Poly Bag	100
Sweet: ½ cup / **Seabrook Farms**	52
Sweet, in butter sauce: 1 cup / **Green Giant**	150
Tiny: 3.3 oz (about ½ cup) / **Birds Eye**	60
and carrots: 3.3 oz (about ½ cup) / **Birds Eye**	50
and carrots: 1 cup / **Kounty Kist** Poly Bag	90
and carrots: ½ cup / **Seabrook Farms**	41
and cauliflower w cream sauce: 3.3 oz (about ½ cup) / **Birds Eye Combinations**	100
w cream sauce: 2.6 oz / **Birds Eye Combinations**	120
Creamed w bread crumb topping: 1 cup / **Green Giant** Bake n' Serve	300
In onion sauce: ½ cup / **Seabrook Farms**	96
w onions and carrots, in butter sauce: 1 cup / **Le Sueur**	160
w pea pods and water chestnuts, in sauce: 1 cup / **Le Sueur**	180
and pearl onions: 3.3 oz (about ½ cup) / **Birds Eye Combinations**	60
and potatoes w cream sauce: 2.6 oz / **Birds Eye Combinations**	140
w sliced mushrooms: 3.3 oz (about ½ cup) / **Birds Eye Combinations**	70
Potatoes, canned	
Au gratin w bacon: 7½ oz can / **Hormel Short Orders**	270

CALORIES

New: 1 cup / **Del Monte**   90
Scalloped w ham: 7½ oz can / **Hormel**
Short Orders   255
Whole: 1 cup / **Stokely-Van Camp**   100
Potatoes, frozen
  Au gratin: 1 cup / **Green Giant**
  Bake n' Serve   390
  Au gratin: ⅓ pkg / **Stouffer's**   135
  Diced, in sour cream sauce: 1 cup /
  Green Giant Boil-in-Bag   270
  French-fried: 2.8 oz / **Birds Eye**
  Cottage Fries   120
  French-fried: 3 oz / **Birds Eye** Crinkle Cuts   110
  French-fried: 3 oz / **Birds Eye**
  Deep Gold Crinkle Cuts   140
  French-fried: 3 oz / **Birds Eye** French
  Fries   110
  French-fried: 3.3 oz / **Birds Eye** Shoestrings   140
  French-fried: 3 oz / **Birds Eye** Steak Fries   110
  French-fried: 3 oz / **Ore-Ida** Cottage Fries   140
  French-fried: 3 oz / **Ore-Ida** Country
  Style Dinner Fries   120
  French-fried: 3 oz / **Ore-Ida** Crispers   230
  French-fried: 3 oz / **Ore-Ida** Golden
  Crinkles   130
  French-fried: 3 oz / **Ore-Ida** Golden Fries   130
  French-fried: 3 oz / **Ore-Ida** Pixie Crinkles   170
  French-fried: 3 oz / **Ore-Ida** Self Sizzling
  Crinkles   160
  French-fried: 3 oz / **Ore-Ida** Self Sizzling
  Fries   160
  French-fried: 3 oz / **Ore-Ida** Self Sizzling
  Shoestrings   220
  French-fried: 3 oz / **Ore-Ida** Shoestrings   170
  Fried: 3 oz (about ½ cup) / **Birds Eye**
  Deep Gold   160
  Fried: 2.5 oz / **Birds Eye** Tasti Fries   140
  Fried: 2.5 oz / **Birds Eye** Tasti Puffs   190

	CALORIES
Fried: 3.2 oz / **Birds Eye** Tiny Taters	200
Hash browns: 4 oz / **Birds Eye**	70
Hash browns: 4 oz / **Birds Eye** O'Brien	60
Hash browns: 3 oz / **Ore-Ida** Southern Style	70
Hash browns w butter sauce: 3 oz / **Ore-Ida** Southern Style	120
Hash browns w butter sauce and onions: 3 oz / **Ore-Ida** Southern Style	130
Hash browns, shredded: 3 oz (about ½ cup) / **Birds Eye**	60
Hash browns, shredded: 3 oz / **Ore-Ida**	60
O'Brien: 3 oz / **Ore-Ida**	60
Parsley: ½ cup / **Seabrook Farms**	104
Scalloped: ⅓ pkg / **Stouffer's**	126
Shoestring, in butter sauce: 1 cup / **Green Giant** Boil-in-Bag	310
Slices, in butter sauce: 1 cup / **Green Giant** Boil-in-Bag	210
Stuffed w cheese-flavored topping: 5 oz / **Green Giant** Oven Bake	240
Stuffed w sour cream and chives: 5 oz / **Green Giant** Oven Bake	230
and sweet peas, in bacon cream sauce: 1 cup / **Green Giant** Boil-in-Bag	240
Tater Tots: 3 oz / **Ore-Ida**	160
Tater Tots w bacon flavor: 3 oz / **Ore-Ida**	150
Tater Tots w onions: 3 oz / **Ore-Ida**	160
Vermicelli: 1 cup / **Green Giant** Bake n' Serve	390
Whole, boiled: ½ cup / **Seabrook Farms**	76
Whole, peeled: 3.2 oz (about ½ cup) / **Birds Eye**	60
Whole, small, peeled: 3 oz / **Ore-Ida**	70
Potatoes, mix, prepared: ½ cup unless noted	
Au gratin / **Betty Crocker**	150
Au gratin / **French's** Big Tate	190
Creamed / **Betty Crocker**	160

CALORIES

Hash browns / **French's** Big Tate	165
Hash browns w onions / **Betty Crocker**	150
Julienne / **Betty Crocker**	130
Mashed / **French's**	120
Mashed / **French's** Big Tate	140
Mashed / **Hungry Jack** (4 serving container)	170
Mashed / **Hungry Jack** (12, 24, 40 serving container)	140
Mashed / **Magic Valley**	110
Pancakes: three 3-in cakes / **French's** Big Tate	130
Potato Buds / **Betty Crocker**	130
Scalloped / **Betty Crocker**	150
Scalloped / **French's** Big Tate	190
w sour cream and chives / **Betty Crocker** Sour Cream 'n Chive	140

Potatoes, sweet, frozen

Candied: 4 oz / **Mrs. Paul's**	180
Candied w apples: 4 oz / **Mrs. Paul's**	160
Candied, orange: 4 oz / **Mrs. Paul's**	180
Glazed: 1 cup / **Green Giant** Boil-in-Bag Southern Recipe	340

Pumpkin, canned: 1 cup / **Del Monte**	80
Pumpkin, canned: 1 cup / **Libby's** Solid Pack	80
Pumpkin, canned: 1 cup / **Stokely-Van Camp**	90

Sauerkraut, canned: 1 cup

Del Monte	50
Libby's	40
Bavarian style / **Stokely-Van Camp**	70
Chopped / **Stokely-Van Camp**	50
Shredded / **Stokely-Van Camp**	50

Soup greens, in jar: 1 jar / **Durkee**	216
Spinach, canned: 1 cup / **Del Monte**	45
Spinach, canned: 1 cup / **Libby's**	45

Spinach, frozen

In butter sauce: 1 cup / **Green Giant**	90
Chopped: 3.3 oz (about ½ cup) / **Birds Eye**	20

CALORIES

Chopped: ½ cup / **Seabrook Farms**	25
Creamed: 3 oz (about ½ cup) / **Birds Eye** Combinations	60
Creamed: 1 cup / **Green Giant**	190
Creamed: ½ cup / **Seabrook Farms**	104
Leaf: 3.3 oz (about ½ cup) / **Birds Eye**	20
Leaf: ½ cup / **Seabrook Farms**	24
Souffle: 1 cup / **Green Giant** Bake n' Serve	300
Souffle: ⅓ pkg / **Stouffer's**	135
Squash, cooked, frozen: 4 oz / **Birds Eye**	50
Squash, cooked, frozen: ½ cup / **Seabrook Farms**	46
Squash, summer, in cheese sauce, frozen: 1 cup / **Green Giant** Boil-in-Bag	120
Squash, summer, sliced, frozen: 3.3 oz (about ½ cup) / **Birds Eye**	18
Stew, vegetable, canned: 7½ oz / **Dinty Moore**	160
Stew, vegetable, frozen: 3 oz / **Ore-Ida**	60
Succotash	
Canned: 1 cup / **Stokely-Van Camp**	170
Frozen: 3.3 oz (about ½ cup) / **Birds Eye**	80
Frozen: ½ cup / **Seabrook Farms**	87
w cream style corn, canned: 1 cup / **Libby's**	190
w whole kernel corn, canned: 1 cup / **Libby's**	150
Tomato paste, canned	
Contadina / 6 oz	150
Del Monte / 6 oz	150
Hunt's / 3 oz	70
Town House / ⅔ cup	150
Tomato puree, canned: 1 cup / **Contadina**	120
Tomatoes, canned: 1 cup unless noted	
Stewed / **Contadina**	70
Stewed / **Del Monte**	70
Stewed: 4 oz / **Hunt's**	30
Stewed / **Libby's**	60
Stewed / **Stokely-Van Camp**	70
Stewed / **Town House**	70

	CALORIES
Wedges / **Del Monte**	60
Whole / **Del Monte**	50
Whole: 4 oz / **Hunt's**	25
Whole / **Libby's**	45
Whole: ½ cup / **S and W Nutradiet**	21
Whole / **Stokely-Van Camp**	50
Whole / **Town House**	50
Turnip greens	
Chopped, canned: 1 cup / **Stokely-Van Camp**	45
Chopped, frozen: 3.3 oz (about ½ cup) / **Birds Eye**	20
Chopped, frozen: ½ cup / **Seabrook Farms**	22
Chopped w diced turnips, frozen: 3.3 oz (about ½ cup) / **Birds Eye**	20
Leaf, frozen: ½ cup / **Seabrook Farms**	22
Zucchini, frozen: 3.3 oz (about ½ cup) / **Birds Eye**	16
Zucchini sticks, in light batter: 3 oz / **Mrs. Paul's**	180
Zucchini, in tomato sauce, canned: 1 cup / **Del Monte**	60

Vegetable Juices

	CALORIES
6 oz glass unless noted	
Sauerkraut, canned / **Libby's**	20
Tomato	
Bottled / **Welch's**	38
Canned / **Campbell**	35
Canned / **Del Monte**	35

CALORIES

Canned / Libby's	35
Canned / S and W Nutradiet	22
Canned / Sacramento Plus	35
Canned: 4 fl oz / Seneca	27
Canned: 1 cup / Stokely-Van Camp	45
Canned / Town House	35
Tomato cocktail, canned / Ortega Snap-E-Tom	38
Tomato-flavored cocktail, bottled or canned / Mott's "Beefamato"	70
Tomato-flavored cocktail, bottled or canned / Mott's "Clamato"	80
Tomato-flavored cocktail, bottled or canned / Mott's "Nutrimato"	70
Vegetable cocktail, canned	
S and W Nutradiet	21
Town House	35
"V-8"	35
"V-8" Spicy Hot	35
Low sodium / "V-8"	35

Wines and Distilled Spirits

The caloric content of all distilled spirits—gin, rum, vodka, whiskey, tequila—is determined solely by the amount of alcohol present. Thus the calorie count is higher or lower depending upon the proof (a measure of the alcohol content). The following figures apply to all plain distilled spirits, all brands: 1½ fl oz (one jigger)

80 proof	100
86 proof	105
90 proof	110
94 proof	115
100 proof	125

4 fl oz

	CALORIES
Altar, red / **Gold Seal**	132
Altar, red / **Henri Marchant**	132
Blackberry / **Manischewitz**	180
Bordeaux	
Red / **B & G** Margaux	83
Red / **B & G** Prince Noir	81
Red / **B & G** St. Emilion	84
White / **B & G** Graves	87
White / **B & G** Haut Sauternes	132
White / **B & G** Prince Blanc	83
White / **B & G** Sauternes	127

Burgundy

Red / **B & G** Beaujolais St. Louis	80
Red / **Gold Seal**	85
Red / **Gold Seal** Natural	82
Red / **Henri Marchant**	85
Red / **Henri Marchant** Natural	82
Red / **Manischewitz**	85
Red / **B & G** Nuits St. George	93
Red / **B & G** Pommard	89
Red / **Taylor**	100
Sparkling / **Gold Seal**	97
Sparkling / **Henri Marchant**	97
Sparkling / **Taylor**	104
White / **B & G** Chablis	80
White / **B & G** Pouilly Fuisse	85
White / **B & G** Puligny Montrachet	81
White / **Gold Seal**	85
White / **Henri Marchant**	85

Catawba

Pink / **Gold Seal**	132
Pink / **Henri Marchant**	132
Pink / **Manischewitz**	130
Pink / **Taylor**	128
Red / **Gold Seal**	130
Red / **Henri Marchant**	130
White / **Gold Seal**	132
White / **Henri Marchant**	132

Chablis

Gold Seal	90
Gold Seal Nature	88
Henri Marchant	90
Henri Marchant Nature	88
Taylor	96
Rose / **Gold Seal**	99
Rose / **Henri Marchant**	99

Champagne

Gold Seal Blanc de Blancs	86
Gold Seal Brut	87

CALORIES

Gold Seal Extra Dry	96
Henri Marchant Blanc de Blancs	86
Henri Marchant Brut	87
Henri Marchant Extra Dry	96
Manischewitz	85
Mumm's Cordon Rouge Brut	87
Mumm's Extra Dry	109
Taylor Brut	100
Taylor Dry	104
Pink / **Gold Seal**	97
Pink / **Henri Marchant**	97
Pink / **Taylor**	108
Claret / **Taylor**	96
Cold Duck / **Gold Seal**	97
Cold Duck / **Henri Marchant**	97
Cold Duck / **Taylor**	120
Concord	
Cream red / **Manischewitz**	160
Cream white / **Manischewitz**	130
Dry / **Manischewitz**	85
Medium Dry / **Manischewitz**	120
Red / **Gold Seal**	132
Red / **Henri Marchant**	132
Labrusca	
Gold Seal	132
Henri Marchant	132
Red / **Henri Marchant**	116
Lake Country	
Taylor Gold	104
Pink / **Taylor**	108
Red / **Taylor**	108
White / **Taylor**	104
Madeira / **Gold Seal**	144
Madeira / **Henri Marchant**	144
Malaga / **Manischewitz** American Extra Dry	180
Moselle / **Julius Kayser's** Graacher Himmelreich	80
Moselle / **Julius Kayser's** Piesporter Reisling	76
Moselle / **Julius Kayser's** Zeller Schwarze Katz	76

	CALORIES
Niagara, cream white / **Manischewitz**	130
Pinot / **Gold Seal** Chardonnay	85
Pinot / **Henri Marchant** Chardonnay	85
Port	
Gold Seal	166
Henri Marchant	166
Taylor	192
Ruby / **Gold Seal**	166
Ruby / **Henri Marchant**	166
Tawny / **Gold Seal**	166
Tawny / **Henri Marchant**	166
Tawny / **Taylor**	184
Pouilly Fume / **B & G**	80
Rhine	
Gold Seal	91
Henri Marchant	91
Julius Kayser's Liebfraumilch Glockenspiel	76
Julius Kayser's Niersteiner	72
Taylor	100
Rhone / **B & G** Chateauneuf du Pape	93
Riesling / **Gold Seal** Johannisberg	92
Riesling / **Henri Marchant** Johannisberg	92
Rose / **Gold Seal** Vin	99
Rose / **Henri Marchant** Vin	99
Rose / **Taylor**	96
Sancerre / **B & G**	81
Sangria / **Taylor**	132
Sauterne	
Gold Seal Dry	97
Gold Seal Haut Altar	109
Henri Marchant Dry	97
Henri Marchant Haut Altar	109
Taylor	108
Sherry	
Gold Seal	147
Henri Marchant	147
Taylor	164
Cocktail / **Gold Seal**	127

CALORIES

	CALORIES
Cocktail / **Henri Marchant**	127
Cocktail / **Taylor**	130
Cream / **Gold Seal**	172
Cream / **Henri Marchant**	172
Cream / **Taylor**	184
Vermouth, dry / **Taylor**	132
Vermouth, sweet / **Noilly Prat**	171
Vermouth, sweet / **Taylor**	176

Y east

	CALORIES
Bakers: 1 oz	24
Brewer's, debittered: 1 tbsp	23
Brewer's, debittered: 1 oz	80
Dry, active: ¼ oz pkg / **Fleischmann's**	20
Dry, active, in jar: ¼ oz / **Fleischmann's**	20
Fresh, active: .6 oz pkg / **Fleischmann's**	15
Household: .5 oz / **Fleischmann's**	15
Torula: 1 oz	79

Yogurt

1 cup unless noted (8 oz = ⅞ to 9/10 cup)

	CALORIES
All flavors: 8 oz container / **Dannon**	200
All flavors w fruit: 8 oz container / **Dannon**	260
All fruit flavors / **Lucerne** Lowfat	260
Apple, spiced / **Borden** Swiss Style	270
Apricot / **Borden** Swiss Style	270
Apricot / **Sealtest Light n' Lively** Lowfat	240
Apricot / **Viva** Swiss Style Lowfat	250
Black cherry / **Sealtest Light n' Lively** Lowfat	240
Black cherry / **Viva** Swiss Style Lowfat	250

CALORIES

Blackberry / **Viva** Swiss Style Lowfat	250
Blueberry	
Borden Swiss Style	270
Europa / 6 oz container	210
Meadow Gold Western Sundae Style Lowfat	270
Sealtest Light n' Lively Lowfat	240
Viva Swiss Style Lowfat	250
Blueberry-vanilla / **Sealtest Light n' Lively** Lowfat	240
Boysenberry / **Borden** Swiss Style	270
Boysenberry / **Meadow Gold** Western Sundae Style Lowfat	270
Boysenberry / **Viva** Swiss Style Lowfat	250
Cherry / **Borden** Swiss Style	270
Cherry: 6 oz container / **Europa**	210
Cherry-vanilla / **Borden** Swiss Style	270
Coffee / **Borden** Swiss Style	270
Cranberry-orange / **Borden** Swiss Style	270
Fruit salad / **Viva** Swiss Style Lowfat	250
Lemon / **Sealtest Light n' Lively** Lowfat	240
Lemon / **Viva** Swiss Style Lowfat	250
Lemon-lime / **Viva** Swiss Style Lowfat	250
Lemon-lime-flavored / **Sealtest Light n' Lively** Lowfat	230
Lime / **Borden** Swiss Style	270
Orange, mandarin / **Borden** Swiss Style	270
Orange, mandarin / **Meadow Gold** Western Sundae Style Lowfat	260
Orange, mandarin / **Sealtest Light n' Lively** Lowfat	240
Orange, mandarin / **Viva** Swiss Style Lowfat	240
Peach	
Borden	261
Europa / 6 oz container	210
Meadow Gold Western Sundae Style Lowfat	260
Sealtest Light n' Lively Lowfat	240
Viva Swiss Style Lowfat	240
Peach Melba / **Sealtest Light n' Lively** Lowfat	240
Pear / **Borden** Swiss Style	270

Pineapple / **Meadow Gold** Western Sundae Style Lowfat	270
Pineapple / **Sealtest Light n' Lively** Lowfat	250
Pineapple-coconut / **Viva** Swiss Style Lowfat	250
Pineapple-orange / **Viva** Swiss Style Lowfat	250
Plain	
Borden Lite-Line Lowfat	140
Borden Swiss Style	167
Dannon / 8 oz container	150
Europa / 6 oz container	130
Lucerne Lowfat	160
Sealtest Light n' Lively Lowfat	140
Prune / **Borden** Swiss Style	270
Prune: 8 oz / **Light n' Lively**	257
Raspberry	
Borden	278
Europa / 6 oz container	210
Meadow Gold Western Sundae Style Lowfat	270
Sealtest Light n' Lively Lowfat	230
Viva Swiss Style Lowfat	250
Red cherry / **Viva** Swiss Style Lowfat	250
Strawberry	
Borden	266
Europa / 6 oz container	210
Meadow Gold Western Sundae Style Lowfat	270
Sealtest Light n' Lively Lowfat	240
Viva Swiss Style Lowfat	250
Strawberry-banana / **Sealtest Light n' Lively** Lowfat	270
Strawberry fruit cup / **Sealtest Light n' Lively** Lowfat	250
Vanilla / **Borden**	276
Vanilla: 8 oz / **Light n' Lively**	195

FROZEN

Danny Flip / 5 fl oz	175
Danny In-A-Cup / 8 fl oz	180

CALORIES

Danny Parfait / 4 fl oz 160
Danny Sampler / 3 fl oz 70
Danny-Yo / 3½ fl oz 110
Fruit: 8 fl oz / **Danny** In-A-Cup 210
Peach: ½ cup / **Sealtest** 110
Red raspberry: ½ cup / **Sealtest** 110
Vanilla: ½ cup / **Sealtest** 120
Bars
    Carob-coated: 1 bar / **Danny** On-A-Stick 125
    Chocolate-coated: 1 bar / **Danny** On-A-Stick 125
    Uncoated: 1 bar / **Danny** On-A-Stick 65
    Yosicle / 2½ fl oz 90

FAST FOODS

Fast Foods

ARBY'S

	CALORIES
Roast Beef Sandwich	350
Beef and Cheese Sandwich	450
Super Roast Beef Sandwich	620
Junior Roast Beef Sandwich	220
Swiss King Sandwich	660
Ham 'N Cheese Sandwich	380
Turkey Sandwich	410
Turkey Deluxe Sandwich	510
Club Sandwich	560

ARTHUR TREACHER'S

Fish—two pieces	360
Chicken—two pieces	370
Shrimp—7 pieces	380
Chips	280
Krunch Pup	200
Cole Slaw	120
Lemon Luvs	280
Chowder	110
Fish Sandwich	444
Chicken Sandwich	410

BURGER CHEF

Hamburger	260
Cheeseburger	300
Double Cheeseburger	430
Big Shef	540
Super Shef	600
Skipper's Treat	600
French Fries	190
Shakes	330

	CALORIES
Mariner Platter	680
Rancher Platter	640

BURGER KING

Whopper	650
Double Beef Whopper	850
Whopper w Cheese	760
Double Beef Whopper w Cheese	970
Whopper Junior	360
Whopper Junior w Cheese	420
Whopper Jr. w Double Meat	490
Whopper Jr. Double Meat Pattie w Cheese	550
Hamburger	310
Hamburger w Cheese	360
Double Meat Hamburger	440
Double Meat Hamburger w Cheese	540
Steak Sandwich	600
Whaler	660
Whaler w Cheese	770
Onion Rings—Large	330
Onion Rings—Regular	230
French Fries—Large Bag	360
French Fries—Regular Bag	240
Chocolate Milkshake	380
Vanilla Milkshake	360
Apple Pie	240

CARL'S JR.

Famous Star Hamburger	480
Super Star Hamburger	660
Old Time Star Hamburger	440
Happy Star Hamburger	290
Steak Sandwich	630
California Roast Beef Sandwich	380
Fish Fillet Sandwich	550

CALORIES

Original Hot Dog	340
Chili Dog	360
Chili Cheese Dog	400
American Cheese	40
11 oz Regular Salad w Condiments	170
2 oz Blue Cheese Dressing	200
2 oz Thousand Island Dressing	190
2 oz Lo-Cal Italian Dressing	48
French Fries	220
Onion Rings	320
Apple Turnover	330
Carrot Cake	380
20 oz Shake	310
20 oz Soft Drink	200

CHURCH'S FRIED CHICKEN

1 average piece, boned, dark	305
1 average piece, boned, white	327

DAIRY QUEEN / BRAZIER

Snacks and Desserts

Cone—Small	110
Cone—Regular	230
Cone—Large	340
Chocolate Dipped Cone—Small	150
Chocolate Dipped Cone—Regular	300
Chocolate Dipped Cone—Large	450
Chocolate Sundae—Small	170
Chocolate Sundae—Regular	290
Chocolate Sundae—Large	400
Chocolate Malt—Small	340
Chocolate Malt—Regular	600
Chocolate Malt—Large	840
Float	330

	CALORIES
Banana Split	540
Parfait	460
"Fiesta" Sundae	570
Freeze	520
"Mr. Misty" Freeze	500
"Mr. Misty" Float	440
"Dilly" Bar	240
"DQ" Sandwich	140
"Mr. Misty" Kiss	70

Fast Foods

Hamburger	260
Cheeseburger	320
Big "Brazier"	460
Big "Brazier" w Cheese	550
Big "Brazier" w Lettuce and Tomato	470
Super "Brazier" / The "Half-Pounder"	780
Hot Dog	270
Hot Dog w Chili	330
Hot Dog w Cheese	330
Fish Sandwich	400
Fish Sandwich w Cheese	440
French Fries	200
French Fries—Large	320
Onion Rings	300

DUNKIN' DONUTS

Cake and Chocolate Cake Donuts (includes rings, sticks, crullers)	240
Yeast Raised Donuts	160
Glazed Yeast Raised Donuts	168
Fancies (includes coffee rolls, danish, etc).	215
with filling and topping	add 45
Munchkins—Yeast Raised	26
Munchkins—Cake and Chocolate Cake	66
with filling and topping	add 13

HARDEE'S

	CALORIES
Hamburger	276
Cheeseburger	321
Huskie	648
Big Twin	447
French Fries—Small	239
French Fries—Large	381
Apple Turnover	282
Milkshake	391
Roast Beef Sandwich	390
Fish Sandwich	468
Hot Dog	346

KENTUCKY FRIED CHICKEN

Chicken Dinner:	
3 pieces chicken w mashed potatoes and gravy, cole slaw, and roll	
Original Recipe Dinner	830
Extra Crispy Dinner	950
Individual pieces, Original Recipe:	
Wing	151
Drumstick	136
Keel	253
Rib	241
Thigh	276

LONG JOHN SILVER'S SEAFOOD SHOPPES

Fish w Batter (2 piece order)	409
Fish w Batter (3 piece order)	613
Treasure Chest (1 piece fish & 3 peg legs)	467
Chicken Planks (4 piece order)	458
Peg Legs w Batter (5 piece order)	514
Ocean Scallops (6 piece order)	257
Shrimp w Batter (6 piece avg order)	269

CALORIES

Breaded Oysters	460
Breaded Clams	465
S.O.S. Super Ocean Sandwich	554
Fryes	275
Cole Slaw	138
Corn on the Cob	174
Hush Puppies	153

MCDONALD'S

Hamburger	260
Cheeseburger	300
Quarter Pounder	420
Quarter Pounder w Cheese	520
Big Mac	540
Filet-O-Fish	400
Egg McMuffin	350
Hot Cakes w Butter and Syrup	470
Scrambled Eggs	160
Pork Sausage	180
English Muffin (Buttered)	190
French Fries	210
Apple Pie	300
Cherry Pie	300
McDonaldland Cookies	290
Chocolate Shake	360
Vanilla Shake	320
Strawberry Shake	340

PIZZA HUT

Serving size: one half of a 10-inch pizza (3 slices)

Thin 'N Crispy Pizza
Beef	490
Pork	520
Cheese	450
Pepperoni	430
Supreme	510

CALORIES

Thick 'N Chewy Pizza

Beef	620
Pork	640
Cheese	560
Pepperoni	560
Supreme	640

STEAK N SHAKE

Steakburger	276
Steakburger w Cheese	352
Super Steakburger	375
Super Steakburger w Cheese	451
Triple Steakburger	474
Triple Steakburger w Cheese	625
Low Calorie Platter	293
Baked Ham Sandwich	451
Toasted Cheese Sandwich	250
Ham & Egg Sandwich	434
Egg Sandwich	275
Lettuce & Tomato	4
French Fries	211
Chili & Oyster Crackers (⅔ oz.)	337
Chili Mac and 4 Saltines	310
Chili—3 Ways & 4 Saltines	402
Baked Beans	173
Lettuce & Tomato Salad (1 oz, 1000 Island dressing)	168
Chef Salad	313
Cottage Cheese (½ cup)	93
Apple Danish	391
Strawberry Sundae	329
Hot Fudge Nut Sundae	530
Brownie Fudge Sundae	645
Apple Pie	407
Cherry Pie	334
Apple Pie a la Mode	549

	CALORIES
Cherry Pie a la Mode	476
Cheese Cake	368
Cheese Cake w Strawberries	386
Brownie	258
Vanilla Ice Cream (1½ Scoops)	213
Vanilla Shake	619
Strawberry Shake	648
Chocolate Shake	608
Orange Freeze	516
Lemon Freeze	548
Coca-Cola Float	514
Orange Float	502
Lemon Float	555
Root Beer Float	529
Orange Drink	83
Lemon Drink	86
Orange Juice	104
Coffee	2
Hot Tea	4
Iced Tea	6
Milk	146
Root Beer	115
Dr. Pepper	137
Hot Chocolate	686

TACO BELL

Bean Burrito	343
Beef Burrito	466
Beefy Tostada	291
Bellbeefer	221
Bellbeefer w Cheese	278
Burrito Supreme	457
Combination Burrito	404
Enchirito	454
Pintos 'N Cheese	168
Taco	186
Tostada	179

WHITE CASTLE

	CALORIES
French Fries	225
Cheeseburger	185
Hamburger	160
Fish (wo tartar sauce)	192

Index

ABOUT THE AUTHOR

JEAN CARPER is a freelance writer, specializing in consumer and health subjects. She has written numerous articles for national magazines (*Reader's Digest, Consumer Reports, Saturday Review, Today's Health*) in the medical field, including articles on food. She is the author of seven other books: *Stay Alive!, Bitter Greetings: The Scandal of the Military Draft, The Dark Side of the Marketplace* (co-written with Senator Warren G. Magnuson), *Not With a Gun, The All-in-One Carbohydrate Gram Counter, The All-in-One Low Fat Gram Counter,* and *Eating May be Hazardous to Your Health.* Ms. Carper writes a syndicated column for Princeton Features and is the national consumer reporter for Westinghouse Broadcasting. She is a graduate of Ohio Wesleyan University and lives in Washington, D.C.

BE A WINNER
IN THE RACE FOR
FITNESS

These physical fitness titles give every member of the family the guidance they need for getting in shape and keeping fit. Choose the program most suited to you whether it be yoga, jogging, or an exercise routine. You'll feel better for it.

☐	20358	THE COMPETITIVE EDGE J. Anderson & M. Cohen	$3.95
☐	14418	DR. SHEEHAN ON RUNNING George A. Sheehan	$2.75
☐	14935	RUNNING FOR HEALTH AND BEAUTY Kathryn Lance	$2.75
☐	20785	JAZZERCISE Missett & Meilach	$2.95
☐	22879	LILIAS, YOGA AND YOU Lilias Folan	$2.95
☐	01296	LISA LYON'S BODY MAGIC Lyon & Hall	$9.95
☐	20992	AEROBICS Kenneth H. Cooper	$3.25
☐	13621	AEROBICS FOR WOMEN Cooper & Cooper	$2.50
☐	20803	THE AEROBICS WAY Kenneth H. Cooper	$3.50
☐	20887	THE NEW AEROBICS Kenneth H. Cooper	$3.25
☐	20705	CELLULITE Nicole Ronsard	$3.50
☐	22776	THE ALEXANDER TECHNIQUE Sara Barker	$2.95
☐	20881	INTRODUCTION TO YOGA Richard Hittleman	$2.95
☐	20999	YOGA 28 DAY EXERCISE PLAN	$3.50
☐	14485	90 DAYS TO SELF-HEALTH Shealy, M.D.	$2.50

Buy them at your local bookstore or use this handy coupon for ordering:

Bantam Books, Inc., Dept. FI, 414 East Golf Road, Des Plaines, Ill. 60016

Please send me the books I have checked above. I am enclosing $_____ (please add $1.00 to cover postage and handling). Send check or money order —no cash or C.O.D.'s please.

Mr/Mrs/Miss _____

Address _____

City_____ State/Zip_____

FI—8/82

Please allow four to six weeks for delivery. This offer expires 12/82.

How's Your Health?

Bantam publishes a line of informative books, written by top experts to help you toward a healthier and happier life.

☐ 01376	THE FOOD ADDITIVES BOOK Nicholas Freydberg & Willis A. Gortnor A Large Format Book	$10.95
☐ 20830	AN ALTERNATIVE APPROACH TO ALLERGIES T. Randolph & R. Moss, Ph.D.	$3.95
☐ 20562	SECOND OPINION Isadore Rosenfeld	$3.95
☐ 20669	HEART RISK BOOK Aram V. Chobanian, M.D. & Lorraine Loviglio	$2.50
☐ 20494	THE PRITIKIN PERMANENT WEIGHT-LOSS MANUAL Nathan Pritkin	$3.95
☐ 20322	HEALTH FOR THE WHOLE PERSON: The Complete Guide to Holistic Health Hastings, et. al.	$3.95
☐ 20163	PREVENTION OF ALCOHOLISM THROUGH NUTRITION Roger Williams	$2.95
☐ 14221	THE BRAND NAME NUTRITION COUNTER Jean Carper	$2.50
☐ 13629	SWEET AND DANGEROUS John Yudkin, M.D.	$2.50
☐ 23066	NUTRITION AGAINST DIESEASE Roger T. Williams	$3.95
☐ 01464	MY BODY, MY HEALTH Stewarts, Hatcher, Guest	$10.95
☐ 14561	NUTRITION AND YOUR MIND George Watson	$2.75
☐ 22801	HOW TO LIVE 365 DAYS A YEAR THE SALT FREE WAY Brunswick, Love & Weinberg	$3.50
☐ 20621	THE PILL BOOK Simon & Silverman	$3.95
☐ 20134	PRITIKIN PROGRAM FOR DIET AND EXERCISE Pritikin & McGrady, Jr.	$3.95
☐ 20052	THE GIFT OF HEALTH: A New Approach to Higher Quality, Lower Cost Health Care Shames & Shames	$2.95
☐ 20130	WHICH VITAMINS DO YOU NEED? Martin Ebon	$2.75
☐ 13259	THE FAMILY GUIDE TO BETTER FOOD AND BETTER HEALTH Ron Deutsch	$2.50
☐ 20530	PSYCHODIETETICS Cheraskin, et al.	$2.75

Buy them at your local bookstore or use this handy coupon for ordering:

Bantam Books, Inc., Dept. HN, 414 East Golf Road, Des Plaines, Ill. 60016

Please send me the books I have checked above. I am enclosing $_____
(please add $1.00 to cover postage and handling). Send check or money order
—no cash or C.O.D.'s please.

Mr/Mrs/Miss _____

Address _____

City_____ State/Zip_____

HN—8/82

Please allow four to six weeks for delivery. This offer expires 2/83.

SAVE $2.00 ON YOUR NEXT BOOK ORDER!

BANTAM BOOKS

Shop-at-Home
Catalog

Now you can have a complete, up-to-date catalog of Bantam's inventory of over 1,600 titles—including hard-to-find books.

And, you can save $2.00 on your next order by taking advantage of the money-saving coupon you'll find in this illustrated catalog. Choose from fiction and non-fiction titles, including mysteries, historical novels, westerns, cookbooks, romances, biographies, family living, health, and more. You'll find a description of most titles. Arranged by categories, the catalog makes it easy to find your favorite books and authors and to discover new ones.

So don't delay—send for this shop-at-home catalog and save money on your next book order.

Just send us your name and address and 50¢ to defray postage and handling costs.

BANTAM BOOKS, INC.
Dept. FC, 414 East Golf Road, Des Plaines, Ill. 60016

Mr./Mrs./Miss_____
                              (please print)
Address_____
City_____State_____Zip_____

Do you know someone who enjoys books? Just give us their names and addresses and we'll send them a catalog too at no extra cost!

Mr./Mrs./Miss_____
Address_____
City_____State_____Zip_____

Mr./Mrs./Miss_____
Address_____
City_____State_____Zip_____

FC—9/81